U.S. LIGHTHOUSE SERVICE TENDERS

EASTWIND PUBLISHING 1-885457-12-X- CORRECTIONS AND ADDITIONS – FIRST EDITION

Addendum to: U.S. LIGHTHOUSE SERVICE TENDERS, 1840-1939

Page 32   WARRINGTON, 1871
add   "In 1869, while still in private service, was wrecked in Lake Huron, but was rebuilt then sold to the Lighthouse Service in 1870."

Page 35   MISTLETOE, 1872
amend   "Main Engines - Steam, Vertical Beam

correct last sentence to read: "It was then registered as the freighter *SS Mistletoe*, but operated as a chartered fishing platform, transporting private anglers for sport fishing. While at anchor 2-1/2 miles south of Ambrose Lightship with 74 passengers on board, a fire broke out. The passengers and crew was all safely evacuated, but the old wooden hull burned quickly to the waterline and she sank quickly on 05 October 1924."

Page 70   MAYFLOWER, 1897
add   "She was completed by the builder and delivered on 09 October 1897."

Page 79   MAGNOLIA class, 1904
correct   Builder   Baltimore Shipbuilding & Dry Dock Co., Baltimore Maryland – Not Ohio.

Page 81   ASPEN, 1906
add   "The machinery was then removed and it was intended to be a floating museum. However, the plans were never fulfilled and it remained in storage. It was sold again in the mid 1970's and partially rebuilt, but again, not completed. It was totally stripped in 1999 and scrapped in Spring 2000."

Page 104   COSMOS, 1919
add   Builder - Jacob Roberts, City Island NY

Page 115   PYXIE, 1923
add   Builder – Fore River Shipyard, Quincy MA
amend   "Design - Built and delivered on 09 Feb 1909 to for the War Department (U.S.Army) Quartermaster Corps as the Tug Boat *General R. B. Ayres*, then used by the Artilliary Corps as a Small Mine Planter."

Page 125   VIOLET class, 1930
add to Violet   "At the start of World War II, she was designated as WAGL-250".

Page 130   HICKORY, 1933
add   "Delivered - 08 March 1933".

U.S. LIGHTHOUSE SERVICE TENDERS
1840 -1939

By Douglas Peterson, USCG (Ret)

EASTWIND PUBLISHING
Annapolis & Trappe, Maryland USA

Published by Eastwind Publishing
Annapolis and Trappe, Maryland, U.S.A.

©2000 Eastwind Publishing

All rights reserved. No part of this book may be used or reproduced
in any manner, including electronic methods without the permission of the publisher,
except in the case of brief quotations embodied in critical reviews or articles.

For information about permission to reproduce
selections from this book write to the publisher,
Eastwind Publishing, P.O. Box 1773, Annapolis, MD 21404
or call: 410-476-4445
www.eastwindpublishing.com

Peterson, Douglas

U.S. Lighthouse Service Tenders, 1840-1939

Includes bibliographical reference and index.

Printed in China

ISBN 1-885457-12-X

First Edition

A Dedication

To all those unsung heroes who served in the Lighthouse Service, particularly those who sailed and labored on the Tenders; you sought not glory, but service to your fellow man! We will not forget! It is to you I dedicate this book.

Crew on *USLHT Rose*, c. 1916.

National Archives

Those who go down to the sea in ships, who do business on great waters; they have seen the works of the Lord, and His wonders in the deep.

Psalms 107:23-24

Table of Contents

De-icing a bouy.   *National Archives*

Acknowledgments vii

Foreward ix

INTRODUCTION xi
    What is a 'Tender'? xii
    Harbor Launches & Buoy Boats xiii

A BRIEF HISTORY xv
    About the Data xviii
    Abbreviations & Designations xix

TENDERS OF THE LIGHTHOUSE SERVICE
    Chapter I. The Early Years, 1840-1869 1
    Chapter II. Under the Lighthouse Board, 1870-1910 27
    Chapter III. With the Bureau of Lighthouses, 1910-1939 91
    Chapter IV. Epilog: Into the Coast Guard, After 1939 147

APPENDIX A - Hired Vessels 149

APPENDIX B - Lighthouse District Maps 152
    Map 1. Lighthouse Establishment Districts as authorized in 1838 153
    Map 2. Lighthouse Service Districts established by the Board in 1852 155
    Map 3. Lighthouse Service Districts modified by the Board up to 1910 .. 157
    Map 4. Bureau of Lighthouses Districts as defined 1910 to 1939 159

BIBLIOGRAPHY 161

INDEX 165

Acknowledgments

While I've been tracking the histories of Coast Guard and Revenue Cutters for over thirty-five years, it was only in the last few years that I realized how little information had been compiled on Lighthouse Service Tenders. So I decided to gather the information on this unsung fleet. The more I dug for information the more I discovered how little had been compiled.

In my search for this illusive data, many people, often with their own busy schedules and knowing as little as I did, would lend a hand or help dig up a nugget of information. Many people, too numerous to name individually, have contributed to this book. They provided information (no matter how obscure, it is all valuable data), encouraged me, or opened new doors or avenues of research into my studies. However, there are a few individuals who deserve a special note here. And for the rest of you if you aren't mentioned, you know who you are and I do too: A big thanks! I couldn't have done it without each of you.

While the U.S. Lighthouse Service merged into the Coast Guard in 1939, their own special rich heritage and history are kept alive today by many friends and supporters of the U.S. Lighthouse Society of San Francisco and their President Wayne "Head Keep" Wheeler. With hospitality legendary of that old service, Wayne and his gang graciously opened all their files and assisted in the data collection of our old Black hull fleet. And on the east coast, the same efforts are underway by Ken Black of the Shore Village Museum in Rockland, Maine, who is also striving to preserve that same heritage.

And to the Historian's Office at Coast Guard Headquarters in Washington, D.C., whose assistance was invaluable in finding and clarifying numerous obscure facts and freely opening up files in support of Coast Guard history. Thanks to Dr. Bob Browning and Scott Price who went the extra mile on numerous occasions in providing information and digging out essential data.

A special appreciation goes to Patrick Hornberger, of Eastwind Publishing, another lover of maritime history and the old Lighthouse Service. He stuck his neck out and said this history had to be published, even though other publishers had rejected it. He helped a "rookie" get the stuff together, chase down photographs and contribute photos from Eastwind Publishing's archives (sharing some rare photos), while proffering words of encouragement when things got challenging.

A special thanks also to Rusty Nelson who created the excellent graphics in Appendix B.

And most importantly, to my wife, who has had to endure my running around to do research, spending hours at the computer, and being confronted repeatedly with "Lighthouse Service talk" at the dinner table. Every ship has a Captain, but we all know that it is the First Mate (or modern day Chief) that keeps things running. A better "First Mate" I couldn't ask for or find anywhere, and I know the next thirty years will be at least as great as the first thirty! Thanks, dear.

And finally, to anyone who enjoys and appreciates the rich heritage and the joys of the Lighthouse Service, and the ships which kept it going. Whether you are an old salt, or a young discoverer of this great organization, keep this in mind: The next time you visit a lighthouse or go boating, remember that it was the Tenders that supported and maintained these wonderful things. Thus, it is your responsibility to protect the past and learn from it, to shape its future, and feel the pride of being part of the best service in the United States.

Foreward

No greater love has a sailor than that for his ship. For we land-lovers this is understandable when we see the yachts of the America's Cup and the ascot-adorned millionaires who own these sleek race-horses of the sea. But just as great a love affair exists by the sailors, whether callused deck-hands or dirty boiler-stokers, for their work-horse buoy tenders.

Envisioning buoy tenders as objects of beauty requires seeing them through the eyes of a "workaholic" because nowhere on the seas are there ships and crews that get less rest. Lightships have little to do during clear, quiet days; warships are bored with routine during times of peace; and even merchant ships are tied up in port during slack commercial periods. But buoys always need tending; and much like traffic lights on land, they seem to breed. Each year there are always more.

Those of us, including myself, who are opposed to "big government" have forgotten about buoy tending (and much else). We take for granted the flow of commerce upon the seas and overlook the tens of thousands of buoys required to bring safety to our waters.

Thirty years ago I had time for aircraft carriers, battleships, and submarines only. Today I know how much the buoy tenders have contributed to the commercial strength of this nation.

Douglas Peterson shares with us his love affair—a history of lighthouse tenders between 1840 and 1939. To simply say that this book fills a void in our knowledge concerning these important ships understates its value. Buried not too deeply within these pages are the stories of rescue and disaster, and yes, above all else, routine because for "workaholics" routine is the cornerstone to success.

Robert L. Scheina
Professor of History,
National Defense University
Washington, D.C.
Former U.S. Coast Guard Historian

Introduction

They were the forgotten fleet of the federal government. They did their jobs with little or no fanfare. But they did it well and consistently to the highest standards, and established traditions which are still upheld today. While very little has been documented about these ships, they were the lifeline for lighthouses and lightships, and essential to the support and maintenance of the aids to navigation system. And those aids guided the merchant ships and navies which were the lifeblood and security of our growing nation. These unsung heroes were the tenders of the U.S. Lighthouse Service.

The Lighthouse Service acquired its first vessel in 1840, the former Revenue Cutter RUSH. During the next seventeen years, other vessels would be chartered or purchased to provide logistical support to the various lighthouses, and tend other aids to navigation. It is from these original duties that the name "tender" was applied, and became synonymous with any vessel of the Lighthouse Service.

The Lighthouse Service built its own tender in 1857, and the fleet of the Lighthouse Service continued to grow in numbers as well as functions and responsibilities. Later, tending buoys and constructing various aids to navigation were included. And, because of the nature of their duties and where they operated (along our coasts), it was only natural that they would also eventually be tasked with life saving.

First, serving along the Atlantic seaboard, the areas of responsibility grew with the nation, expanding into the Gulf of Mexico, the Great Lakes, the Mississippi-Missouri-Ohio river systems and tributaries, the Pacific coast, Alaska, and finally the central Pacific Islands. Some of the early organizational plans and traditions established by the Lighthouse Service in the 1860s are part of the Coast Guard (and Navy) today. Coast Guard (and Naval) District boundaries and numbers, tender names, and pride in the work of the Service are all part of this early heritage.

By the late 1800s, uniformity and standardization within the Lighthouse Service fleet of tenders had been set. All tenders were painted with black hulls, and white superstructures. All tenders flew the triangular Lighthouse Service Flag, and carried a polished brass miniature lighthouses affixed to their bows for identification.

When the Lighthouse Service merged into the Coast Guard in 1939 (on the eve of its 150th anniversary), it almost doubled the Coast Guard's fleet by adding sixty-four tenders and thirty lightships.

In the 1990s, three books have been written detailing the vessels of the United States Coast Guard and one of its predecessor services, the U.S. Revenue Marine/Revenue Cutter Service. But another seagoing service, actually older than the Coast Guard and eventually merged into the Coast Guard in 1939, has yet to be covered in a book detailing its vessels. That service is the U.S. Lighthouse Service, founded in 1789 (a year before the Revenue Marine in 1790). This book is meant as a companion to those other three books.

This book will list the more than two hundred named tenders of the Lighthouse Service from the first one purchased in 1840 (*Rush*) to the last one built prior to the merger into the Coast Guard in 1939 (*Fir*), in chronological order. It is divided

Crew aboard *USLHT Myrtle*, 1896.   *National Archives*

U.S. Lighthouse Buoy depot at Portsmouth, Va. Tenders *Laurel* (left) and *Orchid* (right), c. 1925. *Mariners' Museum*

into three sections, reflecting the various phases of the Lighthouse Service and their tenders. The first section deals with the "early years" (1840-1869) as the tender fleet first became established. The next section (1870-1909) covers tenders built to more standardized designs under the supervision of the Lighthouse Board. And the final section (1910-1939) deals with the Service while under the administration of the Bureau of Lighthouses in the newly formed Department of Commerce. One appendix lists "hired" vessels, chartered by the Lighthouse Service but not owned or commissioned by the government. Another appendix provides various maps of the boundaries of the Lighthouse Districts at different times, to show where the tenders served.

Finally, you may notice gaps of information or data. Many records have been lost due to disposal of old documents, or records falling apart due to age. If you are aware of additional information to further complete these records, help us preserve the heritage of the Lighthouse Service and its Tenders, and send information to the publisher.

WHAT IS A 'TENDER' ?

When the term "Tender" is mentioned, most often it is identified with a black hulled vessel belonging to the U.S. Coast Guard called a Buoy Tender. History buffs, with particular interest in the old Lighthouse Service, will relate the term "Tender" to that of a Lighthouse Tender. But what is the origin of the term "Tender"?

Any commissioned vessel of the Lighthouse Service (other than a Lightship) is referred to as a Lighthouse Tender. This was because their responsibilities were to maintain, support, or "tend" the various lighthouses along America's coasts, providing supplies, fuel, mail, and transportation. These Tenders also towed non-propelled lightships to their stations after maintenance or if they drifted off station. Later, when buoys became a more standard form of aids to navigation, the tenders were tasked with tending them also. So the term Lighthouse Tender became synonymous with any vessel of the Lighthouse Service tasked with the above responsibilities.

By the late 1800s, uniformity and standardization of the Tenders had been established: black hulls and white superstructures. With the exception of local variations, Tenders have almost always had a black hull. It was easier to maintain, particularly when the hull was bumped regularly and banged while tending aids, towing lightships, or handling cargo.

When the Lighthouse Service merged into the Coast Guard in 1939, the Lighthouse Tenders became Coast Guard Cutters, but continued to be classed as Lighthouse Tenders. The title "Buoy Tender" as an official hull classification wasn't enacted until 1943.

The now famous title "Tender" still applies to all classes of vessels in the Coast Guard supporting and maintaining aids to navigation, and are proudly known and identified by the black hulls of the "Tender fleet."

The first tenders were just vessels capable of carrying cargo or construction materials. They were often small tugs or coastal freight type vessels, modified with a boom to lift materials. However, as the Service started building their own vessels to better fulfill the missions of the Lighthouse Service, a distinctive design evolved.

A prolonged forward section would have a large low well deck to handle cargo and buoys. When a foc'sle was included, sometimes that deck was rounded so buoys would not get snagged on the corners. The foremast would also be the main stanchion for a large boom capable of lifting from ten to twenty tons of weight. Above the main deck near the stern, a separate quarters was built and reserved for the District Inspector when he rode on board, performing his duties.

While each tender (up until 1908) was individually custom designed and built for a specific region and duty, a standardized design evolved, including all of the above listed characteristics. However, each tender had its own special characteristics or designs. Looking at pictures of the various tenders from one year to the next (particularly after the 1880s), most tenders look alike with a few differentiating features.

A few differences to look for in tenders are:
- The size and shape of the bridge: Is it square or round? The number of windows.
- Is the main deck enclosed or open the full length of the hull?
- Height, size, and shape of the stack.
- Number, size, and position of ports in the side of the hull.
- Size of the District Inspector's Quarters.
- Placement of any doors or windows above decks.
- Note any differences in the masts, rigging or the boom assembly.
- Railing heights and lengths, particularly near the well deck.
- Location and number of ventilators.
- Is the hull's stem and stern straight up-and-down, or sloped?
- How large is the foc'sle deck (assuming there is one)? Is it flat or rounded?
- The length of the fantail. Is it open, covered, or enclosed?
- If it is a paddle-wheeler (stern or side): How large or predominant is the wheel(s)? What are the patterns of the wheel guards?

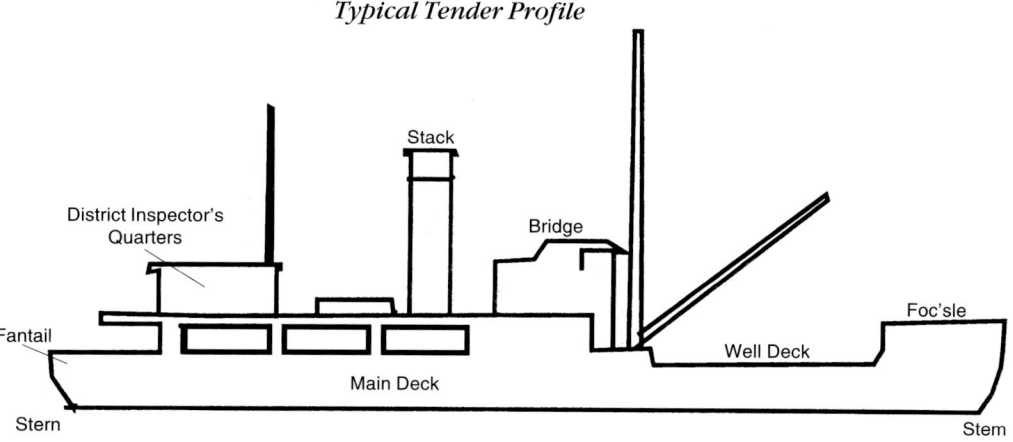

Typical Tender Profile

HARBOR LAUNCHES & BUOY BOATS

Text on Lighthouse Service Tenders would not be complete without the mention of the various small craft (harbor launches and buoy boats). During the time span of the Lighthouse Service, literally thousands of small craft were built, often for specific purposes, and often to no standardized design. Almost every lighthouse had a small boat or two. Each Lighthouse Depot had a collection of launches and boats for various purposes: replacements and spares for the Lighthouses and Tenders, local shallow water aids to navigation support and maintenance, and to ferry workers between the nearest city and the Depot.

Every Lighthouse Tender had at least two boats (acting as lifeboats) assigned to it. These smaller assigned craft were often put to work servicing aids to navigation in shallower waters where the larger tender could not go. These boats were built specifically for each tender. Often, these smaller boats would evolve to become harbor tenders in their own right, operating independently from its "mother" tender. And sometimes, these smaller independent launches would then be assigned their own names.

And because these smaller craft had no permanent crews attached and were property of a larger Depot or Tender, they were not commissioned and specific records on each craft were not kept. More often than not, a one- or two-line mention would occur in an official report about a named "harbor launch," then it would disappear into oblivion with little or no history or specifications ever to be found.

xiv INTRODUCTION

USLHT Holly at Point-No-Point, Chesapeake Bay, c. 1910.

National Archives

Because of the lack of records, small (usually under 50 feet in length), unmanned launches and boats as a collective group will not be addressed; however, those that were named and operated as small tenders or Harbor Launches in many areas will be listed here. The known years of service will be listed and annotated with a question mark for the unknown years (before or after). Other than that, the format is the same for the larger commissioned tenders covered in this book.

The term "Buoy Boat," while synonymous with small non-commissioned craft in the Coast Guard, was in fact a fairly new term within the history of the Lighthouse Service. A 38-foot, open bay auxiliary vessel was designed to support larger tenders in 1927, and became a standardized design that was mass produced for the northeastern seaboard lighthouse districts. The vessel was officially designated as a "Buoy Boat," the first such application of the term, which continued into the 1960s with the Coast Guard.

A Brief History

The United States Lighthouse Service has had a unique pattern of growth and a significant role in the development of the United States since its creation. The oldest agency and the earliest public works in the United States, the Lighthouse Establishment, under the Treasury Department, was created on 07 August 1789, to set up and maintain lighthouses, beacons, buoys and public piers at "any bay, inlet, harbor or port of the United States, for rendering the navigation thereof easy and safe." It was the ninth act passed by the newly formed Congress. The act gave the new Federal government jurisdiction over existing lighthouses and other aids to navigation operated at that time by various state organizations: twelve lighthouses, seven unlit buoys, and a few miscellaneous fog signals.

Old lighthouses were replaced with newer more sturdy structures, and new sites had lights built on them, to guide the maritime trade safely along America's coasts, and to help them avoid the hazards to safe navigation. While some floating navigational markers had been placed in waters as early as 1793, the first "buoys" were authorized by Congress in 1797. By 1820, there were 55 lighthouses, and the first floating lighthouse, or light ship, had been established near Norfolk, Virginia.

The supply and inspection of existing lighthouses, and the construction of new ones, were generally performed by contractors. This method of operations often meant the government had no direct control of the workings of the organization. Control and organization remained fairly loose under this arrangement until the 1840s. Oversight was the responsibility of the Commissioner of the Revenue of the Treasury Department (1792-1820), then later the Fifth Auditor of the Treasury, Steven Pleasanton (1820-1852).

On 07 July 1838, the Lighthouse Service established eight areas of responsibility, also known as "districts." The Atlantic coast was divided into six districts and the Great Lakes into two districts. [See Appendix B for maps of the various Lighthouse Districts.] Revenue Cutters were often assigned to assist in each Lighthouse District, the first indication of a merger that would occur more than a century later.

With many remote lighthouses along the coasts, supplying them was often difficult and sometimes impossible from land. By 1840, there were 234 lighthouses, 30 lightships, and 900 lesser aids to navigation: all of them had to be maintained and supported. So the former Revenue Cutter *Rush* was purchased in 1840 for use as a Lighthouse Tender, bringing fuel, water, and supplies to lighthouses and tending buoys in a major harbor.

By an Act of Congress on 28 Sep 1850, a systematic coloring and numbering of all buoys was established.

Library of Congress

Steven Pleasanton, as Fifth Auditor of the Treasury, oversaw the operation and construction of lighthouses from 1820 to 1852.

Because of the proximity of many lighthouses to areas where ship wrecks often occurred, the Lighthouse Establishment was tasked in 1848 with "rendering assistance to shipwrecked mariners." It was probably because of these similar functions: the Revenue Marine checking on lighthouses and aids to navigation; and the Lighthouse Service rendering assistance to ships down at sea, that Alexander V. Fraser, head of the Revenue-Marine Bureau, proposed the merging of the two Treasury Department agencies. However, due to other circumstances, the attempt failed, and would not occur for almost century.

In 1851, in response to complaints of the lack of quality and consistency of the American aids to navigation system, Congress ordered an investigation of the Lighthouse Establishment. To undertake this study, a special board was created, with membership including Rear Adm. Shubrick USN; Capt. Samuel F. DuPont, USN; Brig. Gen. Joseph G. Totten, US Army Corps of Engineers; Lt. Col. James Kearny, US Topographic Engineers;

and Professor Alexander D. Bache, Superintendent of the Coast Survey. They spent seven months in careful investigation of the Lighthouse organization and submitted a 760-page report recommending the creation of a Lighthouse Board, to oversee the proper level of control and administration of this growing agency.

By direction of the Treasury Secretary Thomas Corwin, this Board was created on 09 Oct 1852 to oversee the organization. The Lighthouse Board consisted of two officers from the Navy, two officers from the Army Corps of Engineers, and two scientists from the civilian community, with junior officers from the Navy and Army to act as secretaries. Notables who served on the Lighthouse Board during its 58-year reign over the Lighthouse Service included Shubrick (its first chairman, serving in that capacity for 19 years), and Joseph Henry (head of the Smithsonian Institution), who also later served as the only civilian Chairman for seven years. Former Superintendents of the Coast Survey (later called the Coast and Geodetic Survey) A.D. Bache, Mendenhall, and Pritchett, were notable civilians on the Board. Naval Officers Jenkins, Dewey, Evans, and Schley, and Army Engineer Officers Totten, Humphreys, Franklin, Meade, Poe, and Casey, all served on the Board. Other board officers that later served in the Confederacy were Cmdr. Semmes and Gens. Rosecrans and Beauregard.

The Board worked quickly to standardize equipment and increase efficiency of the organization. It had over 335 lighted aids (including lighthouses), 49 fog signals, and a thousand buoys to oversee.

This same Act of Congress restructured the coasts of the United States into 12 Lighthouse Districts (seven on the Atlantic coast, two in the Gulf of Mexico, two in the Great Lakes, and one for the Pacific coast). This arrangement of districts was the pattern for the Navy's Naval Districts established in 1903! Each Lighthouse District also had a Navy or Army officer as its Lighthouse Inspector.

In 1857, the U.S. Lighthouse Service built its first Lighthouse Tender, the steam powered *USLHT Shubrick*, at Philadelphia Navy Yard. The wood-hulled, side-wheel tender became the first tender built specifically for the Lighthouse Service (all previous tenders had been chartered or purchased), and the first tender on the Pacific coast.

With the onset of the Civil War, many lighthouses and beacons were destroyed to prevent aiding the enemy. Tenders were seized. Numerous other aids to navigation were ignored and fell into disuse, and were not maintained due to the priorities of the military.

In 1862, a bill was introduced to try and merge the Lighthouse Service into the U.S. Navy, but it was soundly defeated.

After the Civil War, six former Navy vessels were purchased. Four of these vessels, with botanical names, established the tradition of naming tenders for flowers, plants, and trees.

The distinctive triangular flag, with a red border and blue lighthouse on a white field, was first used as the service's flag in 1869. It would later be officially adopted on 03 September 1888.

Over the next three decades, as the nation grew, so did the regions of the nation over which the Lighthouse Service had jurisdiction concerning aids to navigation.

In 1874, the Mississippi, Missouri, and Ohio rivers and their tributaries (also known as the Western rivers) were added. Puerto Rico was added in 1900. The Territory of Hawaii was added in 1903, extending to Guam and American Samoa in 1905.

In 1881, the first lighted buoy in the United States was established at the entrance to New York Bay.

Between 1882 and 1885, attempts were made to consolidate the Lighthouse Service with the Life Saving Service and the Coast and Geodetic Survey, then merge that conglomeration into the Navy. The Navy had argued for the plan on the premise that the three organizations were maritime and had no relationship to the parent Treasury Department; however, that plan was thwarted.

In 1885, the first self-propelled lightship was built. Until this time, lightships were often towed by tenders on and off station for regular maintenance.

On 14 February 1903, when the new Department of Commerce and Labor was created, the Lighthouse Service was transferred effective 01 July 1903 but remained under the control of the Lighthouse Board. When the new department was divided in 1910 into the Department of Commerce and the Department of Labor, the Lighthouse Service remained with the Department of Commerce. The seal of the new Department of Commerce had a lighthouse in it, reflecting one of its major responsibilities (pictured oppostie). On 01 July 1910, the old military Lighthouse Board was disestablished. During the fifty-eight year tenure of the Lighthouse Board, the number of lighted aids had increased from 335 to nearly 4,000, fog signals from 49 to 457, and buoys from about 1,000 to 5,300.

The newly created Bureau of Lighthouses, with a simplified administration, was totally reorganized, and put under the direction of a civilian Commissioner. The first Commissioner was George R. Putnam, who held the position for twenty-five years. Each district was then managed by a District Supervisor (instead of the old title of District Inspector). New districts (or regions of responsibility) were also set up.

The last sail powered Lighthouse Tender, the *Pharos*, was taken out of service in 1908. The first practical lighted buoys were employed about 1910.

During World War I, about twenty of the ocean going tenders served with the Navy or the War Department (Army), then returned to Lighthouse Service duty after the conflict was over.

In the 1920s, the foremost agency in the world dealing with navigation, the U.S. Bureau of Lighthouses, developed and tested the "radio fog signal" (now known as a Radio Beacon), for use with the "Radio Compass" (today called the Radio Direction Finder or RDF). The methodology is still used today.

By 1926, The Lighthouse Service had established an Airways Division, to extend the radio beacon program to aviation, and provide other aids to navigation systems for the aviation community. In 1933, this division became a separate entity as part of the new Civil Aeronautical Administration (precursor to the modern Federal Aviation Administration).

President Roosevelt's Reorganization Order #11 consolidated one of the oldest federal agencies, the Lighthouse Service, moved it out of the Commerce Department and back to the Treasury Department, merging with the United States Coast Guard, effective 07 July 1939, one month shy of its 150th anniversary. The merger was most logical, for many functions of the Lighthouse Service and the Coast Guard were parallel and often duplicated. Both organizations had the same goal: the protection of life and property at sea. With this merger, U.S. Lighthouse Service brought 4,119 full-time civilian employees and sixty-four tenders (from 200-foot ocean going tenders to 72-foot harbor tenders), supporting over 1,400 lighthouses and 39 lightships, and 29,606 aids to navigation, protecting over forty-seven thousand miles of seacoasts and inland waterways. All these resources came under the direction of a newly created Aids to Navigation Division in the United States Coast Guard.

Collection, P. Hornberger

George R. Putnam was the first commissioner of the Lighthouse Service, 1910-1935.

Flag of the U.S. Lighthouse Service flown on all lighthouse tenders and lightships until 1939.

About the Data

Any discussion on the "technical" aspects, or measurements of vessels, regardless of its merchant or federal origins or duties, requires clarification of specifics: gauging the size of a vessel.

In the 1700s, a ships weight or tonnage often determined what the vessel was capable of carrying. By the late 1700s and early 1800s, a standardized means of measuring a ship's size was by its length "between perpendiculars" (again, an interior means of determining its capabilities), or along its waterline (the first consistent external measurement applicable to any kind of ship). In this century, the most common method of measure is a vessel's maximum length, that is, length overall. Trying to reconcile these differences, or find a common mode of measurement, for comparison can sometimes be difficult and confusing.

LBP—Length between perpendiculars, was not consistent in the 1800s, but recently has been codified. It was often (but not always) the overall interior length on the underside of the first deck above the waterline running the full length of the ship. The main deck was commonly the highest deck on the ship that ran the full length of the hull from bow to stern.

LWL—Length at the water line, measured the length of the hull where it met the water, under normal displacement. However, LBP and LWL did not often reflect the actual length of a vessel's hull, either because of the rigging (such as the bowspirit of a sailing vessel), the rake of the bow, or the depth of the counter on the stern.

LOA—The length overall, measures the exterior length of the hull from the extreme forward of the bow (or stem) to the aftmost part of the stern. This method of measure is the most common after the 1920s.

Other measurements of the hull regularly used which often cause confusion are "Depth" and "Draft."

DEPTH—More properly "Depth of Hold," an early method of measuring capacity/size of a ship, was the inside vertical distance of the hull from the underside of the lowest (or cargo) deck to ceiling of the cargo hold (or underside of the main deck).

DRAFT—The outside vertical measure from the surface of the water to the lowest extension of the vessel in the water.

Also, a vessel's weight often can be confusing:

DISPLACEMENT—the weight of a ship is determined by the amount of water the floating hull displaces.

FULL—or LOADED displacement is the weight of a vessel when floating at her maximum allowable draft, fully equipped and provisioned, with the maximum of cargo, passengers, and consumables on board.

MEAN—Also known as STANDARD displacement/draft, measured with the vessel fully manned and engined, ready for sea, with potable water, but without boiler feed-water or fuel.

LIGHT—Ready for sea but with no consumables on board.

For the purposes of this record (unless otherwise noted), the following data perameters will be adhered to:
- Full (or max) Displacement in tons.
- Dimensions (in feet and inches) as follows:
  Length overall x Beam (maximum) x Depth of Hold.
- Maximum Draft is also included (in parenthesis) and noted where known.
- Built (used for private vessels prior to government acquisition) will indicate when construction was completed for its private or commercial use.
- Any other variations or additions to the data will be so noted.

The Lighthouse Service, as indicated in its numerous documents, often had a new tender named and designed, with a probable assignment (often to replace an aging tender at a specific location), before funds were appropriated from Congress and approval was given to build it. Thus, some tenders were listed on the roles for years before they were commissioned.

However, in this book, tenders are listed in chronological order according to the date they were commissioned or placed in service. The only exceptions are tenders that were planned for construction but were later cancelled; which are included by the date they were originally planned or authorized. One other exception is the small named unmanned harbor launches for which we only know some of their years of service.

Abbreviations & Designations

AtoN	Aids to Navigation
bhp	Brake Horsepower
diam	Diameter
CSS	Confederate States Ship (1861-1865)
EPA	Environmental Protection Agency
FNH	Fuervas Naval de Honduras (Honduran Navy)
FS	Freight & Supply Vessel (U.S. Army designation)
FW	Fresh Water
HP	Horsepower
IHP	Indicated Horsepower
IX	Unclassified Vessel (U.S. Navy designation)
lbp	Length between perpendiculars
LHB	Lighthouse Board
LHD	Lighthouse District
LHE	Lighthouse Establishment
LHS	Lighthouse Service
loa	Length overall
lwl	Length at the Water Line
MARAD	U.S. Maritime Administration
max	Maximum (displacement or draft)
MV	Motor Vessel
NA	Not available, or unknown
NFR	No further record or information
NOAA	National Oceanic and Atmospheric Administration
RCS	Revenue Cutter Service
shp	Shaft Horsepower
SP	Navy Section Patrol vessel
SS	Steam Ship
std	Standard (displacement)
USACOE	United States Army Corps of Engineers
USAF	United States Air Force
USCG	United States Coast Guard (1915-present)
USCGC	United States Coast Guard Cutter
USCSS	United States Coast Survey Ship (1789-1865)
USLHS	United States Lighthouse Service (1789-1939)
USLHT	United States Lighthouse Tender
USN	United States Navy (1794-present)
USPHS	United States Public Health Service
USRC	United States Revenue Cutter
USRCS	United States Revenue Cutter Service (1865-1915)
USRM	United States Revenue Marine (1790-1865)
USS	United States Ship (a vessel of the U.S. Navy)
WAGL	Lighthouse Tender (1942-1943), or Buoy Tender (1943-1965)
WAK	Cargo Ship (U.S. Coast Guard)
WAL	Lightship (1942-1967)
WD	Buoy Boat (1939-1967)
WLB	Seagoing Buoy Tender (1965-present)
WLI	Inland Buoy Tender
WLIC	Construction Tender
WLM	Coastal Buoy Tender (1965-present)
WLR	River Tender (1965-present)
WLV	Lightship (1967-1985)
WWI	World War I
WWII	World War II
YAG	Yard Auxiliary Vessel (U.S. Navy designation)
YNT	Net Tender, Small (U.S. Navy designation)

NOTE: Each state is abbreviated to its appropriate two-letter code assigned by the U.S. Postal Service.

CHAPTER I
The Early Years 1840-1869

From almost the time that the Lighthouse Service had been created in 1789, the remote lighthouses along the coasts needed logistical support. Transporting the keepers and their families as well as supplies such as coal, fresh water and lantern oil, food and mail, often took place via water because support by land routes was often impractical or impossible. As more lighthouses were built and light vessel stations were established in the 1820s, vessels were regularly needed to perform the tasks of supporting these vital aids to navigation. And as the system grew in size and complexity, Lighthouse Inspectors would annually travel to each of the lighthouses to insure that the keepers were properly operating and maintaining the lights for which they were responsible.

The first vessels used for this task were rented or chartered for short periods of time, and provided the necessary logistical support for a specific area. Sometimes, these "hired vessels" were employed to transport materials for the construction of a new lighthouse. In the New York City bay area, the local pilots were contracted to tend the buoys, insuring these aids were on station and properly maintained. In at least two regions, as early as 1824, Revenue Cutters (vessels of the Revenue-Marine, the forerunner to today's Coast Guard) were regularly employed to check on the various lights and transport the Inspector along the coast.

However, since this wasn't the primary duties of those individuals, the reliability and consistency of their work was often lacking. It also proved to be expensive and not the most effective use of resources. This would prompt the start of a fleet of vessels which would be owned and operated by the Lighthouse Service, known as Lighthouse Tenders. The Tenders' mission would be to act as supply ships, bringing provisions to the growing number of lighthouses and lightships in the United States. Coal and lantern oil had to be kept in full store. Repair parts, food, medical supplies, and the payroll was often delivered by the Tenders. Personnel was also rotated regularly, transported by Tender. Aids to navigation, such as buoys and daymarks, had to be placed or repaired, and checked semi-annually.

And until the turn of the century when lightships first became self-propelled, they had to be towed into harbor for regular repairs, then towed back on station by the Tenders. Buoys, also growing in number, needed to be serviced regularly (including establishment, periodic repair or maintenance, and occasional replacement).

By 1840, the Lighthouse Service had 234 lighthouses, 30 lightships, and over 900 lesser aids to navigation (shore beacons and some primitive buoys), all requiring maintenance.

The Tenders would also transport the Lighthouse Inspector (the regional supervisor with oversight and authority over a particular Lighthouse District) to various locations to inspect and insure the proper and efficient operation of the light. The District Inspector made annual visits to every light in his region to insure that the light was operating properly and that the keepers were in compliance with the various regulations and maintaining the light. All this required a standard mode of support.

The first vessel actually commissioned as a Lighthouse Tender was the former sailing schooner Revenue Cutter *Richard Rush*, purchased in 1840. During the next seventeen years, other private vessels would be purchased or chartered as needs arose (sometimes for long term use, while others only for a short time, such as for a specific project, construction of a new light or for a single season's supply run), and used as Lighthouse Tenders either to provide service in a new area or as a replacement for a tender that was beyond repair. In many cases, the original names were retained, while in other cases the names were changed to fit a more nautical theme (although no systematic naming scheme had yet been developed).

No matter the source, location, or usage of any tender during this era, any vessel employed was considered only a tool used for supporting lighthouses, lightships, or other aids to navigation. They were not considered a significant resource worthy of detailed record keeping thus records are minimal. The scant information and data on these early tenders is presented in this chapter.

In 1857, the first Tender was built specifically for the service, the *USLHT* (U.S. Lighthouse Tender) *Shubrick*, which served for thirty years on the West Coast (including time during and after the Civil War with the Revenue Cutter Service and the Navy in Alaska). It was also the first Tender to serve on the Pacific Coast. It proved beyond any arguments the importance of steam powered tenders. However it wouldn't be until after the Civil War that these learned lessons would be able to be applied to newer tenders.

The Lighthouse Board was created in 1852 to "modernize" the Lighthouse Service. The initial thrust was to upgrade and improve lighthouses and ensure the keepers were competent. An emphasis was also made to standardize the various other aids to navigation which the maritime community relied upon so heavily. Unfortunately, improvements to the Lighthouse Service came to a halt during the Civil War. Many vessels were seized and lighthouses damaged or destroyed by the Confederates to keep the enemy from using them for a strategic advantage. Some of the tenders seized were considered too

Tenders *Mistletoe* (in the foreground) and *Iris* (left), and two unidentified lightships, c. 1865.

U.S. Coast Guard

small to be useful for the cause, while others were employed as supply or support vessels. Hundreds of lesser aids to navigation were destroyed or neglected during the conflict.

Once the hostilities were over, the Lighthouse Board resumed lighthouse construction and improvements to the system, as well as reconstruction of those aids (lighthouses, beacons, buoys, and lightships) destroyed by the war. The Board also realized that a dedicated fleet of vessels was necessary to service these lighthouses, lightships, and other aids to navigation. Towards this end, and immediately after the War, the Lighthouse Board acquired six former Navy steam vessels as a nucleus for a tender fleet. The U.S. Navy had a practice, during the Civil War, of naming their smaller steaming vessels purchased from private sources for various plants. Four of these vessels (*Heliotrope*, *Cactus*, *Iris*, and *Geranium*), formerly from the Navy's "flowerpot fleet," retained their names when acquired by the Lighthouse Service and commissioned as Lighthouse Tenders. Thus, a tradition was established that continues today, almost one hundred and forty years later, giving botanical names to tenders, for flowers, trees, and shrubs. And one of these tenders, *USLHT Iris*, was the first propeller driven tender.

These first primitive tenders were basically regular ships with no special designs for the jobs for which they were employed. However, they delivered supplies to lighthouses, towed lightships (all were sail powered only) on and off stations, assisted in the construction of new lights, and maintained lesser aids to navigation. They performed their jobs well and established traditions which are still with the Tender fleets of the 1990s.

RICHARD RUSH, 1840

Name	Builder	Built	Acquired	Commissioned	Disposition
Richard Rush	Webb & Allen	1830		1831 (RCS)	Decom 1848
	New York		30 Mar 1840	1840 (LHS)	Sold 1848

Hull
  Displacement (tons) 112   Wood Hull
  Dimensions 73'6"(lbp)/71'(deck) x 20'2" x 6'8"

Rig
  Topsail schooner

Built as one of the "Morris" class cutters for the Revenue Marine in 1830, it was commissioned in 1831 as *USRC Richard Rush*, and operated out of New York City. Severely damaged by ice in January 1840. Transferred to the LHS on 30 Mar 1840, she became the first Lighthouse Tender of the service, being commissioned as *USLHT Richard Rush* (original name retained). Served until 1848, operating primarily in the New York harbor and vicinity, maintaining local aids to navigation.

ACTIVE, 1843

A private schooner acquired in 1843 and served until 1848.

                                                NFR

SUNBEAM, 1852

Name	Builder	Built	Commissioned	Disposition
Sunbeam		1852?	Summer 1852	Decom
		Sold 1870		

Hull
  Displacement (tons) 100   Wood Hull
  Dimensions unknown

Rig
  Schooner

Another private schooner, acquired by the LHS and commissioned as a Lighthouse Tender, it assumed the responsibilities of the previous *USLHT Richard Rush*.
    It served in the region of Long Island Sound and New York Harbor (later to be known as the Third LHD), primarily tending buoys and small shore lights. Laid up in 1869 and sold at auction in early 1870.

FIREFLY, 1852

Name	Builder	Built	Purchased	Commissioned	Disposition
Firefly		NA	1852	1852	Seized 1861

Hull
  Displacement (tons) 85   Wood Hull
  Dimensions 75' x 24' (4'5" draft)

Rig
  Schooner

The private schooner *Firefly* was acquired by the LHE in 1852, and commissioned as *USLHT Firefly* (private name retained), then assigned to the Sixth LHD. Renamed *USLHT Jasper* in 1857. In Sep 1857, ran aground at Shackley Banks, but only slightly damaged. While under repairs in the building ways at Wilmington, NC, in 1861, was seized by the Confederates in North Carolina, but found to be of little use.

WAVE, 1853

Name	Builder	Built	Purchased	Commissioned	Disposition
Wave		1853	1853	1853	Condemned May 1861
	Northport, NY				Sold 1861

Hull
  Displacement (tons)   77   Wood Hull
  Dimensions   65' x 21' x 6'3" (6' draft)

Rig
  Schooner

Built in 1853. Condemned in May 1861, it was sold almost immediately. It was replaced in 1861 by *USLHT Delaware*, which then assumed the name of *USLHT Wave*.

SPRAY, 1853

Name	Builder	Built	Purchased	Commissioned	Disposition
Spray		NA	1853	1853	Condemned 1878
					Sold 15 Mar 1879

Hull
  Displacement (tons)   48   Wood Hull
  Dimensions   76' x 21' x 6'

Rig
  Schooner

Purchased by the LHE in 1853, it served as *USLHT Spray* in the Fourth LHD. Rebuilt at Wilmington, NC, in Jun 1868 for $8,800. In Jan 1874 it was laid up, then sent to the Fifth LHD in Jan 1876. It was then declared unseaworthy in 1876, it was sent to the Seventh LHD in Apr 1876. Finally condemned in Spring of 1878, it was sold on 15 Mar 1879 for $833.

LOOKOUT, 1853

Name	Builder	Built	Purchased	Commissioned	Disposition
Lookout	Doyle & Irwin	1853	1853	1853	
	Elizabeth City, VA				Sold 1858

Cost
  $2,200 (purchase price) + $1,350 (outfitting)

Hull
  Dimensions   unknown   Wood Hull

Rig
  Schooner

A schooner built in 1853 and purchased that same year. Commissioned as *USLHT Lookout*, it was assigned to the Fifth LHD. Sold in 1858.

NFR

FRANKLIN PIERCE, 1853

Name	Builder	Built	Purchased	Commissioned	Disposition
Franklin Pierce		NA	1853	1853	Unsea Dec 1865
					Sold Mar 1866

Cost
  $3,200 (purchase price) + $1,000 (coppering of hull)

Hull
  Displacement (tons) 80   Wood Hull, copper sheathed
  Dimensions   unknown, (5-½' draft)

Rig
  Schooner

The private schooner *Zendrico* was purchased by the LHS at Baltimore in Feb 1853, then the hull was coppered. Commissioned as *USLHT Franklin Pierce*, it was intended for the Seventh LHD but sent to the First LHD instead due to needs there. Declared unseaworthy in Dec 1865 and sold in 1866 at Portland, ME, for $1,800. While in private trade, struck rocks near Green Islands in Maine and sank in May 1891.

WILLIAM R. KING, 1853

Name	Builder	Built	Purchased	Commissioned	Disposition
William R. King		1849	Jun 1853	1853	Seized Mar 1861
				1862	Sold 1863

Cost
  $3,500 (purchase price) + $1,500 (outfitting costs)

Hull
  Displacement (tons) 81   Wood Hull
  Dimensions   unknown, (4' draft)

Rig
  Center board schooner

The private schooner *The Knight* was built in 1849. Purchased in Baltimore in Jun 1853 and refitted by Fardy & Auld of Baltimore for $1,500. It was then commissioned as *USLHT William R. King* and assigned to the Eighth LHD. It was reassigned to the Ninth LHD in Jul 1858. Seized by the Confederates in Mar 1861, it was refitted in Jul 1861 and served in Louisiana as the *CSS William R. King*. Recaptured by the USN in 1862 and returned to duty in the LHS in 1862. Disposed of in 1863.

  William R. D. King was a Congressman from North Carolina (1811-1816) and Senator from Alabama (1819-1844 and 1848-1852). Elected to serve as Vice-President in 1853, he was seriously ill at the time and died before he could assume office.

HEROINE, 1853

Name	Builder	Built	Purchased	Commissioned	Disposition
Heroine		NA	Jun 1853	1853	Trans USA Feb 1855

Cost
  $1,500 (purchase price) + $1,600 (outfitting costs)

Hull
  Displacement (tons) unknown
  Dimensions   unknown, (4-½' draft)

Rig
  Schooner

A 70-ton schooner with a draft of 4-½', purchased from the U.S. Army Engineers Department in Jun 1853 for $1,500. An additional expense of $1,600 was necessary to outfit the vessel as a Lighthouse Tender. Commissioned as *USLHT Heroine* (Army name retained), it was assigned to the Eighth LHD. In Dec 1853, it was reassigned to the Seventh LHD and exchanged with the *USLHT William R. King*. In Feb 1855, it was transferred back to the U.S. Army.

ELIZA, 1853

Name	Builder	Built	Chartered	Purchased	Commissioned	Disposition
Eliza		NA	1851	Nov 1853	1853	Lost 1857

Cost
  $6,300

Hull
  Dimensions   140'   Wood Hull, copper sheathed

Rig
  Schooner

Built as the private schooner *Eliza*. Chartered in 1851 for $675 a month, and used as a Supply Tender. Ran aground on a reef in Florida in Jan 1853, but refloated. Purchased by the LHE in Nov 1853 and commissioned as *USLHT Eliza* (original name retained). Ran aground on Long Island in Mar 1857, and lost.

ELIZABETH, 1854

Name	Builder	Built	Purchased	Commissioned	Disposition
Elizabeth		NA	1854	1854	Sold 1855

Hull
  Displacement (tons)   45   Wood Hull
  Dimensions   unknown

Rig
  Schooner

A small schooner purchased in 1854 and commissioned as *USLHT Elizabeth* (original name retained) and used in the Second LHD through 1855.
                    NFR

FAIRY, 1854

Name	Builder	Built	Purchased	Commissioned	Disposition
Fairy		NA	May 1854	May 1854	Lost Sep 1854

Cost
  $4,500

Hull
  Displacement (tons)   30   Wood Hull
  Dimensions   unknown, (4-½' draft)

Rig
  Schooner

The small private schooner *Fairy* was purchased by the LHE at New Orleans in May 1854 and served as *USLHT Fairy* (original name retained) in the Eighth LHD. Ran aground at Pass Carvallo and lost in a violent gale in Sep 1854. The *USLHT Essayons* was purchased as a replacement.

PHAROS, 1854

Name	Builder	Built	Purchased	Commissioned	Disposition
Pharos	Port Jefferson, NY	NA	30 Apr 1854	May 1854	Decom 1907 Sold 18 Aug 1908

Cost
  $6,630 (purchase price)

Hull
  Displacement (tons)   213 (max) / 168 (std)   Wood Hull
  Dimensions   100'(loa) / 96'(lbp) x 24' x 7'6" (6'6" draft)

Rig
  Two masted 'lugger' schooner

Complement
  2 officers, 9 men (1907)

Built as the private schooner *H.H. Talman*, it was purchased on 30 Apr 1854 as *USLHT Pharos* and used as a Supply Tender, serving out of the Second LHD, and delivering supplies to lights along the entire Atlantic coast. Relieved by the new *USLHT Fern* in 1873, and sent to the Eighth LHD where it was laid up at Mobile, AL, and ordered sold in 1874. Instead, it was rebuilt in 1877 and assigned to the Fifth LHD. In 1890, it was reassigned to the Sixth LHD. Declared unseaworthy in 1907, it was condemned and sold for $3,601 in 1908. This was the last sailing Lighthouse Tender to be in service.

Pharos is a small peninsula at Alexandria, Egypt, and the site of a large lighthouse of ancient times, one of the seven wonders of the ancient world. The study of lighthouses is also known as Pharology.

USLHT Pharos, the last sailing lighthouse tender to serve, c. 1854.

National Archives

GEORGE STEERS, 1854

Name	Builder	Built	Purchased	Commissioned	Disposition
George Steers	Steers	NA	Jun 1854	Jun 1854	Laid up Feb 1861 Sold 1861

Cost
  $4,000

Hull
  Displacement (tons)   61   Wood Hull
  Dimensions   63' x 18' x 6' (8' draft)

Rig
  Schooner

Originally the pilot boat *George Steers*, it was purchased in Jun 1854 and commissioned as *USLHT George Steers* (original name retained). While assigned to the Second LHD for all of its career, it briefly served in the Seventh LHD in early 1857. Laid up at Brooklyn, NY, in Feb 1861 and sold later that same year.

GOVERNOR AIKEN, 1855

Name	Builder	Built	Purchase	Commissioned	Disposition
Governor Aiken		NA	1855	1855	Condemned 09 Aug 1858 Sold Sep 1858

Hull
  Displacement   unknown   Wood Hull
  Dimensions   unknown

Rig
  Schooner

A schooner purchased in 1855 and commissioned as *USLHT Governor Aiken*, and serving in the Sixth LHD at Charleston, SC. It was condemned on 09 Aug 1858, and the hull sold in Sep 1858 for $321.60, and rigging and sails sold for $375.88. The now civilian boat was captured by the Confederates at Charleston, SC, at the start of the Civil War on 20 Dec 1860, but found to be of little value and was discarded.

William Aiken was the Governor of South Carolina (1844-1846), and an influential member of Congress (1851-1857).

USLHT Governor Aiken (1855-1861) is a different vessel than the Revenue Cutter *William Aiken* (1855-1861), although both are named for the same person, served at the approximate same time, and both were seized by the Confederates at the start of the Civil War.

NORTH WIND, 1855

Name	Builder	Built	Purchased	Commissioned	Disposition
North Wind		NA	Feb 1855	1855	Seized Apr 1861

Cost
  $3,600

Hull
  Displacement (tons)   86   Oak Hull
  Dimensions   unknown, (5' draft)

Rig
  Schooner

Originally a small private schooner *North Wind*. Purchased in Feb 1855 as *USLHT North Wind* (private name retained), and used in the Fifth LHD. Seized by the Confederates in Virginia in Apr 1861.

BOWEN, 1855

Name	Builder	Built	Purchased	Commissioned	Disposition
Bowen	Baltimore, MD	1847	Feb 1855	Feb 1855	Sunk Aug 1872

Cost
  $6,000 (purchase price)

Hull
  Displacement (tons)   75 (full), 30 (light)   Wood Hull
  Dimensions   77' x 21'6" x 7'1" (5' draft)

Rig
  Schooner

The private schooner *G.L. Bowen* was built in 1847. Purchased in Feb 1855 at Key West and commissioned as *USLHT Bowen*, it was assigned to the Seventh LHD as an Engineering Tender. It was renamed *USLHT Florida* on 12 Mar 1855. In Jun 1872, it was reassigned to the Second LHD. It suddenly capsized and sunk in Ipswich Bay, east of Gloucester, MA, in Aug 1872, with no lives lost.

ALERT, 1855

Name	Builder	Built	Purchased	Commissioned	Disposition
Alert		NA	Mar 1855	May 1855	Seized 18 Jan 1861

Hull
  Displacement (tons)   95   Oak Hull, copper sheathed
  Dimensions   unknown, (7' draft)

Rig
  Center board schooner

The private schooner *Lookout*, purchased in Mar 1855 and commissioned as *USLHT Alert*, for use in the Eighth LHD. Seized by the Confederates at Mobile, AL, on 18 Jan 1861. Subsequently served in the Confederate Navy as *CSS Alert*, operating out of Mobile, from 1861 until early 1862, with a crew of 31 and armed with a 32-pounder gun. Recaptured by the *USS Roanoake* in Oct 1862, but found to be of no use.
  This is not the same vessel as the Revenue Cutter *Alert*, which served during the same time period.

ESSAYONS, 1855

Name	Builder	Built	Purchased	Commissioned	Disposition
Essayons		NA	1855	1855	Condemned Oct 1859
					Sold 01 Dec 1859

Hull
  Displacement (tons)   40   Wood Hull
  Dimensions   42' x 14'6"

Rig
  Schooner

A small schooner purchased by the LHE in Feb (or May) of 1855, to replace *USLHT Fairy* in the Ninth LHD. Declared unseaworthy in Oct 1859 and sold at auction on 01 Dec 1859 for $308.70.

DELAWARE, 1856

Name	Builder	Built	Purchased	Commissioned	Disposition
Delaware		NA	1856	1856	Unsea 30 Jun 1879
					Sold 15 Oct 1879

Hull
  Displacement (tons)   138   Wood Hull
  Dimensions   unknown

Rig
  Schooner

A schooner, purchased in 1856 as USLHT *Delaware*. Used as an Engineering Tender in the Fourth LHD to repair the Brandywine Shoals Light. Also used in the Fifth and Seventh LHDs. In Jun 1858, it was repaired at a cost of $1,462.73, then sent to Key West. Reassigned to the Fifth LHD in Sep 1860. It was moved again in May 1861 to the Second LHD to replace the old USLHT *Wave*. On 24 May 1861, having replaced that old tender, USLHT *Delaware*'s name was changed to USLHT *Wave*. It then served the First and Second LHDs until 1879, when it was then found unseaworthy and sold for $159.

LENOX, 1856

Name	Builder	Built	Purchased	Commissioned	Disposition
Lenox		1850	NA	1856	Sold Jan 1857

Cost
  $6,250

Hull
  Displacement (tons)   unknown   Wood Hull
  Dimensions   unknown

Rig
  Schooner

A 710-ton schooner, built in 1850. Employed in the Fourth LHD in 1856 for the repair of Brandywine Light. Also used in the Fifth and Seventh LHDs. Sold at Beaufort in Jan 1857.
It possibly was also chartered and served intermittently from 1859 through 1865.

CHALLENGE, 1856

Name	Builder	Built	Purchased	Commissioned	Disposition
Challenge		NA	May 1856	1856	Laid up May 1862
					Sold 1862

Cost
  $6,250

Hull
  Displacement (tons)   120   Wood Hull
  Dimensions   unknown

Rig
  Schooner

Originally built as the small private schooner *Challenge*, and purchased in May 1856 for use as a Lighthouse Tender. Commissioned as USLHT *Challenge* (original name retained), and assigned to the Tenth LHD in the Great Lakes as a Supply Tender. This was the first Lighthouse Tender in the Great Lakes. Renamed as USLHT *Lamplighter* on 29 Apr 1857. On 11 Sep 1857, it was wrecked off Isle Royale. It was towed to Detroit on 13 Nov 1857 and repaired at a cost of about $1,000. In Sep 1859, it ran aground again, this time on a reef near Mackinaw Straits, with minimal damage. In Apr 1862, with wear and tear showing, it was estimated it would cost $4,000 to rebuild and repair the aging tender. Instead, it was recommended in May 1862 that it be disposed of, and was laid up, replaced by chartered vessel USLHT *Dream*. It was sold in 1862, serving as a merchant ship until 1874.

ACTIVE, 1856

Name	Builder	Built	Purchased	Commissioned	Disposition
Active		NA		11 Sep 1856	Sold 30 Jun 1866

Cost
  NA

Hull
  Displacement   unknown
  Dimensions   unknown

Rig
  Schooner

A 50-ton schooner Tender, named *USLHT Active*. Place in service on 11 Sep 1856, it was assigned to the Second LHD as an Inspection Tender. In Feb 1865, it was involved in a collision with *USLHT Ranger*, but was repaired. In 1866, due to age, major repairs were recommended but not approved. Instead, it was sold on 30 Jun 1866 for $2,251.06 at New Bedford.

NFR

VIGILANT, 1856

Name	Builder	Built	Purchased	Commissioned	Disposition
Vigilant		1856	20 Nov 1856	1856	Wrecked 07 Feb 1866
					Sold Jun 1866

Cost
  $4,400 (purchase price) + $800 (alterations)

Hull
  Displacement (tons)   86   Wood Hull
  Dimensions   70'6" x 21'4" x 6'8" (8' draft, loaded)

Rig
  Schooner

The private schooner *Mirror*, built in 1856. It was purchased that same year on 20 Nov, and commissioned as *USLHT Vigilant*. It was used in the First and Seventh LHDs. Wrecked near Key West, FL, on Feb 1866, the hull was sold in Jun 1866.

SKYLARK, 1856

Name	Builder	Built	Purchased	Commissioned	Disposition
Skylark		1854	Dec 1856	Dec 1856	Sold 16 Oct 1867

Cost
  $6,600

Hull
  Displacement (tons)   146   Wood Hull
  Dimensions   unknown

Rig
  Schooner

The private schooner *Skylark* was built in 1854, and purchased in Dec 1856 for use as the *LHT Skylark* (original name retained). It was assigned to the Tenth LHD in the Great Lakes. Renamed *USLHT Watchful* in 29 Apr 1857. Sold at auction on 16 Oct 1867 for $3,050. It was replaced by *USLHT Haze*.

USLHT Minot alongside Minot's Ledge Light under construction, 1857. *U.S. Coast Guard*

MINOT, 1857

Name	Builder	Built	Purchased	Commissioned	Disposition
Minot		NA	NA	1857	Decom 30 Nov 1860

Hull
    Displacement (tons)   unknown
    Dimensions   unknown

Rig
    Schooner

A small 60-ton schooner, employed at the construction of the Minots Ledge Lighthouse outside Boston Harbor until Sep 1858, then transferred to the Fifth LHD, serving until 30 Nov 1860.

NFR

RANGER, 1857

Name	Builder	Built	Purchased	Commissioned	Disposition
Ranger		NA	1857	1857	Decom Sold 01 Nov 1865

Hull
    Displacement (tons)   77   Wood Hull
    Dimensions   unknown

Rig
    Schooner

Purchased in 1857, commissioned as *USLHT Ranger* and assigned to the Second LHD. In Feb 1865, involved in a collision with *USLHT Active*. Sold at New Bedford for $4,375.85 on 01 Nov 1865.

USLHT Van Santvoort was renamed *USLHT Coeur de Leon* in 1860. In this 1863 photo, during the Civil War, *USS Coeur de Leon* was on loan to the Navy from the Lighthouse Board.

VAN SANTVOORT, 1857

Name	Builder	Built	Purchased	Commissioned	Disposition
Van Santvoort		1853	1857	1857	Decom 1866
	Coxsackie, NY				Sold 16 Nov 1866

Cost
  unknown

Hull
  Displacement (tons)   110 (full) / 60 (std)   Wood Hull
  Dimensions   100' x 20'6" x 4'10" (4'6" draft, light)

Machinery
  Main Engine   One Hight Pressure Steam Donkey
  Main Boiler   Single   Coal fired
  Propulsion   Side paddle wheels

The commercial steamer *Alfred Van Santvoort* (named for its owner, who owned many ships in the New York area) was built in 1853. Acquired in 1857 and placed in service in the Second LHD as *USLHT Van Santvoort*. In Sep 1858, it changed places with the *USLHT Minot*. Name changed to *USLHT Coeur de Leon* in Sep 1860. In Nov 1860, it was used for the construction of Minots Ledge Lighthouse. Loaned to the USN in Apr 1861 and commissioned on 02 Oct 1861 as *USS Coeur de Lion*, and used as a small gunboat. Repaired by the Navy in Jul 1862 for a cost of $2,211.34. It served as a tug boat in the Chesapeake Bay with the Potomac & James River Squadrons for the duration of the Civil War, enforcing blockades. It was disabled on 18 Apr 1865 while involved with naval operations on the Nansemond River. It was ordered by the Navy to be repaired on 31 May 1865, but if not completed on time, it was to be returned to the LHS as is. Decommissioned from the Navy on 02 Jun 1865 and returned to the LHS the next day. It was sent to Philadelphia in Feb 1866 and found to be worthless as a tender. Its sale was authorized on 22 Sep 1866 and was sold at Wilmington, DE, in Nov 1866 for $1,800. It became the merchant ship *Alice*, operating until 1873.

USLHT Shubrick after its rebuild in the late 1860s. The most obvious change is the pilot house which was raised above the main deck. *Columbia River Maritime Museum*

SHUBRICK, 1857

Name	Builder	Contracted	Launched	Commissioned	Disposition
Shubrick	Navy Yard Philadelphia, PA	18 Aug 1856	08 Aug 1857	25 Nov 1857 (LHS) 15 Oct 1861 (RCS)	Decom Jan 1886 Sold 20 Mar 1886

Cost
  $60,000

Hull
  Displacement (tons)   305   Wood Hull
  Dimensions   140'8" x 22'6" x 11' (draft 9')

Machinery
  Main Engine   Single expansion steeple steam   BHP 284
  Main Boilers   Single   Coal fired
  Propulsion   Side paddle wheels (19' in diam.)

Armament
  2 Dahlgren guns
  1 24-pounder

USLHT Shubrick was the first steam powered Lighthouse Tender, and the first Tender on the Pacific Coast. Authorized for construction on 18 Aug 1856 for $60,000, and completed on 25 Nov 1857. This was the only Lighthouse Tender built with armament, to protect the light keepers and citizens from Indian attacks. She was armed with 2 Dahlgren guns and one 24-pounder on the foc's'le. After completion, *USLHT Shubrick* sailed "round the Horn" and arrived in San Francisco on 27 May 1858, ready for duty.

Transferred to the RCS on 23 Aug 1861 for duty in Alaska during the Civil War, serving as *USRC Shubrick* (LHS name retained). From 15 Feb until 15 May 1865, it served with the USN as *USS Shubrick*. Returned to the LHS on 24 Dec 1866 and recommissioned in Jan 1867. It served exclusively on the west coast. Ran aground near Point Arena, CA, in dense fog on 08 Sep 1867, then rebuilt at San Francisco Navy Yard at a cost of $162,399.12 and placed back in service in 1869.

With the arrival of the new *USLHT Manzanita* to San Francisco in Jan 1880, *USLHT Shubrick* was reassigned to the Thirteenth LHD. She was placed out of service in Dec 1885 and stored at the Mare Island Navy Yard. Decommissioned in Jan 1886 due to old age and replaced by *USLHT Madrono*. Sold for $3,200 at Astoria, OR, two months later, she was stripped and burned for the copper in her hull in San Francisco Bay.

Admiral William B. Shubrick was a prominent officer in the USN. He was the head of the special congressional board that investigated the LHS and created the LHB, and was appointed the first chairman of the newly formed LHB (the governing body for the LHS), serving in that position from 1852 until 1871.

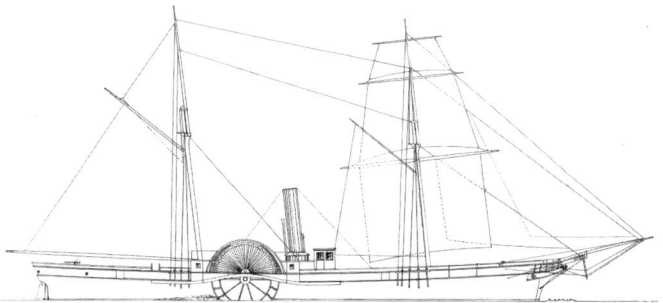

Plan for *USLHT Shubrick*, 1857. The first vessel specifically built for the LHS and the first steam tender. *National Archives*

HOWELL COBB, 1857

Name	Builder	Built	Commissioned	Disposition
Howell Cobb	New York, NY	1857	05 Sep 1857	Seized 1861

Cost
  $8,831.47 (construction)
  $2,906.59 (outfitting)

Hull
  Displacement (tons)   90   Wood Hull
  Dimensions   unknown

Rig
  Schooner

Built for the LHS as *USLHT Howell Cobb* and used as a Supply Tender. Although it operated out of New Bedford, it was supplying lights along the entire Atlantic coast. In Jul 1857, it was transferred to the Sixth LHD at Charleston. Ran aground in the Bahamas on 13 Dec 1857, it was initially considered to be a total loss, but was repaired. Seized by the Confederates in South Carolina in 1861.
   Although commissioned before *USLHT Shubrick*, this was the second Tender built for the LHS (its contract and construction started after work on *Shubrick* had already begun).
   Mr. Howell Cobb was the Secretary of the Treasury (1857-1860), under which the LHE was part.
Concurrently, the USRM (forerunner of today's USCG) also had a 63-foot schooner named *USRC Howell Cobb*, which ran aground and sank in Dec 1861.

HELEN, 1858

Name	Builder	Built	Purchased	Commissioned	Disposition
Helen		NA	Apr 1858	1858	Seized Jan 1861
					Sunk 02 Apr 1863

Cost
  $5,250

Hull
  Displacement (tons)   145   Wood Hull
  Dimensions   unknown

Rig
  Schooner/Sloop

A private schooner purchased at New York City in Apr 1858 and commissioned as *USLHT Helen* (original name retained), and used as a supply vessel for six months. It was then fitted out and used as a Tender and assigned to the Sixth LHD. Seized by the Confederates in South Carolina in Jan 1861. As the *CSS Helen*, it served as a supply ship along the Florida coast. Captured by a boat from *USS Sagamore*, it was burned and sunk near Bayport, Cedar Keys, FL, on 02 Apr 1863.

BUCHANAN, 1858

Name	Builder	Built	Purchased	Commissioned	Disposition
Buchanan		NA	May 1858	1858	Seized 18 Apr 1861

Hull
  Displacement   ¾ ton   Wood Hull
  Dimensions   unknown

Rig
  Schooner

A small schooner, purchased in May 1858 and commissioned as *USLHT Buchanan* (named for then U.S. president). It was assigned to the Fifth LHD. While on an Inspection Patrol with the Inspector of the Fifth LHD on board, the ship was boarded and seized by Confederate troops on the James River in Virginia on 18 Apr 1861, it was then taken to Richmond. The Inspector and the tender crew were released, but the vessel was retained by the local authorities sympathetic to the Southern cause.

NFR

GRANITE, 1860

Name	Builder	Built	Purchased	Commissioned	Disposition
Granite		NA	1860	USLHS 1860	Decom USN 29 Jun 1865
				USN 1862	Sold by LHS Dec 1866

Hull
  Displacement (tons)   75   Wood Hull
  Dimensions   unknown

Rig
  Sloop rigged schooner

The private schooner *Granite* was purchased in 1860 as *USLHT Granite* (original name retained). It was first used in the construction of Minots Ledge Lighthouse. Transferred to the Navy on 19 Jan 1862 for the duration of the Civil War. As the *USS Granite*, it served with distinction, operating on the sounds of North Carolina until decommissioned by the Navy on 29 Jun 1865. It was returned to the LHS on 29 Jun 1865 and was sold at Philadelphia in Dec 1866 for $2,092.99.

CHASE, 1861

Name	Builder	Built	Purchased	Commissioned	Disposition
Chase		NA	1861	Apr 1861	Unsea. Jun 1867
					Sold May 1868

Hull
  Displacement (tons)   57   Wood Hull
  Dimensions   unknown

Rig
  Schooner

A small private schooner, acquired by the LHS in 1861 as *USLHT Chase*, and used in the Fifth LHD. In May 1866, it was transferred to the Sixth LHD. Declared unseaworthy in 1867. It was sold at Charleston on May 1868 for $1,253.85.

MARTHA, 1862

Name	Builder	Built	Purchased	Commissioned	Disposition
Martha		NA	1862	1862	Captured 16 Jul 1864

Hull
  Displacement (tons)   unknown
  Dimensions   unknown

Rig
  Schooner

A small, light draft, 40-ton schooner, acquired from the War Department (Army war prize?) sometime in 1862. Used in Jan 1863 for the reconstruction of the Head of Passes Light in Louisiana. As the *USLHT Martha*, it served on the lower Mississippi River region below New Orleans tending buoys and shore lights. While en route to Pensacola, FL, it was captured and burned in Chandeleur Sound by the Confederates on 16 Jul 1864. The crew was taken as prisoners to Mobile where the Master and his son escaped.

DUPONT, 1863

Name	Builder	Built	Captured	Commissioned	Disposition
DuPont		NA	13 May 1862	Jan 1863	Decom 1869
					Sold 04 Aug 1870

Cost
  $1,200 (to repair and fit out)

Hull
  Dimensions   unknown   Wood Hull

Rig
  Schooner

The rebel schooner *Anna Deane* (sometimes referred to as *Annie Dean*) was captured by Admiral Dupont, USN in 13 May 1862, while attempting to run supplies to the Confederates. The war prize was then given to the LHS in Jan 1863 and repaired for $1,200. It was commissioned as *USLHT DuPont* (named for its captor), and served in the Sixth LHD. It was sold at New Orleans on 04 Aug 1870 for $1,734, with the furniture sold separately for $42.
  Samuel F. DuPont, while a captain in the USN, served as a member of the LHB (1852-1857). Later, Adm. Dupont served with great distinction during the Civil War.

BELLE, 1863

Name	Builder	Built	Purchased	Commissioned	Disposition
Belle		1861	1863	1863	Decom 10 Jul 1874
	St. Joseph, MI				Sold May 1875

Hull
  Displacement (tons)   115   Oak Hull
  Dimensions   88' x 21'3" x 6'10" (6' draft)

Rig
  Schooner

Built as a private vessel *Belle Stevens* in 1861, it was purchased in 1863 and commissioned as *USLHT Belle*. From 1869 to 1872, in addition to its regular duties, it also transported materials for the construction of Spectacle Reef Light. While serving in the Eleventh LHD in the Great Lakes as an Engineering Tender, it ran aground and was badly damaged on 10 Nov 1873. Ordered sold on 10 Jul 1874, the sale was completed in May 1875 for $470, and it was replaced by *USLHT Dahlia*. This was the last sailing tender operated on the Great Lakes.

BIBB, 1864

Name	Builder	Launched	Commissioned	Disposition
Bibb	Freeman, Knap & Totten	10 Apr 1845	1846 (RCS)	Decom 19 Sep 1877
	Pittsburgh, PA		20 Jul 1864 (LHS)	Sold 19 Apr 1878

Cost
  $ 50,000 (construction bid for initial construction)
  $145,604.13 (completed, including alteration)

Hull
  Displacement (tons)   409 (full) / 360 (std)   Wood Hull
  Dimensions   160'(loa)/150'(lwl)/143'(lbp) x 23' x 10'

Machinery
  Main Engines   2 high pressure side-lever steam
  Main Boilers   Coal fired
  Propulsion   Hunter's horizontal side wheel (as designed)
                  Conventional side wheel (as modified)

Originally authorized in 1843 for the U.S. Revenue-Marine as one of its first iron hulled steam driven cutters, with the proposed name of *USRC Tyler*. However, it proved unsuccessful due to its engineering design with horizontal paddle wheels (also called Hunter's Wheels). Commissioned in 1846 as *USRC George M. Bibb*, and much modified and converted to more conventional side paddle wheels in Cincinnati. It was transferred to the Coast Survey on 09 Jan 1847. It was totally rebuilt, including a new wooden hull (but using some of the original machinery) and later in 1853, became the first steam powered oceanographic vessel in the United States. At the start of the Civil War, *USCSS Bibb* was briefly loaned to the RCS from 31 May to 26 Aug 1861. Loaned to the Federal LHE in Jul 1864 and commissioned as *USLHT Bibb*, it served in the Sixth LHD for six months. Returned to the Coast Survey, it served until 1879.

USS Putnam and *USS Satelite* with the Navy during the Civil War. Lithograph from *Harper's Weekly*, July-December 1861. *U.S. Naval Historical Center*

GENERAL PUTNAM, 1865

Name	Builder	Built	Purchased	Commissioned	Disposition
General Putnam		1857	24 Jul 1861 (USN)	Sep 1861 (USN)	Decom 28 Sep 1891
	Brooklyn, NY		02 Jun 1865 (LHS)	1865 (LHS)	Sold 05 Jul 1893

Cost
  $8,000 (purchase price)
  $9,450 (alterations and refit)

Hull
  Displacement (tons)   Wood Hull
    [1865]:   149 (full), 126 (mean)
    [1889]:   220 (full)
  Dimensions
    [1865]:   120'0"(loa) / 103'6"(lwl) x 22' x 8'0" (5'6" draft)
    [1889]:   135'3"(loa)

Machinery
  Main Engines   Single acting steam   BHP 176
  Main Boilers   Coal fired
  Propulsion   Side paddle wheels

The private steam tug *William G. Putnam* was built in 1857. Purchased by the USN in New York City on 24 Jul 1861 for $14,000 and commissioned as *USS General Putnam* (renamed for Revolutionary War hero and patriot Israel Putnam). *USS Putnam* (as it was also known) served with the Navy along the coasts of North Carolina and Virginia, an had its boiler replaced in 1863.

Decommissioned by the Navy on 02 Jun 1865, it was sold at auction to the LHS on the same day and commissioned as *USLHT General Putnam* (Navy name retained), then assigned to the Third LHD. Rammed by the *SS Major Reybold* and sunk in a collision in Nov 1867 shortly after being assigned to the Second LHD. At this time, the *Martha Washington* was chartered for a year to cover the duties of the disabled *USLHT General Putnam*. Raised in Jul 1868 and repaired at a cost of $4,738 at Wilmington, DE, it was reassigned to the Third LHD.

The tender's name was shortened to *USLHT Putnam* in Sep 1869. Rebuilt and lengthened from 120 feet to 135 feet (loa) in 1877. In Jun 1883, it was transferred back to the Second LHD. Overhauled at New York in Aug 1880, it was totally rebuilt again in 1889 at a cost of $18,500. In Mar 1891, it was reassigned to the Seventh LHD at Key West. Placed out of service in 1891 and laid up, it was sold in 1893 for $1,825. It became the merchant ship *SS Putnam* operating until 1896.

HELIOTROPE, 1865

Name	Builder	Built	Purchased	Commissioned	Disposition
Heliotrope		1863	16 Dec 1863 (USN)	24 Apr 1864 (USN)	Decom 01 Sep 1881
	Hunters Point, NY		17 Jun 1865 (LHS)	1865 (LHS)	Sold 10 Nov 1881

Cost
   $6,000

Hull
   Displacement (tons) 239 (max) / 218 (std)   Wood Hull
   Dimensions   134' x 24'6" x 6'8" (5'0" draft)

Machinery
   Main Engine   One inclined beam steam
   Main Boilers   Coal fired
   Propulsion   Side paddle wheels

Originally built as the private steamer *Maggie Baker* in 1863, it was purchased by the Navy on 16 Dec 1863 for $38,000 and commmissioned on 24 Apr 1864 at New York City as *USS Heliotrope* for use as a tug and ordinance boat in the upper Chesapeake Bay. Decommissioned from the Navy on 12 Jan 1865, it was transferred to the LHS on 17 Jun 1865 at Washington, DC, and commissioned as *USLHT Heliotrope* (Navy name retained), and assigned to the Fifth LHD as an Inspection Tender. Declared unfit in 1879, it was decommissioned and sold at auction for $1,400 on 10 Nov 1881, replaced by *USLHT Holly*. The former *Heliotrope* later became the merchant barge *John Bolgiano*, operating through 1893.

CACTUS, 1865

Name	Builder	Built	Purchased	Commissioned	Disposition
Cactus		1863	07 Dec 1863 (USN)	04 May 1864 (USN)	Decom 31 Jan 1909
	Brooklyn, NY		20 Jun 1865 (LHS)	1865 (LHS)	Sold Jul 1909

Cost
   $10,000

Hull
   Displacement (tons) 242 (max) / 200 (full) / 176 (std)   Wood Hull, Copper Sheathed
   Dimensions   140'7" (loa) / 129' (lwl) x 22'6" x 8'4" (7'6" draft full, 5' light)

Machinery
   Main Engine   One low pressure steam engine   IHP 160   BHP 200
   Main Boilers   Coal fired
   Propulsion   Side paddle wheels

Complement
   4 officers, 11 men (1907)

Built as the private steamer *Polar Star* in 1863, it was acquired by the USN at Brooklyn Navy Yard on 07 Dec 1863 for $38,000. It was commissioned on 04 May 1864 as *USS Cactus*, and used as a supply ship. After the Civil War, it was decommissioned by the Navy on 08 Jun 1865 and purchased by the LHS on 20 Jun 1865 and commissioned as *USLHT Cactus* (Navy name retained), serving in the Second LHD as a Supply and Inspection Tender. It received a new boiler in 1867. Declared unfit in 1869, it was replaced by the new *USLHT Verbena*. But was totally rebuilt in 1870 by James Dean of New York for $20,000 and assigned to the Third LHD. In May 1882, *USLHT Cactus* underwent major repairs at the cost of $17,534.15. It was rebuilt again in Jan 1887 for $19,150. In Spring of 1893, it received a new boiler. Condemned and decommissioned in 1909, replaced by the new *USLHT Orchid*. The old tender put up for sale, with a bid of $315 rejected by the government on 16 Jun 1909. Rebid for $1,025, it was finally sold in Jul 1909, evenutally becoming the merchant ship *Prospect*, operating until 1921.

USLHT Cactus.   Mariners' Museum

USLHT Iris, c. 1865. *Mariners' Museum*

IRIS, 1865

Name	Builder	Built	Purchased	Commissioned	Disposition
Iris		1863	16 Oct 1863 (USN)	Nov 1863 (USN)	Decom 1892
	Brooklyn, NY		18 Oct 1865 (LHS)	1865 (LHS)	Sold 15 Dec 1892

Cost
    $13,500 (purchase price)

Hull
    Displacement (tons)   281 (full) / 159 (std)   Wood Hull
    Dimensions
      [1865]:   87' (loa) / 85' (lbp) x 23'2" x 11'2" (9'6" draft, loaded)
      [1871]:   115' (loa)

Machinery
    Main Engine   Overhead LP condensing independent slide valve   BHP 70
    Main Boiler   Single; Flue Water Leg   Coal fired
    Propulsion   Single propeller

Built in 1863 as the small private steaming tug *Willet Rowe*, it was acquired by the USN on 16 Oct 1863 for $32,500. The cost to alter it for Navy service was $5,605, and it was commissioned in Nov 1863 as *USS Iris* and used as an armed tug at Charleston, SC. Decommissioned by the Navy on 15 Jul 1865, it was sold to the LHS on 18 Oct 1865 (with *Geranium*). It was commissioned as *USLHT Iris* (Navy name retained) and assigned to the First LHD. It was the first propeller driven Tender in the Service, and was used as an Engineering Tender. It was rebuilt by Dialogue & Wood of Camden, NJ, in 1871 at a cost of $27,945, and lengthened to 115 feet. In the Fall of 1879 and in Oct 1888, it received a new boiler. It continued to serve in the First LHD at Portland, ME, until sold for $2,200 in 1892. It was replaced by *USLHT Lilac*. The old lighthouse tender then became the merchant ship *SS Iris* operating in Texas until about 1910.

CHAOS, 1865

Name	Builder	Built	Purchased	Commissioned	Disposition
Chaos		NA	12 July 1865	1865	Lost Aug 1866

Cost
    $4,055 (purchase price) + $1,914 (fitting out costs)

Hull
    Dimensions   unknown, (6' draft)   Wood Hull

Rig
    Schooner

A schooner captured during the Civil War, and sold at auction as a war prize in Jul 1865. Purchased by the LHS in 1865 and commissioned as *USLHT Chaos*, and served in the Eighth and Ninth LHDs. Ran aground at Revenue Shoal and lost in Aug 1866. A private tug and *USLHT Geranium* failed to save it. The hull was not saved, but the rigging and sails were salvaged and sold for $177.50.

USLHT Geranium after it was lengthened, c. 1907.

Mariners' Museum

GERANIUM, 1865

Name	Builder	Built	Purchased	Commissioned	Disposition
Geranium		1863	05 Sep 1863 (USN)	15 Oct 1863 (USN)	Condemned 29 Nov 1909
	Newburgh, NY		18 Oct 1865 (LHS)	1865 (LHS)	Sold 19 Jan 1910

Cost
   $13,500 (purchase price)

Hull
   Displacement (tons)   356 (full) / 251 (mean)   Wood Hull
   Dimensions
     [1863]   128'6" (loa) / 125' (lwl) x 23'3" x 8'3"
     [1879]   155'6" (loa) x 23'3" x 10'6" (8'0" max / 7'6" mean / 6'6" light)

Machinery
   Main Engine   Single beam steam engine   IHP 300   BHP 210
   Main Boiler   One return tubular   Coal fired
   Propulsion   Side paddle wheels

Complement
   4 officers, 14 men (1907-10)

Built as the private steaming tug *John A. Dix* in 1863, and purchased for $42,000 by the USN on 05 Sep 1863. It was commissioned as *USS Geranium* on 15 Oct 1863 at the New York Navy Shipyard, and served as a tug off the South Carolina coast during the Civil War. Decommissioned by the Navy on 15 Jul 1865, it was sold to the LHS on 18 Oct 1865 (with *Iris*).

   Commissioned as *USLHT Geranium* (Navy name retained), it was assigned to the Eighth LHD out of New Orleans as an Inspection Tender. Rebuilt by William E. Woodall & Co. in 1879 for $14,500 and lengthened to 155 feet. In 1884, it was reassigned to the Fourth LHD. In Jan 1889, it was relieved by the new *USLHT Zizania* at Wilmington, DE, and reassigned to the Second LHD in 1890. In Oct 1892, it received a new boiler. *USLHT Geranium* went to the First LHD in 1907. Condemned in 1909 at Portsmouth, ME, it was sold in 1910 and replaced by *USLHT Aster*.

J. N. SEYMOUR, 1867

Name	Builder	Built	Purchased	Commissioned	Disposition
J. N. Seymour	B.C. Terry Camden, NJ	1860	26 Oct 1861 (USN) 20 Jun 1865 (LHS)	Nov 1861 (USN) 1867 (LHS)	Decom 01 Oct 1881 Sold 10 Nov 1881

Cost
  $6,000 (purchase price)
  $7,041.60 (new boiler)

Hull
  Displacement (tons) 169 (full) / 133 (std)   Wood Hull
  Dimensions   120'3"(loa) / 100'(lbp) x 20'6" x 7'3" (draft 6'6" max/ 5'9" std)

Machinery
  Main Engine   Single Beam Steam
  Main Boiler   Single   Coal fired
  Propulsion   Side paddle wheels

Originally built as the private steamer *Isaac N. Seymour* in 1860. Acquired by the USN for $18,000 on 26 Oct 1861, it was commissioned in Nov 1861 as *USS I.N. Seymour*, and served on the North Atlantic Blockade Squadron. It was sunk after hitting a submerged object in Hatteras Inlet on 20 Feb 1862, but was raised and repaired. It sank again when it struck a bank in the Neuse River on 24 Aug 1862, but was again raised and repaired. Decommissioned by the Navy on 16 May 1865, it was transferred to the LHS at Washington, DC, on 20 Jun 1865.

Commissioned in 1867 as *USLHT J.N. Seymour* (Navy name retained, with initials probably changed due to a typographical error). In 1867, it was transferred to the Fifth LHD. Name changed to *USLHT Tulip* in 1869. Repaired by Dialogue & Wood in 1871 at a cost of $16,350. Served in the Fifth LHD until 1879 when it was declared unfit, and decommissioned in 1881, replaced by *USLHT Jessamine*. After it was sold at auction for $7,100 on 10 Nov 1881, it was redocumented on 07 Jun 1882 as the merchant ship *SS Magnolia*, and sold into Canadian hands in 1888. Sold again, it was burned for the scrap metal at Sydney, Nova Scotia, in 1897.

SUNRISE class, 1867

Three 12-ton, two-masted, half-deck luggers, built by the LHS and used as freight launches in the Eighth LHD. All were placed in service in 1867.

Sunrise
Placed in service in 1867. Sale authorized on 07 Sep 1875 and sold on 25 Oct 1875 for $265.

Sunset
Placed in service in 1867. Sale authorized on 07 Sep 1875 and sold on 25 Oct 1875.

Susan
Placed in service in 1867. Sale authorized on 26 Mar 1873 and finally sold on 25 Oct 1875 for $52.50.

NFR

HAZE, 1867

Name	Builder	Built	Purchased	Commissioned	Disposition
Haze	Henry Mallory Mystic, CT	1861	06 Jun 1867	16 Oct 1867	Decom 15 Mar 1905 Sold 1905

Cost
  $27,000 (purchase price)

Hull
  Displacement (tons) 328 (full) / 281 (mean) / 274 (light)   Wood Hull
  Dimensions   137'0"(loa) / 124'(lwl) x 24'7" x 16'2" (8'4" draft)

Machinery
  Main Engine   Single expansion steam   BHP 292   IHP 196
  Main Boilers   Coal fired
  Propulsion   Single propeller

The former private coastwise freight steamer *Merchant*, built in 1861, was purchased from T.S. Winslow of New York City in Jun 1867 and commissioned as *USLHT Haze*, to replace the aging *USLHT Watchful* in the Twelfth LHD in the Great Lakes. This was the first steam propeller driven Lighthouse Tender in the Great Lakes. In 1869, it was reassigned to service the Tenth and Eleventh Districts, servicing Lake Erie and the Detroit River. Rebuilt by Gibson & Craig of Buffalo, NY, from May to Jul 1876 at a cost of $29,608.75 with new engines installed. *USLHT Haze* continued to operate out of Detroit in the Tenth LHD until it was laid up on 15 Mar 1905 when it was sold for $800. The crew was tranferred to the new *USLHT Crocus*.

NARRAGANSETT, 1867

Name	Builder	Built	Purchased	Commissioned	Disposition
Narragansett	Port Jefferson, NY	1862	1867	1867	Sunk 21 Sep 1887

Hull
  Displacement (tons) 130   Wood Hull
  Dimensions   60' x 24'6" x 5'6" (4'6" draft)

Rig
  Schooner

The private schooner *Narragansett* was built in 1862. Acquired by the LHS in 1867 and commissioned as *USLHT Narragansett* (original name retained) and rebuilt in 1868 at City Island, NY, before being assigned to the Sixth LHD for use as an Engineering Tender. Name changed to *USLHT Mignonette* on 07 Oct 1871. On 08 Nov 1877, it sank at anchor near Stratford Shoal during a gale, but was raised and repaired for $1,000. It was then ordered to Key West, FL, in Jun 1878 for duty in the Seventh LHD. It was swept from its moorings and sunk with all 16 souls on board in a hurricane off Brazos Santiago, TX, on 21 Sep 1887.

MARTHA WASHINGTON, 1867

Name	Builder	Built	Contracted	Commissioned	Disposition
Martha Washington		NA	1867	Nov 1867	Decom Jan 1869

Cost
  $40/day (Nov 1867-Sep 1868)
  $30/day (Sep 1868-Jan 1869)

Hull
  Displacement (tons) unknown
  Dimensions   40' (loa)

The private 44-foot (loa) steamer *Martha Washington*, chartered from Nov 1867 to Jan 1869 for buoy service at $40 a day (contract renewed in Sep 1868 for $30 a day) and commissioned as *USLHT Martha Washington* (private name retained). Used for construction, and to fill in for *USLHT General Putnam* in the Third LHD while it was undergoing repairs after a collision and sinking.

Note: See Appendix A for additional information on commissioned and hired vessels.

MAGGIE, 1868

Name	Builder	Built	Purchased	Commissioned	Disposition
Maggie		1853	03 Jan 1868	1868	Unsea. 30 Aug 1879
	Cambridge, MD				Sold 01 Oct 1879

Cost
  $7,000 (purchase price) + $2,190 (outfitting)

Hull
  Displacement (tons)   95   Wood Hull
  Dimensions   81'6" x 24' x 5'9" (4'6" draft)

Rig
  Center board schooner

A private schooner, purchased at Baltimore on 03 Jan 1868 and commissioned as *USLHT Maggie*. It was rebuilt at Baltimore in 1869, then served in the Sixth LHD. It was then moved to the Fifth LHD in 1870. Totally rebuilt at Baltimore in Dec 1873. Declared unseaworthy on 30 Aug 1879 and sold on 01 Oct 1879 for $145. It then became the private pilot boat *Irene*, operating until 1914.

CORINNE, 1868

Name	Builder	Built	Purchased	Commissioned	Disposition
Corinne		1865	1868	1868	Decom
	New Orleans, LA				Sold 15 Apr 1879

Hull
  Displacement (tons)   12 (full) / 7 (light)   Wood Hull
  Dimensions   42'7"(lbp) x 12'4" x 3'0"

Rig
  Schooner

A small, two-masted, 12-ton lugger, built in 1865. Acquired by the LHB in 1868 and commissioned as *USLHT Corrine* (original name retained), and used as a freight boat in the Eighth LHD. Authorized for sale on 08 Sep 1875, but continued to serve. Ordered sold on 06 Mar 1879, it was finally sold on 15 Apr 1879 for $250. It then became the private vessel *Mahala Francis*, operating until about 1920.

GUTHRIE, 1869

Name	Builder	Built	Purchased	Commissioned	Disposition
Guthrie		1856	1869	1869	Sunk 17 Nov 1873
	Brooklyn, NY				

Hull
  Displacement (tons)   141 (full) / 133 (mean) / 64 (light)
  Dimensions   89' x 22' x 8'3" (10' draft)

Rig
  Schooner

A private schooner built in 1856. Acquired by the LHS in 1869 as *USLHT Guthrie*. Used as a Supply Tender in the Second LHD. In Spring 1873, it was relieved by *USLHT Fern*, and was reassigned to the Eighth LHD to transport materials for the construction of the Trinity Shoals and Timbalier Lighthouses. Grounded and sunk in a hurricane on 17 Nov 1873 off Trinity Shoals in Louisiana.
  Note: There is no similarity between the *USLHT Guthrie* (1869-1873) and Revenue Cutter *James Guthrie* (1868-1882), which served concurrently in their respective services. Both were named for Treasury Secretary James Guthrie.

BACHE, 1869

Name	Builder	Built	Purchased	Commissioned	Disposition
Bache		NA	NA	May 1869	Decom late 1869

Cost
  $7,000 (purchase price) + $2,190 (outfitting)

Hull
  Displacement (tons)   95   Wood Hull
  Dimensions   81'6" x 24' x 5'9" (4'6" draft)

Rig
  Center board schooner

The Coast Survey schooner *USCSS A.D. Bache*, transferred to the LHS in May 1869 and commissioned as *USLHT Bache* (original Coast Survey name retained). It was used for buoy service in the Seventh LHD for about six months. The schooner was then returned to the Coast Survey where it served until 1870.

Professor Alexander Dallas Bache, LLD (1806-1867), had been the Superintendent of the Coast Survey (1843-1867) and a member of the Lighthouse Board (1852-1867).

CHAPTER II
Under the Lighthouse Board 1870 -1910

Although the Lighthouse Board had been established in 1852, the primary initial actions were the standardization of all the assorted navigation aids (lighthouses, lightships, beacons, and buoys). Then the Civil War from 1861-1865 disrupted things, with destruction of or neglect to over half the lights and other aids to navigation in the country. However, by 1870, with the lights and other aids to navigation under restoration and standardization, emphasis was being placed on the Tenders that supported the missions of the Lighthouse Service. In 1870, after the post Civil War recovery, the service was maintaining 528 lighthouses and beacons, 33 lightships (all non-propelled), 2446 buoys, and 315 assorted other unlit shore aids (beacons and day marks), plus 49 fog signals. The service also was operating a growing fleet of 19 tenders (6 sailing and 13 steam powered tenders). Less than half these tenders were designed or built for Lighthouse Service duties.

Congress was urged to provided funding for newer vessels built to Lighthouse Service standards: the results were apparent. Funding was appropriated and construction or purchases were authorized, for vessels specifically designed to meet the needs of the service. The tender fleet was expanding as never before.

New tenders were individually procured as replacements for specific aging tenders that were surveyed and decommissioned. Their designs varied to suit the regions in which they would serve whether on open waters of the ocean or bays, inland or shore work, the Great Lakes, or on the major rivers in the central United States. For example, if a tender servicing the upper Chesapeake Bay was getting old and beyond repair, a new tender would be designed specifically for that region (and often a name assigned), funding would then be sought and appropriated from Congress (this often took two or three years), then a contract would be let and the tender built and commissioned, replacing the old tender.

In the meantime, to increase the efficiency of the Tenders in service, the vessels were classified according to their normal functions. Engineering Tenders were generally used to support the construction of new aids. They would haul construction materials, house construction crews, and provide whatever logistical support was necessary for the building and repair of aids to navigation. Supply Tenders were used to transport freight and supplies from the main support depot to outlying bases along the coast. But the majority of the tenders were assigned to the various District Inspectors and were classed as Inspection Tenders. These were the working vessels that made the routine supply and support runs to the various lighthouses, tended minor aids to navigation, and towed unpropelled lightships to and from their stations. The Inspection Tenders usually had additional special quarters for the Inspector to live in while he was on board. He inspected the various aids and lights, insuring that the local keepers were complying with the Lighthouse Service regulations and properly maintaining the aid to navigation on which the maritime community depended. This starts the tradition of equipping all Tenders built for the Lighthouse Service with special quarters to be set aside for use by the District Inspector.

Smaller craft without a permanent crew assigned, known as "launches," were also being built and assigned to lighthouses, depots, and post lanterns. By and large, the majority of these launches were built locally without a standard design, and were assigned only a number (not a name) for identification. The launches were also built to be used in conjunction with specific Tenders, to maintain aids in waters that were too shallow for the larger vessels. Some of these eventually got their own names and became independent of the bigger "mother" Tenders. However, in most cases, named or unnamed, the launches were mostly ignored and records on these smaller craft are almost nonexistent.

All tenders would eventually have similar features which would distinguish them from ordinary vessels. The design would evolve, allowing form to fit function. Hulls made only of wood gave way to composite construction (iron frames with wood planking), then to totally metal hulls (iron, and later steel) but with wood superstructures, and finally all metal construction. Sail power was phased out (the last sail powered tender, *USLHT Pharos*, acquired in 1854, was taken out of service in 1908), as steam propulsion plants became standard and more sophisticated. Derricks or booms were added forwards for the handling of buoys. In 1887, one of the functions of Lighthouse Tenders was actually described as a "buoy tender" for the first time. But that wasn't to become an official hull designation for another 75 years!

Names assigned to tenders were also standardized. After 1875, all new tenders built for the service were assigned botanical names, for plants, trees, and shrubs often indigenous to the area where the new tender was to be assigned. There were only a few variances from the norm. *Shubrick*, *Joseph Henry*, *General Poe*, and *John Rodgers* were all named for notables on the Lighthouse Board and the only other exception was the tender *Grace Darling*, which was named for the heroine and daughter of an English lighthouse keeper.

For the first time, tender design was somewhat standardized. While, in most cases, tenders continued to be built individually, "Classes"

Steam Launch *USLHT Anemone* at work.

National Archives

(two or more vessels of the same design) started appearing, for economy and ease of support.

By the late 1800s, a common practice in the design and construction of a tender was the rounding of the deck on the foc'sle (a style known as a "turtleback") to prevent the buoys (their cages or lanterns) from hanging up or snagging on the hull of the tender when they were side-by-side during servicing.

By the late 1890s, paint schemes and markings for Lighthouse Tenders had been standardized: black for hulls, stacks and deck machinery; white for deckhouse superstructures and railings; tan (officially called "straw") for masts and booms and deck fittings; and gray for decks. The name of the tender would be affixed with brass letters on the stern, and a miniature brass lighthouse would be attached on the bow. The Lighthouse Service flag was flown from the foremast.

In 1898, during the Spanish-American War, four tenders served "with distinction" in the U.S. Navy leading to the addition of another task for Lighthouse Tenders: military readiness.

Shortly after the turn of the century, with the move to the new Department of Commerce and Labor, funding for the Lighthouse Service tightened. The planned construction of new tenders was deferred or canceled, and some existing tenders were laid up.

By 1910, the military Lighthouse Board was replaced by a more simplified civilian administration to operate the reorganized Bureau of Lighthouses. However, the Board had done its job. The Lighthouse Establishment was now bigger than anyone had ever dreamed, and the most modern in the world.

USLHT Verbena, 1870. *U.S. Lighthouse Society,*

VERBENA class, 1870

Name	Builder	Contracted	Launched	Commissioned	Disposition
Verbena	Wm. Cramp & Sons Philadelphia, PA	03 Mar 1869	1869	1870	Decom NA Sold Spring 1911
Alanthus	Wm. Cramp & Sons Philadelphia, PA	03 Mar 1869		1870	Decom 1881 Sold 15 Feb 1882

Cost
  $44,100 (each)

Hull
  Displacement (tons)   295 (mean)   White Oak Hull
  Dimensions   135'(lbp) x 25'5" x 9'0" (9'0" max / 7'6" mean / 6'6" light draft)

Machinery
  Main Engine   Condensing beam steam   IHP 300
  Main Boiler   Single tubular   Coal fired
  Propulsion   Side paddle wheel

Complement
  4 officers, 12 men (1907)
  6 officers, 15 men (1915)

Alanthus
Authorized under an appropriation on 03 Mar 1869 for $50,000. Commissioned in 1870 with sister *Verbena*. Assigned to the Sixth LHD at Charleston, SC. Overhualed and a new boiler installed in 1875. Declared unfit in 1880, decommissioned in 1881, and sold in 1882 for $1,025. Any usable old fittings from the *Alanthus* were transferred to the new *USLHT Wistaria* which took its place.

Verbena
Authorized under an appropriation of 20 Jun 1868 for $40,000. Assigned to the Second LHD at New Bedford for its entire career as an Inspection Tender, replacing the old *USLHT Cactus*. It tended aids in Vineyard Sound and Buzzard's Bay. It was rebuilt and a new boiler installed in Oct 1883. Sold in 1911, the hull was gutted and it became the unpowered barge *Dandy*, and was in use until 1923.

IVY, 1870

Name	Builder	Built	Purchased	Commissioned	Disposition
Ivy	Chester, PA	1865	1870	1870 Sold 25 Oct 1875	Laid up 01 May 1875

Cost
$13,000 (purchase price)

Hull
| Displacement (tons) | 231 (full) | Wood Hull |
| Dimensions | 60' x 14' x 6'6" | |

Machinery
Main Engine	Steam
Main Boiler	Coal fired
Propulsion	Single propeller

Built in 1865 as the private steam tug *Commodore*. Purchased from the Delaware & Chesapeake Canal & Towage Co. in 1870 and commissioned as *USLHT Ivy*, serving in the Seventh and Eighth LHDs as an Engineering Tender. Repaired in 1871 at a cost of $3,500. Laid up on 01 May 1875, it was decommissioned and sold on 25 Oct 1875 for $5,850.

GENERAL POE, 1870

Name	Builder	Built	Launched	Commissioned	Disposition
General Poe	Birely, Hillman & Streaker Philadelphia, PA	1870	1870	1870	Decom NA

Cost
$10,950 (purchase price) + $300.39 (outfitting)

Hull
| Displacement (tons) | unknown | Wood Hull |
| Dimensions | 64' x 16' | |

Machinery
Main Engines	Steam
Main Boilers	Coal fired
Propulsion	

Built in 1870 as a LHS Tug and commissioned as *USLHT General Poe* in 1870. It was then sent to the Eighth LHD where additional alterations and additions were done at Mobile for $472.25. In Oct 1871, it was transferred to the Fourth LHD.

Brigadier General Orlando M. Poe, U.S. Army Corps of Engineers, served on the LHB in numerous capacities from 1865 to 1884.

NFR

ROSE, 1870

Name	Builder	Built	Purchased	Commissioned	Disposition
Rose		NA	May 1870	1870	Unfit 06 Jan 1878 Sold 01 Mar 1881

Cost
$10,950 (purchase price)

Hull
| Displacement (tons) | 36 | Wood Hull |
| Dimensions | 64' x 16'6" x 6'6" | |

Machinery
Main Engine	Steam
Main Boiler	Coal fired
Propulsion	Single propeller

A steam tug, purchased for the LHS in May 1870. *USLHT Rose* served in the Fourth LHD. Declared unfit in 1878 and sold in 1881, for $1,750.

NFR

MARY, 1870

Name	Builder	Built	Purchased	Commissioned	Disposition
Mary		1860	1870	1870	Decom 1887
	Brunswick, NJ				Sold Jul 1887

Cost
  $3,000

Hull
  Displacement (tons) unknown
  Dimensions 44' x 17'

Machinery
  Main Engine Steam
  Main Boiler unknown
  Propulsion Propeller

Funds for purchase were authorized by an appropriation on 15 Jul 1870. A small steam launch purchased in 1870 as *USLHT Mary*, and assigned to the First LHD. Condemned in Jul 1887 and abandoned on the beach at Fort Preble, it was then sold as condemned property at Portland, ME.
                                                                                      NFR

VIOLET, 1871

Name	Builder	Built	Purchased	Commissioned	Disposition
Violet		1864	1870	1871	Decom NA
	Elizabethport, Staten Island, NY				Sold 1910

Cost
  $11,800 (hull) + $5,027 (machinery): $16,827 (total purchase price)

Hull
  Displacement (tons) 231 (full) / 116 (std)   Wood Hull
  Dimensions [1870] 107' x 21'6" x 7'3" (4'2" draft)
                [1887] 143'(lbp) x 23'6" x 8'8" (7'6" max / 7'0" mean draft)

Machinery
  Main Engines Steam   IHP 400 BHP 300
  Main Boilers Coal fired
  Propulsion Side paddle wheel

Complement
  5 officers, 16 men (1908-10)

Originally built in 1864 as the 107-foot steamer *Martha Washington*. Purchased in New York City in 1870 and rebuilt in 1871 at a cost of $16,827 ($11,800 for hull, $5,027 for machinery). Commissioned as *USLHT Violet*, serving in the Fourth LHD. It underwent a major overhaul in New York in 1877 at the cost of about $12,000. Rebuilt again in 1886 by Wm. E. Woodall of Baltimore for $19,950 and lengthened to 143-feet. It was then reassigned to the Fifth LHD where it served as an Inspection Tender. Sold in 1910, becoming the private steamboat *Charles H. Werner*, operating out of Baltimore. It was abandoned due to old age in 1919.

    Rumors persist, but with no significant evidence, that this *Martha Washington* may have been the same as the one chartered in 1867. However, their descriptions are totally dissimilar.

WARRINGTON, 1871

Name	Builder	Built	Purchased	Commissioned	Disposition
Warrington	J.M. Jones Shipyard Detroit, MI	1868	1870	1871	Sold 1910

Cost
  $25,000

Hull
  Displacement (tons)   410 (full) / 300 (std)   White Oak Hull
  Dimensions   260' (loa) / 152' (lbp) x 25'6" x 11'6"
  (12'6" max /11'0" mean / 8'0" light draft)

Machinery
  Main Engine   Steam   IHP 250 BHP 400
  Main Boilers   Coal fired
  Propulsion   Single propeller

Complement
  5 officers, 15 men (1907)
  5 officers, 19 men (1910)

Built as the private Great Lakes freight steamer (a style locally known as a steam barge) *Henry Warrington* in 1868, and purchased and outfitted by the LHS in 1870 for use as a Supply and Construction Tender. Commissioned as *USLHT Warrington* (original name retained), and served in the Eleventh LHD. In Spring 1879 there was a fire on board which destroyed the cabin and caused other damage, which was repaired at a cost of $16,000. In the 1890s, it continued to operate in the Great Lakes out of Detroit, working on construction of Spectacle Reef Light near Mackinac Straits in 1896. In Feb 1898, the engine and boiler were replaced, then it was transferred to the Tenth LHD out of Buffalo, NY, and used as an Engineering Tender.

Placed out of service in 1910, she was sold that same year to the Hines Lumber Company of Chicago, to haul lumber. The former tender ran aground near Charlevoix, MI, on 21 Aug 1911 and was considered a total loss.

USLHT Warrington, c. 1889, is an example of a typical design of a vessel unique to the Great Lakes, known as a Steam Barge. Other Great Lakes Tenders were of a similar design.

National Archives

MINNIE, 1871

Name	Builder	Built	Purchased	Commissioned	Disposition
Minnie	John Mahoney New Orleans	early 1871	Apr 1871	late 1871	Decom NA Sold 1875

Cost
 $1,500 (purchase price)

Hull
 Displacement (tons) 12
 Dimensions unknown

Machinery
 Main Engine Steam
 Main Boiler Coal fired
 Propulsion Single screw

A small, 12-ton, half-decked steam launch, built in early 1871. Purchase was authorized on 10 Apr 1871, and it was commissioned as USLHT *Minnie*. It was used as a Freight Tender in the Eighth LHD. On 27 Aug 1875, authority to sell was requested by the District Inspector.

MAGNOLIA, 1871

Name	Builder	Built	Purchased	Commissioned	Disposition
Magnolia	St. Michaels, MD	1869	Apr 1871	1871	Sold May 1882

Cost
 $10,000 (purchase price)

Hull
 Displacement (tons) 118   Wood Hull
 Dimensions 97' (loa) / 92' (lbp) x 27'5" x 6'6" (4'6" draft)

Rig
 Schooner

Built as the *George E. Smoot*, it was purchased by the LHS in Baltimore in Apr 1871, then rebuilt. Commissioned as USLHT *Magnolia*, it served in the Eighth LHD. It was sold at New Orleans in May 1882 for $3,600, and became the merchant vessel *Magnolia*, operating until 1903.

ARBUTUS, 1871

Name	Builder	Built	Purchased	Commissioned	Disposition
Arbutus	B. C. Terry Keyport, NJ	1862	17 Nov 1862 (USN) Jun 1871 (LHS)	Nov 1862 (USN) Oct 1871 (LHS)	Unfit 29 Jan 1874 Sold 13 Apr 1875

Cost
 $12,800 (purchase price) + $4,500 (repairs)

Hull
 Displacement (tons) 173 (std)   Wood Hull
 Dimensions 125'(loa)/110'6'(lbp) x 22'6" x 7'3" (5'6" dft)

Machinery
 Main Engine Single beam steam engine
 Main Boiler One   Coal fired
 Propulsion Side paddle wheels

Built in 1862 as the merchant ship *Jonas Smith*. Acquired by the USN for $25,000 on 17 Nov 1862 as USS *Daffodil*, for use as a coastal tug in the South Atlantic Blockade Squadron in South Carolina during the Civil War. Sold at auction for $5,313.75 on 13 Mar 1867 back into merchant service as SS *Aaron Wilbur*. Purchase by the LHS authorized was in 1870 and completed in 1871, it was then repaired in Oct 1871 at a cost of $4,500, and then commissioned as USLHT *Arbutus*, serving as an Engineering Tender in the Seventh LHD.

 Declared unfit on 29 Jan 1874. It was sold at Key West for $4,424.30 the next year, the sale being delayed due to bureaucracy. It become the merchant ship *Cora*, serving until 1880.

USLHT Fern, 1891.

National Archives

FERN, 1871

Name	Builder	Contracted	Launched	Commissioned	Disposition
Fern	Delamater & Steack of NY Newport, RI	Jul 1870	1871	27 Dec 1871	Decom Trans USN 30 Jan 1891

Cost
  $84,750

Hull
  Displacement (tons)   548   Steel Hull
  Dimensions   160'(loa)/155'(lwl) x 27'4" x 13'0" (11'9" draft)

Machinery
  Main Engine   Inverted compound condensing steam
  Main Boilers   Coal fired
  Propulsion   Single propeller

Complement
  12 men

Authorized on 15 July 1870 as a tender for the Pacific coast with an appropriation of $90,000. It was commissioned in 1871 as *USLHT Fern* and arrived in San Francisco in the Twelfth LHD in Mar 1872, and used as a Supply Tender. However, due to the needs of the service, it was reassigned to the Third LHD in 1873, relieving *USLHT Pharos* and *USLHT Guthrie*. In the fall of 1878, *USLHT Fern* was rebuilt at a cost of $17,437.

  Fern was transferred to the USN on 30 Jan 1891 and commissioned as USS FERN on 22 Aug 1891, and used as a Freight Boat. Decommissioned on 22 Oct 1898 and used by the Washington, DC, Naval Militia as a training ship. Laid up in 1904 and renamed *USS Gopher* on 27 Dec 1905, thence assigned to the Minnesota Naval Militia. Recommissioned on 30 May 1917 at the start of WWI and used as a practice ship at the Great Lakes Naval Training Center. Recommissioned on 01 Oct 1922 as a Navy Reserve ship, it sank in the Gulf of St. Lawrence while under tow enroute to Boston, on 21 Aug 1923.

USLHT Mistletoe, 1872. At a glance, *Mistletoe* and *Cactus* (1865) look almost identical, however, on closer examination, distinguishing features include Mistletoe's rounded bridge (compared to the square bridge of Cactus), the patterning on the wheel guards, and the main deck superstructure window arrangements and length.

Mariners' Museum

MISTLETOE, 1872

Name	Builder	Contracted	Launched	Commissioned	Disposition
Mistletoe	Robinson Hoffman & Co. Chester, PA	1871	1871	1872	Decom NA Sold 27 Apr 1922

Cost
  $45,833

Hull
  Displacement (tons)   476 (full) / 352 (mean) / 299 (light)   Oak Hull
  Dimensions   [1871]   137'(lbp) x 25'5" x 9' (7'0" max / 6'9" mean draft)
               [1881]   160'(loa) / 153'(lbp)

Machinery
  Main Engines   Steam   IHP 190 BHP 156
  Main Boilers   Coal fired
  Propulsion   Side paddle wheels

Complement
  4 officers, 13 men (1907)
  4 officers, 16 men (1911-15)
  4 officers, 18 men (1917)

Authorized by appropriation of $50,000 on 03 Mar 1871 and built as an Engineering Tender. *USLHT Mistletoe* served on Long Island Sound in the Third LHD. In 1881, it was rebuilt, the boiler was replaced, and it was lengthened 16 feet. It was overhauled again in 1892. After WWI, it was homeported at Newport News, VA. It was the second to last side-wheel tender in the LHS. It served until 1922 when sold. It then became the merchant freighter *SS Mistletoe*, operating briefly until 1924.

USLHT Myrtle, 1896. *National Archives*

MYRTLE, 1872

Name	Builder	Contracted	Launched	Commissioned	Disposition
Myrtle	Birely, Hillmand & Streaker Philadelphia, PA	1871	1872	1872	Decom Sold 14 Dec 1922

Cost
  $44,500

Hull
  Displacement (tons)   542 (full) / 348 (mean) / 230(light) Oak Hull
  Dimensions   140'(loa) / 130'(lbp) x 25'8" x 11'3" (10'9" max / 9'6" mean draft)

Machinery
  Main Engine   Inverted cyclinder locomotive crank steam   IHP 181   BHP 162
  Main Boiler   single steel   Coal fired
  Propulsion   Single propeller   Steam winch

Complement
  5 officers, 14 men (1907-10)
  4 officers, 16 men (1911)
  4 officers, 17 men (1915-17)

Appropriation of $50,000 authorized on 03 Mar 1871, it was built as an Engineering Tender in the winter of 1871. It served in the First and Second LHDs on a shared basis, homeported out of Boston. In Apr 1914 it was transferred from the Third LHD at New York to the Ninth LHD in Puerto Rico, relieving *USLHT Ivy*. But in Feb 1917, it was sent back to New York. Sold in the Third LHD in 1922 for $1,200, it was replaced by *USLHT Spruce*, and the old ship became the merchant vessel *SS Myrtle*, operating until 1943.

DANDELION, 1872

Name	Builder	Built	Purchased	Commissioned	Disposition
Dandelion	Boston, MA	1863	May 1871	1872	Decom 08 May 1878 Sold 10 Jul 1878

Cost
   $16,800 (purchase price)

Hull
   Displacement (tons)   264
   Dimensions   132'6" x 22' x 8' (draft 4' fwd, 5' aft)

Machinery:
   Main Engines   Steam
   Main Boilers   Coal fired
   Propulsion   Side paddle wheels

The private steamer *C.W. Thomas* was built in 1863, and rebuilt in 1870 as the *Sunbeam*. Purchased from the Norwich, New London & Watch-hill Steamboat Co. on May 1871 by the LHS. Commissioned as *USLHT Dandelion*, it served in the Fourth LHD at Philadelphia. In Jan 1874, a new boiler was installed by Neafie & Levy of Philadelphia for $7,300. Declared unfit on 16 Mar 1878, it was authorized for sale on 08 May 1878 and sold later that year for $1,300, replaced by the new *USLHT Pansy*. The former *Dandelion* then became the passenger ship *SS S.A. McCall*, operating until about 1910.

LYRA class, 1872

Name	Builder	Contracted	Launched	Commissioned	Disposition
Lyra	William Foster Mobile, AL	NA	1872	1872	Laid up 01 May 1875 Sold 04 Apr 1876
Polaris	John Mahoney Mobile, AL	NA	NA	1872	Laid up 01 May 1875 Sold 25 Oct 1875
Arcturus	John Mahoney New Orleans, LA	NA	1872	1872	Sold 20 Nov 1880
Orion	John Mahoney New Orleans, LA	NA	1872	1872	Laid up 1880 Sold 20 Nov 1880

Cost
   $1,100 (each)

Hull
   Displacement (tons)   15   Wood Hull
   Dimensions   45' x 15'3" x 4'6" (3' draft)

Rig
   Schooner rigged launch

Design
Built as schooner rigged launches, all employed as freight boats in the Eighth LHD. This was one of the few attempts by the LHS to name a class of tenders for something other than flowers, plants, and trees. Instead, these were named for stars and constellations. All were funded under appropriations for the building of Trinity Shoals and Timbalier Lights in Louisiana, and possibly built as replacements for the *Susan* class launches which had previously served in this region.

Lyra
Used as a freight boat in the Eighth LHD. Laid up in May 1875 and sold in Apr 1876 for $429.75.

Polaris
Used as a freight boat in the Eighth LHD. Laid up in May 1875 and sold in Oct 1875 for $500.

Arcturus
Used by the Engineer of the Eighth LHD for construction. Sold in Nov 1880 for $1,200.

Orion
Used by the Engineer of the Eighth LHD. Laid up in 1880. Sold in Nov 1880 for $975.

PHAROS, 1872

Name	Builder	Contracted	Launched	Commissioned	Disposition
Pharos		NA	NA	1872	Decom NA
					Sold 23 Oct 1875

Hull
    Displacement (tons)   unknown
    Dimensions   unknown

A small, two-masted, 12-ton lugger, used as a Freight Boat in the Eighth LHD. Authorized for sale on 26 Mar 1873 and sold two years later on 25 Oct 1875 for $70!

ATLANTIC, 1873

Name	Builder	Contracted	Launched	Commissioned	Disposition
Atlantic		NA	NA	1873	Decom
					Sold 1873 ?

Hull
    Displacement (tons)   unknown
    Dimensions   unknown

Machinery
    Main Engines   Steam
    Main Boilers   Coal fired

No data available as to specs or service other than that it was in the Sixth LHD in 1873.

DAISY, 1873

Name	Builder	Built	Purchased	Commissioned	Disposition
Daisy		1869	Jun 1873	1873	Decom
					Trans USC&GS 1885

Cost
    $11,000 (purchase price)

Hull
    Displacement (tons)   43.66
    Dimensions   91'6" x 18' x 7'6" (draft 5' fwd, 6' aft)

Machinery
    Main Engine   Low press. surface condensing steam
    Main Boiler   Tubular   Coal fired
    Propulsion   Single propeller

Built in 1869 as the private steam launch *On Time*, and purchased by the LHS in Jun 1873. After its purchase, it was refitted and commissioned as *USLHT Daisy* and assigned as an Inspection Tender in the Second LHD at Boston, tending aids north of Cape Cod. In Jun 1883, it was sent to the Third LHD at New York City and swapped with *USLHT Warrington*.
On 09 May 1885, it was sold at auction for $1,010, but the sale was not approved by the Treasury Secretary. Instead, it was transferred to the Coast & Geodetic Survey on 22 May 1885. Later sold into private hands and became the private merchant *SS Clarence*, serving until 1904.

CROCUS, 1874

Name	Builder	Contracted	Launched	Commissioned	Disposition
Crocus	Neafie & Levy Phildadelphia, PA	NA	1873	1874	Decom Sold 15 Jun 1878

Cost
  $4,600

Hull
  Displacement (tons)   unknown   Oak Hull
  Dimensions   35' x 10' x 3'0" (2'2" draft)

Machinery
  Main Engines   Two direct acting link motion steam
  Main Boiler   One locomotive type   Coal fired
  Propulsion   Twin propellers

A steam launch built for the LHS and assigned to the Sixth LHD as an Engineering Tender. In Dec 1873, the hull was coppered and it was reassigned to Charleston, SC, to assist with the construction of the Morris Island Lighthouse. In Jan 1875, USLHT *Crocus* transferred to Lazaretto Point in the Fifth LHD. It was sold at auction for $650 in 1878.

DAHLIA, 1874

Name	Builder	Contracted	Launched	Commissioned	Disposition
Dahlia	Neafie & Levy Philadelphia, PA	11 Jun 1873	16 Feb 1874	May 1874	Decom 1909 Sold 17 Feb 1909

Cost
  $81,800 (contract)

Hull
  Displacement (tons)   426 (full) / 333 (mean)   Iron Hull
  Dimensions   141'6"(loa) / 129'6"(lbp) x 25' x 10'6" (5'7" draft)

Machinery
  Main Engine   Steam   IHP 225 BHP 80 (1892)
  Main Boiler   Coal fired
  Propulsion   Single propeller, iron

Complement
  6 officers, 15 men

The first tender built specifically for the Great Lakes, it was also the first iron-hulled tender in the region. Authorized on 03 Mar 1873 with a special appropriation of $90,000. Commissioned in 1874 as USLHT *Dahlia*, it was also the first Great Lakes tender with a botanical name. In the Spring of 1882, repairs and alterations were completed, costing $9,812.40. Assigned to the Eleventh LHD as an Inspector's Tender (later renamed to the Ninth LHD in 1890) on Lake Michigan. Sold for $5,400 on 17 Feb 1909, it became the passenger steamer *Flora M. Hill* in upper Lake Michigan. It was later crushed by ice and sunk off Chicago Harbor on 11 Mar 1912.

USLHT Dahlia, 1874.   Mariners' Museum

LAMPLIGHTER, 1874

Name	Builder	Built	Purchased	Commissioned	Disposition
Lamplighter		NA	1874	1874	Decom NA
					Sold NA

A steamer, acquired in 1874, and used as a Supply Tender.
NFR

MARIE, 1875

Name	Builder	Built	Purchased	Commissioned	Disposition
Marie		NA	NA	1875	Decom NA
					Sold NA

A small steam launch in service in the First LHD in 1875.
NFR

ALICE, 1875

Name	Builder	Built	Purchased	Commissioned	Disposition
Alice		1870	Nov 1874	1875	Decom 22 Jul 1880
					Sold 09 Aug 1880

Cost
  $18,000 (purchase price, including alterations)

Hull
  Displacement (tons)   615 (full)
  Dimensions   222' x 35'6" x 2'6"(draft)   Wood Hull

Machinery
  Main Engines   2 steam engines
  Main Boilers   3 boilers   Coal fired
  Propulsion   Side paddle wheels

The longest vessel commissioned into the LHS, purchased at St. Louis in Nov 1874 and commissioned as *USLHT Alice* in 1875. It was the second vessel to serve as a River Tender, operating in the Fifteenth LHD. Authorized for sale on 22 Jul 1880, it was sold and dismantled on 09 Aug 1880 for $892, and replaced by *USLHT Joseph Henry*. She was originally built as a sidewheel packet and placed the first government lights on the Ohio River. In the spring of 1878, enroute from St. Louis to New Orleans servicing lights along the Mississippi she was snagged, breaking eight of her timbers and returning to St. Louis for repairs.

USLHT Lily, 1875.

U.S. Coast Guard

LILY, 1875

Name	Builder	Contracted	Launched	Commissioned	Disposition
Lily		NA	1874	28 Jul 1875	Sunk 23 Nov 1911
	Jeffersonville, IN				Decom 24 Nov 1911

Cost
 $25,000

Hull
 Displacement (tons) 507 (full) / 275 (std)   Wood Hull
 Dimensions 178'(loa) / 163'(lwl) x 28' x 4'4" (draft 3'0" mean / 2'8" light)

Machinery
 Main Engines Steam IHP 307 BHP 90
 Main Boilers Coal fired
 Propulsion Side paddle wheels

Complement
 4 officers, 10 men (1888)
 5 officers, 20 men (1907)
 7 officers, 19 men (1910)
 7 officers, 17 men (1911)

The first tender specifically built for river service was built in Jeffersonville, IN, just across the Ohio River from Louisville, KY. *USLHT Lily* was commissioned in 1875, for service in the Fourteenth LHD on the upper Mississippi River. It was gutted by fire while at the dock in Cincinnati on 20 Sep 1884. It was then totally rebuilt by Madison Marine Railway at a cost of $10,850. It was back in service in Jan 1885. Allegedly, it was painted maroon with gold trim one season, and was nicknamed "Black Lily" by the locals. It served in the Fourteenth LHD until Mar 1888, when it was replaced by *USLHT Goldenrod* and transferred to the Fifteen LHD to replace the wrecked *USLHT Ivy*. In 1909, *USLHT Lily* was reassigned to Rock Island, IL, on the Missouri River.

On 17 Oct 1911, it sank near Washington, MO. Refloated, it hit a snag and sank a month later in Nov 1911 near St. Albans, MO (near St. Louis), and was declared a total loss on 24 Nov 1911. An island has since formed where sand filled in around the hulk, and the location is known today as Lily Island.

LAUREL, 1876

Name	Builder	Contracted	Launched	Commissioned	Disposition
Laurel	Columbian Iron Works Baltimore, MD	1875	1876	1876	Decom NA Sold 19 Jan 1909

Cost
　$40,000

Hull
　Displacement (tons)　320 (full) / 217 (light)　　Oak Hull
　Dimensions　134'(lbp) x 25' x 10' (7' draft)

Machinery
　Main Engines　Vertical Direct Acting Steam　IHP 250　BHP 180
　Main Boilers　Surface Condensing　Coal fired
　Propulsion　Twin propellers

Complement
　5 officers, 12 men

Appropriations for $50,000 authorized 03 Mar 1875. Relocated in Summer 1876 to the Eighth LHD at New Orleans and used as an Inspection Tender. Overhauled in New York City in Aug 1883. Reassigned to the Seventh LHD at Key West in 1890. Sold in 1909 for $1,050.

USLHT Pansy, 1925.　　　　　　　　　　　　　　　　　　　　　　　　　　　　U.S. Coast Guard

PANSY, 1878

Name	Builder	Contracted	Launched	Commissioned	Disposition
Pansy	Baird & Huston Philadelphia, PA	1876	1877	May 1878	Decom NA Sold 29 Jan 1933

Cost
　$48,739.14

Hull
　Displacement (tons)　　454 (full) / 431 (mean) / 314 (light)　Iron Hull
　Dimensions　　　　　　152'(loa) x 25' x 10'6" (7'11" max / 7'7" mean draft)
　　　　　　　　　　　　147'(lwl) / 144'(lbp)

Machinery
　Main Engines　　2 independent steam　　　　　　　IHP 254　BHP 132
　Main Boiler　　　1 return tubular　　　　　　　　　Coal fired
　Propulsion　　　 Twin propellers

Complement
　4 officers, 7 men (1907)
　4 officers, 17 men (1910)
　4 officers, 19 men (1917)
　4 officers, 18 men (1925)

Authorized under an appropriation of $50,000 on 31 July 1876. Built as an Inspection Tender and assigned to the Eighth LHD, replacing *USLHT Dandelion*. In 1904, it was transferred to Puerto Rico. Then on 10 Oct 1907, it was laid up briefly, then reassigned to the Third LHD and operated out of Staten Island, NY. Rebuilt in 1915, it received a new boiler and machinery at a cost of $10,868.

　Sold into private hands in 1933, becoming the passenger excursion ship *SS Mayfair*, and replaced by *USLHT Hickory*. During WWII, it was acquired by the USCG and commissioned as *USCGC Mayfair* and used as a training vessel at the Merchant Marine Training School at Hoffman Island, NY, from May to Aug 1942. Following WWII, it resumed its private career as the passenger ship *Mayfair*, operating into the early 1980s, when it was finally given up due to old age.

USLHT Nettle launch, 1885.

National Archives

NETTLE, 1879

Name	Builder	Contracted	Launched	Commissioned	Disposition
Nettle		NA	1878	1879	Decom 1911
	New York, NY				Sold Spring 1911

Cost
  $3,900

Hull
  Displacement (tons)   22 (full) / 18 (std) / 11 (light)   Wood Hull
  Dimensions   58'0"(loa) / 51'(lbp) x 9'10' x 4' (4'6" max / 4'4" mean draft)

Machinery
  Main Engines   Double steam engines   IHP 25 BHP 37
  Main Boiler   Single Scotch type   Coal fired
  Propulsion   Single propeller

Complement
  2 officers, 2 men (1880)
  2 officers, 3 men (1910)

Built as a small Engineering Tender, and assigned to the Fifth LHD, it built and tended unmanned lights on Lake Champlain. In 1879 it was assigned to the Seventh LHD, then in 1883 reassigned to the Fifth LHD to assist *USLHT Jessamine* in the North Carolina sounds. *USLHT Nettle* was rebuilt in 1882. In 1885 it received a new boiler, and in 1889 a new engine. In Jul 1890, relieved by *USLHT Thistle*, it was transferred to the Third LHD and worked the aids along the Hudson River and in Lake Champlain. It received a new boiler in 1893 and in 1900. Decommissioned and sold in 1911, it became the freighter *Nettle*, operating until 1923.

PINK, 1878

Name	Builder	Built	Purchased	Commissioned	Disposition
Pink	Quincy, IL	1875	12 Nov 1878	1878	Sunk 02 Jun 1881 Sold 1881

Cost
  $1,800

Hull
  Displacement (tons) 23   Wood Hull
  Dimensions   73'6" x 16'7" x 2'10"

Machinery
  Main Engines   Steam
  Main Boilers   Coal fired

Former 73½-foot steam yacht *Louisa*, built in 1875. Purchase authorized on 23 Oct 1878 and completed on 12 Nov 1878, and commissioned as *USLHT Pink*. Assigned to the Fifteenth LHD as an Inspection Tender. Capsized and sunk while moored in St. Louis on 02 Jun 1881. The hulk was raised and sold later the same year.

BRAMBLE, 1879

Name	Builder	Contracted	Launched	Commissioned	Disposition
Bramble	H.A. Ramsey & Co. Baltimore, MD	24 Dec 1878	1879	Jun 1879	Decom 1904 Sold 15 May 1905

Cost
  $5,935

Hull
  Displacement (tons) 32 (max) / 30 (std) / 15 (light)   Steel Hull
  Dimensions   46'8"(loa) / 45'0"(lbp) x 11'10" x 4'7"

Machinery
  Main Engines   Steam   IHP 40 BHP 45
  Main Boilers   Coal fired
  Propulsion   Twin propellers

Served as a steam launch in the Fifth LHD in Albermarle and Currituck sounds for its entire career, tending gas buoys in North Carolina. In 1901 it was considered useless, but wasn't placed out of service until 1904, being replaced by *USLHT Juniper*. Sold in 1905, it became the private tow boat *Brandon*, operating until 1921.

USLHT Arbutus, 1879.
National Archives

ARBUTUS, 1879

Name	Builder	Contracted	Launched	Commissioned	Disposition
Arbutus	William J. Malster & Co. Baltimore, MD	18 Oct 1878	01 Jul 1879	Sep 1879	Decom 08 Apr 1924 Sold 03 Mar 1925

Cost
  $49,769.16

Hull
  Displacement (tons)   545 (full) / 398 (mean)   Wood Hull
  Dimensions   153' (loa) x 25' x 10'7" (9'6" max / 8'3" mean / 7'1" light draft)
                        144'6" (lwl) / 145' (lbp)
  Schooner rigged

Machinery
  Main Engines   Steam   IHP 320 BHP 400
  Main Boilers   Coal fired
  Propulsion   Twin propellers

Complement
  5 officers, 14 men (1907)
  6 officers, 15 men (1910)
  6 officers, 19 men (1915)
  5 officers, 20 men (1917)
  7 officers, 23 men (1922)

Authorized by a special appropriation of $50,000 on 20 Jun 1878 and built as an ocean-going Engineering Tender in 1878. In 1888, *USLHT Arbutus* received a new boiler. Operated out of the Fourth LHD until 1890, then the Seventh LHD at New Orleans until 1912, and finally assigned to the Fifth LHD at Portsmouth, VA, and Baltimore. In the summer of 1918, it was rebuilt and radio equipment installed. Inspector's quarters and a raised foc's'le were added and the main deck was enclosed from the bridge to the fantail. Laid up in Jan 1921 due to lack of funds, it was decommissioned in 1924 and sold in 1925, becoming the merchant ship *SS Arbutus* in 1929, operating as a towboat and freighter until 1934.

LOTUS, 1880

Name	Builder	Built	Launched	Commissioned	Disposition
Lotus	Detroit Automotive Works Standardville, MI	1880	1880	1880	Laid up Spring 1899 Sold 19 Jul 1901

Cost
$4,000 (hull) + $967.81 (outfitting)

Hull
Displacement (tons)	15	Oak Hull
Dimensions	40'0"(loa) / 30'03"(lwl) / 27'0"(lbp) x 7'6" x 4' (4' draft)	

Machinery
Main Engine	HP fore & aft vertical steam	BHP 20
Main Boiler	upright	Coal fired
Propulsion	Single Propeller	

Built in 1880 as a Harbor Launch with funds from the appropriations to build the Stannard Rock Light Station in Michigan, and commissioned as USLHT *Lotus*. The machinery was built at the Detroit Locomotive Works. It served in the Eleventh LHD in the Great Lakes. Declared unfit at Detroit in Spring 1899 and laid up, it was decommissioned and sold in 1901.

JOSEPH HENRY, 1880

Name	Builder	Contracted	Launched	Commissioned	Disposition
Joseph Henry	Howard & Co. Jeffersonville, IN	22 Jan 1880	22 Jun 1880	01 Sep 1880	Decom 03 Mar 1903 Sold 05 Jan 1904

Cost
$13,300 (hull)
$43,291.15 (total, including outfitting)

Hull
Displacement (tons)	453 (full), 340 (standard)	White Oak Hull
Dimensions	180'(lbp) x 32' x 5'10"	

Machinery
Main Engines	Steam	IHP 255 BHP 277
Main Boilers	Coal fired	
Propulsion	Side paddle wheels	

Built as a replacement for USLHT *Alice*, and served in the Fifteenth LHD at Memphis, TN. In Jan 1881, assigned to the newly created Sixteenth LHD. The steam launch USLHT *Ivy* was assigned to it for shallow water work. Incandescent lighting was installed throughout the ship in Aug 1888, powered by a 10 HP steam generator.

Condemned in early 1900, USLHT "*Joe Henry*" (as it was known by the locals) served another four years until 1904 when sold, and was replaced by USLHT *Oleander*. After it was sold, it was renamed *Louisiana*, and eventually became the passenger ship *Pattona*, operating until 1916.

Professor Joseph Henry (1797-1878) was a reknown scientist of electricity, and served as the first Director of the Smithsonian Institution. He was also responsible for laying the foundation for our current Weather Bureau. In 1852, he became a member of the LHB, the governing body which had oversight of the LHS. He later served as its Chairman (1871-1878), the only civilian to hold that position.

USLHT Manzanita, 1880.
U.S. Coast Guard

MANZANITA, 1880

Name	Builder	Contracted	Launched	Commissioned	Disposition
Manzanita	H.A. Ramsey Shipbuilding Brooklyn, NY	23 Oct 1878	1879	Sep 1880	Decom 1905 Sold 30 Jun 1906

Cost
  $53,000 (contract)

Hull
  Displacement (tons)   484 (max)   Wood Hull
  Dimensions   152'0" (lbp) x 26'0" x 11'8"

Machinery
  Main Engine   Inverted Cylinder Direct Action Steam IHP 300 BHP 250
  Main Boiler   Single Overhead return flue   Coal fired
  Propulsion   Single propeller, cast iron 4 blade, 9'9" diam.

Although authorized for construction as a replacement for the aging *USLHT Shubrick* on the West Coast in 1869, the actual funding of $60,000 wasn't appropriated and contract approved until 20 Jun 1878. Completed on 29 Sep 1879 and commissioned in 1880 as *USLHT Manzanita*. It was only the second Lighthouse Tender in the Pacific, arriving on the west coast in 1880 and serving in the Twelfth LHD until Jan 1886, then the Thirteenth LHD for the rest of its career. It was rebuilt in spring 1887 at a cost of $24,695.28. In July 1902 it received a new boiler.

USLHT Manzanita foundered and sank on 06 Oct 1905 near Warrior Rock on the Willamette River in Oregon, and was abandoned as a total wreck, and decommissioned. Because the wreck was a hazard to navigation, Kern & Kern of Portland won the salvage rights and raised the hulk seven years later. Later rebuilt, becoming a private tug known as the *Daniel Kern* (named for the head of the salvage company that raised it), serving as the flagship of the Bellingham Tug & Barge Company until 1936, when it was abandoned due to old age. It was then run aground north of Seattle and burned for its scrap metal in 1944.

USLHT Holly, c. 1881.
National Archives

HOLLY class, 1881

Name	Builder	Contracted	Launched	Commissioned	Disposition
Holly	Malster & Reaney Baltimore, MD	20 Jul 1880	26 May 1881	01 Sep 1881	Decom 01 Aug 1931 Sold 04 Dec 1931
Jessamine	Malster & Reaney Baltimore, MD	20 Jul 1880	18 Jun 1881	01 Oct 1881	Decom 20 May 1921 Sold 1922

Cost
 $37,500 (contract price, each)
 $41,911 (actual cost, each)

Hull
 Displacement (tons) 499 (full) / 431 (std) / 367 (light)   Composite Hull (iron hull, wood deck)
 Dimensions   156' (loa) / 146'4" (lbp) x 39'0"(over guards) / 24'2" (hull) x 9'6"
                     (8'6" full / 7'0" light draft)

Machinery
 Main Engine   Marine condensing beam steam   IHP 186   BHP 400
 Main Boiler   Return flue 'Lobster back'   Coal fired
 Propulsion   Side paddle wheels

Complement
 5 officers, 16 men (1907-1917)
 5 officers, 18 men (1925)

Design
  Both these vessels were built as Bay and Sound Tenders for service in the Chesapeake Bay region, as authorized by appropriations of 16 Jun 1880.

Holly
Built in 1880 with a composite hull (wood frame, iron sheathed) as *USLHT Holly* and assigned as an Inspection Tender in the Fifth LHD at Baltimore, MD, and Portsmouth, VA, servicing aids to navigation in the Chesapeake Bay. Pulled as a tender in Jun 1893 and used as a lightship on Wolftrap Shoal 1893 and at Bush Bluff in 1894, then placed in reserve as a relief lightship. In 1898, it was rebuilt and restored to duty as a Bay and Sound Tender. Laid up due to lack of funds in Jan 1921, but later put back into service. Decommissioned and sold for $691 in 1931 after fifty years of service. It later had its engine removed and became the barge *Wright No.1*, in use until 1944 when it was discarded due to old age.

USLHT Jessamine, 1885.
Collection, P. Hornberger

HOLLY class, 1881 (CONT.)
Jessamine
Built at the same time and place as sister-ship *Holly*, and completed on 24 Sep 1881, replacing the old *USLHT Tulip*. Operated out of Fifth LHD in Baltimore as an Engineering Tender during its entire career. In Mar 1884 and May 1889, new boilers were installed. Due to a lack of funding *USLHT Jessamine* was laid up in Jan 1921 and sold in 1922, replaced by *USLHT Hawthorn*. Eventually the old *Jessamine* became the merchant ship *Queenstown*, then renamed *Victor Lynn* in the mid 1920s. It was eventually sold to new owners in Honduras in 1957.

IVY, 1881

Name	Builder	Built	Purchased	Commissioned	Disposition
Ivy		1880	07 Oct 1881	1881	Wrecked 23 Jan 1888
	Port Harmon, OH				Sold 10 Feb 1888

Cost
$5,500

Hull
Displacement (tons) 47.8   Steel Hull
Dimensions 100'8" x 15'6" x 3'5"

Machinery
Main Engine   Steam
Main Boiler   Coal fired
Propulsion   Single propeller

Complement
3 officers, 6 men (1887)

Built as the private steam launch *La Belle* in 1880. Purchase authorized on 24 Sep 1881 and completed on 07 Oct 1881. Commissioned as *USLHT Ivy*, and assigned to the Fifteenth LHD at St. Louis. Hit a snag and sank in Sep 1887. Raised at a cost of $800 and repaired for another $600. Totally wrecked and crushed by the steamer *Baton Rouge* while at the dock in St. Louis in winter quarters as a result of ice flows in Jan 1888. It was declared a total loss and the engines were sold on 10 Feb 1888 for $205. Replaced by *USLHT Lily*.

USLHT Wistaria, 1882. *Mariners' Museum*

WISTARIA, 1882

Name	Builder	Contracted	Launched	Commissioned	Disposition
Wistaria	Pusey & Jones Co. Wilmington, DE	02 Jul 1881	1882	1882	Decom Feb 1911 Trans to USPHS 24 Feb 1911

Cost
  $52,000 (contract)
  $54,455.65 (actual)

Hull
  Displacement (tons)   450 (full) / 393 (mean) / 260 (light)   Iron Hull, Wood deck
  Dimensions   167'6"(loa) / 150(lbp) x 25'6"(hull) / 41'04"(extended) x 10'0"
                        (8'8" full / 8'2" mean / 7'6" light draft)

Machinery
  Main Engine   Condensing beam steam   IHP 250 BHP 355
  Main Boiler   Return flue   Coal fired
  Propulsion   Side paddle wheels   Wood derrick

Complement
  6 officers, 17 men (1907)
  4 officers, 16 men (1910)

Authorized by appropriation of $55,000 on 03 Mar 1881, and built as an Inspection Tender, serving in the Sixth LHD at Charleston, SC, replacing *USLHT Alanthus*. When a major earthquake on 31 Aug 1886 devastated Charleston, SC, *USLHT Wistaria* (later spelled Wisteria) and *USLHT Pharos* both provided assistance and shelter to many distressed families in the area. In 1887 and 1892, new boilers were installed. And two new engines were installed in 1899. In 1910, it was reassigned to the First LHD in Portland, ME. After 29 years of service (an exceptionally long period of time in those days), *USLHT Wistaria* was decommissioned in 1911 and replaced by the new *USLHT Cypress*.

  Authorization was granted on 16 Feb 1911 and the old hull was transferred on 24 Feb 1911 to the Treasury Department for use as a floating hospital with the Public Health and Maritime Hospital Service (forerunner of today's Public Health Service) at Key West, FL, where it was finally moored. It was used as a disinfecting steamer and in 1914 as a detention barge. Although sunk in an upright position on Frankfort Bank near Key West during a hurricane in 1919, it continued to be used. In the mid 1920s was abandoned by the USPHS, then the hulk was used as a platform by the fishing industry for skinning sharks and curing hides. Destroyed by fire on 10 Feb 1933, the remains of the iron hull along with dredgings from the harbor became Wisteria Island, later nicknamed Christmas Island because of the pine trees growing on it.

USLHT John Rogers at the Thompkinsville lighthouse depot, Staten Island, NY, 1884.

National Archives

JOHN RODGERS, 1883

Name	Builder	Contracted	Launched	Completed	Disposition
John Rodgers	Ward, Stanton & Co. Newburgh, NY	07 Aug 1882	12 Apr 1883	01 June 1883	Decom 1921 Sold 1922

Cost
$54,000 (contract)
$59,986.70 (actual)

Hull
Displacement (tons)   571 (full) / 455 (mean) / 260 (light)   Iron Hull
Dimensions   160' (loa) / 151'(lbp) x 27'(hull) / 44'(extended) x 8'8"
(7'9" max / 6'6" light draft)

Machinery
Main Engine   Marine condenser beam steam   IHP 235 BHP 260
Main Boiler   Marine return tubular   Coal fired
Propulsion   Side paddle wheels (20'8" diam, 6' wide)   44-foot wood derrick with manila hemp rigging

Complement
4 officers, 14 men (1907)
4 officers, 15 men (1910)
4 officers, 16 men (1916)
4 officers, 18 men (1918)

Authorized on 07 Aug 1882 in an appropriation of $60,000 and completed in 01 Jun 1883 as *USLHT John Rodgers*, it was used as an Inspection Tender in the Third LHD on the New York and New Jersey coast. In Jan 1889, it ran aground at Noank, CT, but was refloated with no major damage. Electric lighting installed in May 1896. In the early 1900s, it was homeported at New London, CT. It was sold in 1922 for $909.

Named for Rear Admiral John Rodgers, USN (1812-1882), a prominent naval officer and hero, who was the recently deceased chairman of the Lighthouse Board (1878-1882).

GRACE DARLING, 1883

Name	Builder	Built	Purchased	Commissioned	Disposition
Grace Darling		1873	13 Feb 1883	1883	Unfit 25 Aug 1899
	Boothbay, ME				Sold 25 Sep 1899

Cost
  $4,850

Hull
  Displacement (tons)   107 (full) / 80 (mean) / 60 (light)   Oak Hull
  Dimensions (1873)   77' x 17'7" x 6'6" (8'6" max / 7'0" light draft)
           (1892)   92' x 17'7" x 6'6"

Machinery
  Main Engine   Keel condensing steam   IHP 200 BHP 34
  Main Boiler   Upright tubular   Coal fired
  Propulsion   Single propeller (6' diam.)

Built as a private 77-foot boat in 1873, its purchase was authorized on 03 Jan 1883 and completed by the LHS on 13 Feb 1883 and commissioned as *USLHT Grace Darling* (see note below on name source). Assigned to the Third LHD. Renamed *USLHT Rose* in Aug 1892, it was rebuilt with a new boiler and engine and lengthened 15 feet to 92 foot length. In 1894, it was found unfit, but was re-engined the next year by H. Ramseuy of Perth Amboy, NJ, with a new fore and aft compound steam engine and a return flue tubular scotch type boiler. Finally, the sale was authorized on 25 Aug 1899 and it was sold at auction on 25 Sep 1899 for $3,625.

   Grace Darling was the daughter of a lighthouse keeper on a rocky coast in England. On the night of 07 Sep 1838, at the age of 23, and with her father, under the most arduous of conditions, saved the lives of many of the survivors of the steamer *Forfashire* which had run aground in a storm. As a result of this gallant action, she and her father received gold medals from the British Humane Society. This young girl became celebrated in poetry and prose, and became the standard of bravery associated with keepers of lighthouses throughout the world. In 1996, the U.S. Coast Guard launched a new 175-foot buoy tender, *USCGC Ida Lewis* (WLM-551), named for America's equivalent of Grace Darling.

SHARPIE, 1885

Name	Builder	Built	Launched	Commissioned	Disposition
Sharpie		1885	1885	1885	Decom 1907
					Sold NA

Cost
  $450

Hull
  Displacement (tons)   unknown   Wood Hull
  Dimensions   40' x 11' x (14" draft)
  Rig   Flat bottom sail boat with center board

Authorized on 20 Jul 1885, and built in 1885 as a flat bottomed center board sail boat. It was used as a Supply Tender in the sounds of North Carolina of the Fifth LHD. Declared unfit in early 1904, but served until 1907.

USLHT Madroño, 1885.   *Mariners' Museum*

MADROÑO, 1885

Name	Builder	Contracted	Launched	Commissioned	Disposition
Madroño	John H. Dialogue Camden, NJ	1884	1884	14 Sep 1885	Decom Sold 11 Oct 1927

Cost
  $73,300 (contract)
  $87,871.76 (actual)

Hull
  Displacement (tons)   806 (full) / 557 (std) / 411 (light)   Iron Hull
  Dimensions   180'(loa) x 27'6" x 14'8" (11'6" draft full, 9'10" light)
                        163'8" (lwl) / 162'0"(lbp)

Machinery
  Main Engine   Compound inverted fore and aft surface condensing steam   IHP 685 BHP 700
  Main Boilers   Two return flue   Coal fired
  Propulsion   Single propeller, cast iron, 4 blade, 10'2" diam.

Complement
  5 officers, 21 men (1907)
  6 officers, 22 men (1910)
  6 officers, 19 men (1915-17)
  7 officers, 21 men (1925)

Authorized on 07 Jul 1884 with an appropriation of $85,000, to be built as a replacement for *USLHT Shubrick*, and used as an Inspection Tender on the West Coast. Only the third tender on the West Coast (after *Shubrick* and *Manzanita*), arriving in San Francisco in Jan 1886, relieving the *USLHT Manzanita* (which was then sent to replace the aging *USLHT Shubrick* in the Thirteenth LHD).

Sold in 1927 due to old age, it became the salmon cannery freighter M/V *Madrono*. Acquired by the War Department in 1938, before the start of WWII, it was reeingined with deisels. It became the Army freight transport *Colonel Charles L. Willard* until the end of the war.

At various times, two different launches were built specifically for *USLHT Madroño*, but eventually became independent harbor launches. Details on those two launches, *USLHT Hazel* and *USLHT Madroño*, may be found elsewhere in this book.

USLHT Gardenia, 1916.
National Archives

GARDENIA, 1888

Name	Builder	Built	Purchased	Commissioned	Disposition
Gardenia	East Deering, ME	1879	16 Jun 1888	1888	Condemned 19 Sep 1919 / Sold 19 Sep 1919

Cost
  $11,000 (purchase price) + $1,600 (alterations) + $3,000 (outfitting & equipment): $15,600 (total)

Hull
  Displacement (tons)   245 (full) / 217 (mean) / 153 (light)   Wood Hull
  Dimensions   117'(lbp) x 20'2" x 9'4" (6'6" max /6'0" mean draft)

Machinery
  Main Engine   Steam   IHP 200 BHP 130
  Main Boilers   Coal fired
  Propulsion   Single propeller

Complement
  4 officers, 11 men (1907-17)

Built as the private steamer *George W. Beale* in 1879. Purchase authorized on 06 Jun 1888 and the sale completed at Greenport, NY, on 16 Jun 1888 by the LHS and commissioned as *USLHT Gardenia*. Its entire career was spent in the Third LHD as an Inspection Tender working New York harbor. In 1892, it received a new boiler. While at New Haven, CT, *USLHT Gardenia* extinguished a fire on board the tug *Whistler* preventing the spread of the fire to other vessels. It was laid up on 01 Mar 1917 and acquired by the Navy on 04 May 1917 for service in WWI, and commissioned on 13 Sep 1917 as *USS Gardenia*. It served as a harbor control and guard ship at New York harbor until May 1919. It completed its naval service on 01 Jul 1919 and was returned to the LHS in 28 Jul 1919. It was condemned and sold at New York on 19 Sep 1919 for $1,065.

USLHT Goldenrod, sternwheeler, 1888.   U.S. Coast Guard

GOLDENROD, 1888

Name	Builder	Contracted	Launched	Commissioned	Disposition
Goldenrod	Sweeney & Brothers Jeffersonville, IN	22 Nov 1887	27 Aug 1888	12 Dec 1888	Decom 20 Jun 1924 Sold 05 Dec 1924

Cost
  $26,400 (contract)
  $33,221.44 (actual)

Hull
  Displacement (tons)[F.W.]   283 (full) / 144 (std)   Steel Hull
  Dimensions   169'(loa) / 150'(lbp) x 26'6" x 3'8"
                              (3'4" max / 2'6" mean / 2'4" light draft)

Machinery
  Main Engines   2 High press. Non-condensing steam   BHP 152
  Main Boilers   2 locomotive type   Coal fired
  Propulsion   Stern paddle wheel

Complement
  5 officers, 17 men (1907)
  6 officers, 17 men (1910)
  3 officers, 15 men (1915)
  2 officers, 12 men (1924)

Authorized and $40,000 appropriated on 03 Mar 1887 for a "tender for the Western Rivers" with a proposed name of *Nymphaea* ("Water Lily"). Built as a River Tender, (and planned as a replacement for *USLHT Lily,*) specifically for service on the Ohio River, and commissioned as *USLHT Goldenrod*. It was the first stern wheel tender built for the LHS. It was homeported out of Cincinnati, OH, in the Fourteenth LHD. Used by the U.S. Army Corps of Engineers during WWI. When decommissioned and sold in 1924, it was replaced by *USLHT Greenbrier*.

ZIZANIA, 1888

Name	Builder	Contracted	Launched	Commissioned	Disposition
Zizania	Ramsey & Son Baltimore, MD	12 Feb 1887	1887	12 Nov 1888	Decom 18 Nov 1924 Sold 15 Jan 1925

Cost
  $66,900 (contract)
  $66,173.30 (actual)

Hull
  Displacement (tons) 643 (full) / 458 (std) / 331 (light)   Mild Steel Hull
  Dimensions   161'0"(loa) / 157'3" (lwl) / 150' (lbp) x 27'0" x 12'0"
                       (9'6" max / 8'9" mean / 6'9" light draft)

Machinery:
  Main Engines   2 fore & aft double expansion steam   IHP 327 BHP 53
  Main Boiler   One marine return flue   Coal fired
  Propulsion   Twin propellers

Complement
  5 officers, 16 men (1907)
  5 officers, 17 men (1910)
  5 officers, 22 men (1917)
  6 officers, 22 men (1922)

Authorized on 08 Apr 1886, $68,300 was appropriated by Congress on 04 Aug 1886, and contracted the following year. However, due to problems with the contractor, construction was delayed and unfinished, and the vessel finally taken over and completed by the government. The Inspection Tender was commissioned as *USLHT Zizania* in 1888. First assigned to the Fourth LHD, it relieved *USLHT Geranium* at Wilmington in Jan 1889. It was moved to Portland, ME, in the First LHD in Jul 1912. In winter of 1917-1918, it performed icebreaking duties on the Kennebec River.

Decommissioned in 1924, it was replaced by *USLHT Ilex*. The old *Zizania* was sold in 1925, becoming the private vessel *SS Zizania*. Its old steam engines were replaced with a 650 SHP diesel engine in the 1930s. Reacquired by the USN at the start of WWII, it became *USS Adario* (YNT-25) and was used as a net tender at Portsmouth, VA. After WWII, it resumed its previous civilian role as the private freighter *Zizania*, operating until 1951.

BOUQUET, 1889

Name	Builder	Contracted	Launched	Commissioned	Disposition
Bouquet	Frank W. Ofeldt South Brooklyn, NY	25 May 1889	1889	10 Aug 1889	Wrecked 29 Aug 1893

Cost
  $1,126

Hull
  Displacement (tons) unknown   Oak Hull, copper sheathed
  Dimensions   25' x 5'6" x 3'

Machinery
  Main Engine   Compound condensing steam
  Main Boiler   Ofeldt spiral coil   Coal fired
  Propulsion   Single propeller

A 25-foot steam launch built in 1889 for the LHS, completed on 10 Aug 1889 and commissioned as *USLHT Bouquet*. Originally equipped as a "naphtha launch" (naphtha is a petroleum distillate similar to kerosene), it was converted to a coal burning boiler in Spring 1891. Served in the Third LHD and stationed at Sandy Hook, NJ, to tend the experimental electric buoys in lower New York Bay, at Gedney's Channel. These electric buoys were all linked to an electrical power source on the shore by an underwater electrical cable. However, the experiment proved unreliable, expensive, and impractical, and the project ran from 1888 until 1903 when it was terminated. *USLHT Bouquet* was wrecked in a storm at moorings at Sandy Hook on 29 Aug 1893, and declared a total loss. A newer boat was purchased as a replacement and commissioned as *USLHT Daisy*.

CLOVER, 1889

Name	Builder	Contracted	Launched	Commissioned	Disposition
Clover	William McKie East Boston, MA	1889	1889	Sep 1889	Laid up 30 Jan 1900 Sold 1900

Cost
  $20,600 (construction) + $1,150 (boiler & winch)

Hull
  Displacement (tons)   440 (full) / 268 (std)   White Oak Hull, Yellow Pine Planking
  Dimensions   126'4" (loa) / 115'0" (lbp) x 29'0" x 9'0" (7'6" draft)

Rig
  Two masted center-board schooner
  Wood derrick and steam hoist winch

Authorized on 30 Mar 1888 with an appropriation of $27,000 as a tender for the Gulf Coast and replacement for *USLHT Mignonette*. This was the last sail powered Lighthouse Tender specifically built for the LHS. Built and completed in Sep 1889, and commissioned as *USLHT Clover* in 1889, it was assigned to New Orleans in the Seventh LHD. Furnished with a small naptha launch *USLHT Bluebell*. Transferred to the Fourth LHD in Dec 1891. Loaned to the Coast Survey on 20 Feb 1894 and returned on 16 Oct 1894. Stripped and sold in 1900. It then became the merchant vessel *Clover*, sailing until 1903.

BLUEBELL, 1889

Name	Builder	Contracted	Launched	Commissioned	Disposition
Bluebell	Frank W. Ofeldt South Brooklyn, NY	1889	1889	Oct 1889	Sold <1910

Cost
  $1,500

Hull
  Dimensions   25'3" x 5'10"   Wood Hull

Machinery
  Main Engine   Naptha
  Propulsion   Single propeller

A small 25-foot launch, built for the LHS in 1889 as *USLHT Bluebell*, and assigned to *USLHT Clover*.

USLHT Clover
National Archives

RUBY, 1890

Name	Builder	Built	Purchased	Commissioned	Disposition
Ruby		NA	NA	05 May 1890	Decom 21 Nov 1890
				Jun 1891	Nov 1891

Cost
$27/day

A steam barge *J.S. Ruby*, chartered on 05 May 1890, at $27 a day, and commissioned as *USLHT Ruby*. Used in construction of fog signals and repair duties in the Ninth and Eleventh LHDs in the Great Lakes. Decommissioned and released from charter on 21 Nov 1890. *Ruby* was rechartered for six months from June to Nov 1891.

THISTLE, 1890

Name	Builder	Built	Purchased	Commissioned	Disposition
Thistle	John C. Froehlich & Co. Baltimore, MD	1890	1890	13 May 1890	Condemned 1912 Sold 06 Dec 1912

Cost
$9,000 (purchase price) + $600 (sheathing and alterations): $9,600 (total)

Hull
- Displacement (tons) 32 (max) / 16 (std)   Oak Hull
- Dimensions 60' (loa) / 55'10" (lwl) / 50' (lbp) x 15'4" x 7'0" (7'9" max / 7'6" mean / 7'0" light)

Machinery
- Main Engine   Keel condensing steam   IHP 45
- Main Boiler   Marine return flue   Coal fired
- Propulsion   Single propeller, cast iron

Complement
- 3 officers, 3 men (1907)
- 2 officers, 3 men (1910)
- 2 officers, 4 men (1911)

Built as the private steam tug *Cynthia* in 1890, and purchased in May 1890 in Baltimore by the LHS. Original proposed name of *Daffodil* not used. Instead, commissioned as *USLHT Thistle* and used as an Engineering Tender in the Fifth LHD at Baltimore, relieving the underpowered *USLHT Nettle*. Its career was mainly uneventful, except for when it was driven ashore at Black River, NJ, in a storm in 1903.

After it was sold in 1912, it became the private towboat *Cynthia*, operating until 1937.

USLHT Thistle, 1890.

National Archives

USLHT Armeria with inverted ensign, distress signal flags and upside down U.S. flag on 20 May 1910, off Cape Hinchinbrook when it wrecked while bringing in supplies and construction materials for the Cape Hinchinbrook Lighthouse. Boats remove the crew from the wrecked tender.

Collection, James A. Gibbs

ARMERIA, 1890

Name	Builder	Contracted	Launched	Commissioned	Disposition
Armeria	John H. Dialague Camden, NJ	06 Feb 1889	20 Nov 1890	04 Dec 1890	Wreck 20 May 1912 Sold 1914

Cost
  $172,745 (contract)
  $178,930.09 (actual)

Hull
  Displacement (tons) 1052 (full) / 632 (mean) Mild Steel Hull
  Dimensions 201'8" (lbp) x 34'9" x 17'7" (13'4" max/ 11'0" light draft)
  Schooner rigged

Machinery
  Main Engines Independent vertical compound steam IHP 1350 BHP 1200
  Main Boilers Two HP cylindrical (Scotch type) Coal fired
  Propulsion Twin propellers

Complement
  7 officers, 27 men (1908)
  8 officers, 25 men (1910)

Appropriations on 03 Mar 1887 for $147,500, and on 02 Oct 1888 for $32,500 authorized construction to replace *USLHT Fern*. The keel was laid on 25 May 1889 and it was commissioned as *USLHT Armeria* in Dec 1890. Built as a Supply Tender for the Gulf and Atlantic coasts, and homeported in the Third LHD at New York. Served with the USN in the Spanish-American War, 05 May-16 Sep 1898, hauling ammunition for the U.S. Army in West Indies. In 1903, *USLHT Armeria* was used to transport and assist the District Inspector for the local Life Saving Service Stations along the southern Texas coast. Moved to the Thirteenth LHD (Washington state) in 1907, it was further moved to Ketchikan, AK, (the new Sixteenth LHD) in 1911, becoming the first LHT permanently assigned to the Alaska territory. On 20 May 1912, while coaling Cape Hinchinbrook Light in Alaska, it struck a submerged uncharted rock and was wrecked. The tender was considered a total loss, and the hulk was hastily sold for $2,500 at auction in 1914. At the time of the accident, it was considered the most expensive loss in the history of the LHS. Its replacement, *USLHT Cedar*, was funded in 1915 by a special appropriation.

USLHT Azalea, 1891.

AZALEA, 1891

Name	Builder	Contracted	Launched	Commissioned	Disposition
Azalea	Jonson Foundry & Machine New York, NY	10 Feb 1890	29 Nov 1890	25 Jun 1891	Decom 30 Jun 1933 Sold 13 Dec 1933

Cost
   $77,125.00 (contract)
   $79,792.40 (actual)

Hull
   Displacement (tons)   516 (full) / 423 (std) / 330 (light)   Mild Steel Hull
   Dimensions   154'0" (loa) / 145'6" (lbp) x 24'3" x 12'4" (9'0" max / 6'6" light draft)

Machinery
   Main Engine   One inverted condensing fore & aft compound steam   IHP 400
   Main Boiler   One cylindrical single ended (Scotch type)   Coal fired
   Propulsion   Single propeller, cast iron, 8'0" diam.

Complement
   5 officers, 14 men (1908)   5 officers, 21 men (1916)
   5 officers, 17 men (1910)   6 officers, 22 men (1922)
   5 officers, 19 men (1911-15)

Authorized by an appropriation of $80,000 on 02 Mar 1889 and built as an Inspection Tender. Laid on 24 May 1890, it was delivered on 18 Jun 1891, and assigned to the Second LHD at Woods Hole, MA. In 1921, damaged in collision with schooner *Lavinia M. Snow* in dense fog off Pollock Rip, but was repaired. Declared beyond economical repair in 1932, it was replaced by *USLHT Myrtle* and sold in 1933, becoming the *M/V Christiana*. It was rebuilt in 1941 with a new 770 SHP diesel engine. It was acquired by the USN in Aug 1942 and commissioned 09 Nov 1942 as *USS Christiana* (IX-80), serving as a seaplane tender in the British West Indies. It was redesignated as *USS YAG-32* (with no name) on 20 Nov 1943 and used as a District Auxiliary. Decommissioned by the Navy on 28 Jul 1945, it was sold on 25 Feb 1946 to the Wilson Line and used as a passenger ship.

LAUREL, 1891

Name	Builder	Contracted	Launched	Commissioned	Disposition
Laurel		NA	25 Jun 1891	1891	Decom 1898

A small steam launch, launched on 25 Jun 1891. Served until 1898.

NFR

USLHT Marigold, 1891. *National Archives*

MARIGOLD, 1891

Name	Builder	Contracted	Launched	Commissioned	Disposition
Marigold	Detroit Dry Dock Co. Wyandotte, MI	04 Mar 1890	15 Nov 1890	04 Oct 1891	Decom 03 Dec 1945 Sold 19 Oct 1946

Cost
  $77,000 (contract)
  $84,870.68 (actual)

Hull
  Displacement (tons)[F.W.]   587 (full) / 454 (std)   Iron Hull
  Dimensions   159'6" (loa) / 150'0" (lwl) x 27'0" x 12'4" (11'7" max / 8'6" mean draft)

Machinery
  Main Engine   1 triple expansion inverted cylinder steam   IHP 550
  Main Boilers   2 cylindrical tubular (Scotch type)   Coal fired
  Propulsion   Single Propeller, 8'6" diam.
  Wood derrick (1890)
  Steel derrick (1919)

Complement
  2 officers, 24 men (1890)
  7 officers, 20 men (1909)
  5 officers, 19 men (1911-15)
  5 officers, 20 men (1917)
  6 officers, 20 men (1920)
  6 officers, 24 men (1937)

Authorized by appropriation on 02 Mar 1889 for $85,000, and planned for the Eleventh LHD in the Great Lakes. Built as an Inspection Tender, providing logistical support to lighthouses. Composite construction with an iron hull. Assigned to the Eleventh LHD at Detroit for its entire career, servicing aids to navigation in Lake Superior and Lake Huron. Rebuilt in 1919, new Marine Type boilers and a steel derrick were installed. In 1923, "Radio Compass" equipment, now known as RDF (radio direction finder), was added. Later classed as a Bay and Sound Tender.

When the LHS merged into the Coast Guard in 1939, this was the oldest active tender still on the roles. Scheduled to be replaced by the new *USCGC Walnut* and decommissioned in 1940, it was instead retained due to the impending war, and overhauled, increasing her gross tonnage to 696. At the start of WWII, *USCGC Marigold* was designated WAGL-235. When it was decommissioned in 1945, it had served longer than any other Lighthouse Tender: 54 years 1 month 30 days! After it was sold in 1946, it was renamed *Miss Mudhen II*, and totally rebuilt into a 106-foot diesel dredge, operating out of Bay City, MI, into the 1980s.

USLHT Amaranth, 1892. *National Archives*

AMARANTH, 1892

Name	Builder	Contracted	Launched	Commissioned	Disposition
Amaranth	Cleveland Ship Bldg. Co. Cleveland, OH	21 May 1891	18 Dec 1891	14 Apr 1892	Decom 29 Sep 1945 Sold 19 Oct 1946

Cost
  $71,500 (contract)
  $74,993.70 (actual)

Hull
  Displacement (tons)[F.W.]   1053 (full) / 743 (std) / 597 (light)   Steel Hull
  Dimensions   166'(loa) / 150'8"(lwl) x 28' x 14'
                              (12'6" max / 11'6" mean / 8'6" light draft)

Machinery
  Main Engine   1 compound inverted reciprocating steam   IHP 672 SHP 600
  Main Boilers   2 cylindrical (Scotch type)   Coal fired
  Propulsion   Single Propeller, steel, 4 blade, 10'0" diam.
  10 ton wood derrick with steam winch

Complement
  5 officers, 17 men (1907)
  6 officers, 20 men (1910-25)
  6 officers, 24 men (1937)

Authorized by an appropriation of $75,000 by Congress on 30 Aug 1890 as an Engineering Tender, its construction was contracted the following year. Assigned to the Eleventh LHD at Detroit after commissioning, servicing lighthouses and buoys on Lake Superior. On 05 Oct 1901, *USLHT Amaranth* rescued a steamer near the rocks at Copper Harbor, MI, in Lake Superior. While supplying Passage Island Light Station in Jul 1920, the Bay and Sound Tender (as it was now classed) was holed and it lost its rudder. It was repaired and also received new boilers. At the start of WWII, it was the second oldest tender still in service, and assigned at Duluth. With the merger of the LHS into the CG in 1939, it was now a CG Cutter and was designated as WAGL-201 in Jan 1942. Decommissioned in 1945 and sold the next year. Re-engined with a 900 HP diesel in 1947, it became the private freighter *South Wind*, operating in the Great Lakes until laid up in 1954.

LILAC class, 1892

Name	Builder	Contracted	Launched	Commissioned	Disposition
Lilac	Globe Iron Works Cleveland, OH	09 May 1891	1891	03 Aug 1892	Decom 18 Nov 1924 Sold 03 Mar 1925
Columbine	Globe Iron Works Cleveland, OH	09 May 1891	1891	Sep 1892	Decom May 1927 Sold 22 Jul 1927

Cost
$92,000 (contract, each)
$92,124.89 (actual, Lilac); $ 93,992.83 (actual, Columbine)

Hull
Displacement (tons) 643 (full) / 434 (std) / 212 (light)   Steel Hull
Dimensions 155'(loa) / 145'(lbp) x 26'6" x 15'2" (12'3" max / 10'6" light draft)

Machinery
Main Engines   2 compound inverted fore & aft steam   IHP 800
Main Boilers   2 cylindrical single ended (Scotch type) Coal fired
Propulsion   Single propeller, cast iron, 9'4" diam.
               Wood derrick with steam hoisting engine

Complement
5 officers, 16 men (1907-10)
5 officers, 19 men (1915-16)
6 officers, 20 men (1922)
6 officers, 22 men (1925)

Design
Built as Sea-Going Tenders, both were authorized by an appropriation of $95,000 each on 30 Aug 1890 and contracted in 1891.

Lilac
Assigned to the First LHD upon completion, and used as an Inspection Tender, replacing the old *USLHT Iris* at Portland, ME. In Jun 1900, it was overhauled and a new boiler installed. After the turn of the century, reassigned to the Ninth LHD at Puerto Rico where it served the rest of its career. In Jun 1915, it was transferred to the Third LHD, but laid up in 1916 due to a lack of funds, and later restored to duty. It was laid up again in Jun 1920 due to a shortage of funds, then reactivated again. It was sold in early 1925, becoming the freighter *Elma*, and operating until 1938.

Columbine
First assigned to the Thirteenth LHD as an Engineering Tender. In 1915, it was transferred to the Nineteenth LHD in Hawaii. A "Wireless Radio" set was installed in 1916. Then in 1918, it moved to Baltimore and Portsmouth, VA, in the Fifth LHD. Besides its normally hectic work serving aids to navigation, *USLHT Columbine* also received two Life Saving Medals and a Letter of Commendation from the President of the United States, Woodrow Wilson, for its heroism in numerous instances of saving lives. Rebuilt in 1920 at a cost of $54,000. Laid up in 1923, but restored to duty in 1925 and assigned to the Ninth LHD at Puerto Rico. It was finally condemned for scrapped in 1927, replaced by *USLHT Acacia*. However, the old hulk was sold and became the *SS Columbine*, operating until 1942, when it was finally abandoned due to old age.

USLHT Lilac, 1892.   Mariners' Museum

USLHT Columbine, 1892.   National Archives

USLHT Hazel, c. 1898. *National Archives*

HAZEL, 1893

Name	Builder	Contracted	Launched	Commissioned	Disposition
Hazel	San Francisco, CA	Jan 1890	1893	1893	Laid up 19 Oct 1901 Sold late 1902

Cost
$1,750 (contract)

Hull
Displacement (tons) 6.7   Wood Hull
Dimensions   45' x 8' x 4'6"

Machinery
Main Engine   Single condensing steam
Main Boiler   Steel marine
Propulsion   Single propeller, 37-½" diam.

A small, 45-foot, wood-hulled, steam-powered, single-screw launch, contracted in Jan 1890 and placed in service in 1893. Originally built to be used by *USLHT Madrono*, but used independently in the Twelfth LHD in northern California waters. Name *USLHT Hazel* assigned in 1894. Laid up in Oct 1901 at Lighthouse Base Goat Island (now known as Yerba Buena Island in San Francisco Bay), and dismantled and sold in 1902.

ARUM, 1893

Name	Builder	Contracted	Launched	Commissioned	Disposition
Arum		1893	1893		Sold 1908

Cost
$1,135.50

Hull
Displacement (tons) unknown   Wood Hull
Dimensions   25' x 6' x 3' (1'6" max draft)

Machinery
Main Engine   Internal combustion   5 BHP
Propulsion   Single Screw

A small, 25-foot, gas-engined, single-screw, wood-hulled launch, built by the LHS in 1893, and originally assigned to *USLHT Pharos* as a support vessel. After *Pharos* was sold in 1908, it was used independently for inspection, repair and construction work of aids in the Charleston, SC, vicinity. It served past 1910.

USLHT Maple after its 1901 rehabilitation when the superstructure was replaced.

Mariners' Museum

MAPLE, 1893

Name	Builder	Contracted	Launched	Commissioned	Disposition
Maple	Samuel L. Moore & Sons Co. Elizabethport, NJ	1891	1892	Jun 1893	Decom Sold 29 Oct 1933

Cost
$81,800 (contract)
$93,888.90 (actual)

Hull
   Displacement (tons)   799 (full) / 567 (std) / 392 (light)   Steel Hull
   Dimensions   164'(loa) / 156'6"(lwl) / 155'(lbp) x 30' x 11'10"
                      (9'5" max / 8'6" mean / 7'3" light draft)

Machinery
   Main Engines   2 compound fore & aft steam   IHP 650
   Main Boilers   2 steel cylindrical Scotch type   Coal fired
   Propulsion   Twin propellers, cast iron, 4 blade, 6'9" diam.
   Schooner rigged   Wood derrick with steam winch

Complement
   5 officers, 21 men (1910)
   6 officers, 22 men (1911-22)
   5 officers, 20 men (1920)
   7 officers, 25 men (1924-30)

Appropriations of $95,000 authorized for construction on 03 Mar 1891, it was built an Inspector's Tender and delivered on 26 May 1893. It was assigned to the Fifth LHD at Baltimore for its entire career, tending aids on the Virginia coast. It served with the USN (23 Apr-20 Sep 1898) during the Spanish-American War, then was repaired and returned to duty on 06 Feb 1899. In 1901, new boilers were installed and the wood deckhouse was replaced with a steel deckhouse. Later designated as a Bay and Sound Tender, it was still operating in the Fifth LHD. Sold in 1933 into private hands, its engines were removed and it served as an unpowered sail barge under various names (including *McClain* and *Nichols No. 6*) until 1948, and was dismantled in 1949.

The *Drift* as the lightship *Bush* at Bush Bluff, 1914.
U.S. Coast Guard

LEAL, 1894

Name	Builder	Built	Purchased	Commissioned	Disposition
Leal		1894		1894	Decom 1907

A small, steam naphtha launch, built for the LHS in July 1894, and assigned to the Fourth LHD. Placed out of service and laid up in 1907.

DRIFT, 1894

Name	Builder	Built	Purchased	Commissioned	Disposition
Drift		1876	20 May 1893	Mar 1894	Condemned 15 Jan 1918
	Baltimore, MD				Sold 03 May 1920

Hull
- Displacement (tons) 87
- Wood Hull
- Dimensions 80'6" (loa) / 76'0" (lbp) / 60'0" (lwl) x 19'6" x 12'0" (10'8" draft)

Rig
Schooner

Crew
5 officers, 14 men (1907)

Originally built in 1876 for the Coast & Geodetic Survey (now known as N.O.A.A.) as the *USCSS Drift*. Acquired by the LHS in 1893 as *USLHT Drift* (original name retained). Assigned to the Fourth LHD, it was extensively modified and was used as a replacement Light Ship at Bush Bluff, and designated Light Vessel #97, serving in that capacity starting in 1895. Later it was restored and used as a Lighthouse Tender until condemned in 1918.

Authorized for sale on 27 Apr 1920, the sale was completed in May 1920 and it was sold for $150. It then had an engine installed and it became the private vessel *M/V W.J. Townsend*, until 1945 when it was scrapped due to old age.

USLHT *Daisy* loaded with typical "Nun" and "Can" buoys.

National Archives

DAISY, 1895

Name	Builder	Built	Purchased	Commissioned	Disposition
Daisy	Edward Clark & Co. New Bedford, MA	1892	Feb 1895	1895	Decom Sold 19 Mar 1928

Cost
  $6,500 (purchase price)

Hull
  Displacement (tons)   84 (full) / 61 (std) / 35 (light)   Oak frame, Pine planking
  Dimensions   54' x 13'8" x 5'8" (draft 6'0" max / 5' mean / 3'10" light)

Machinery
  Main Engine   Compound condensing steam   BHP 60
  Main Boiler   Upright tubular   Coal fired
  Propulsion   Single propeller

Complement
  2 officers, 4 men (1907-17)
  2 officers, 5 men (1925)

Built as the private launch *Genevieve* in 1892. Purchase authorized on 23 Jan 1895 by the LHS, and completed in Feb 1895 as a replacement for the wrecked *USLHT Bouquet*, to service buoys in Gedney's Channel in lower New York Bay in the Third LHD. Commissioned as *USLHT Daisy*, and assigned to Staten Island, NY, to be used as an Inspector's Launch. Sold in 1928 and replaced by *USLHT Beech*.

USLHT *Water Lily*. *National Archives*

WATER LILY class, 1895

Name	Builder	Contracted	Launched	Commissioned	Disposition
Water Lily	Gas Engine & Power Co. Morris Heights, NY	31 Jul 1895	NA	31 Oct 1895	Decom 1929 Sold 02 Jul 1930
Snowdrop	Gas Engine & Power Co. Morris Heights, NY	Dec 1896	1896	Jan 1897	Decom 1922 Sold 1924

Cost
   $9,700 (contract, each)
   $9,260.50 (actual, Water Lily); $9,670 (actual, Snowdrop)

Hull
   Displacement (tons)   39 (full) / 33 (std) / 29 (light)   White Oak Hull, Cedar planking
   Dimensions   69' (loa) / 64' (lwl) / 61'1" (lbp) x 10'6" x 5'
      (3'8" max / 3'3" mean / 2'11" light draft)

Machinery
   Main Engines   Internal combustion, naphtha   IHP 24
   Propulsion   Twin Propellers   BHP 32 (Water Lily)
                                    36 (Snowdrop)

Complement
   (Water Lily)   (Snowdrop)
      1 officer, 3 men (1896-1910)   1 officer, 5 men (1897)
      2 officers, 2 men (1915-16)   2 officers, 2 men (1907-17)
      2 officers, 3 men (1925)

Design
   Built as small launches.

Water Lily
Authorized in Oct 1895 and built for the LHS, it served as an Inspector's launch at Charleston, SC, in the Sixth LHD for its entire career. In 1896, it was working the Indian River in Florida. Changed from naptha to gasoline, rated at 36 HP in 1912. In 1927, it was transferred to the Sixth LHD. In 1929, it was declared beyond economical repair and laid up, and replaced by *USLHT Althea*. Sold for $401, it became the passenger boat *M/V Water Lily*, operating until 1944 when it was abandoned due to old age.

Snowdrop
Built in Dec 1896 as a small engineering launch and assigned to Charleston, SC, operating out of the Sixth and Seventh LHDs. The engine was converted to burn gasoline in the early 1910s.

MADRONO, 1896

Name	Builder	Contracted	Launched	Commissioned	Disposition
Madrono	San Francisco, CA	29 Jan 1896	1896	Jun 1896	Decom 1907

Cost
  $2,000

Hull
  Displacement (tons) unknown   Wood Hull
  Dimensions 32'8"(loa) / 30'6"(lbp) x 7'8-½" x 5'01"   Coal fired

Machinery
  Main Engine   Vertical Inverted non-condensing compound steam
  Main Boiler   Return tubular

A small, wood-hulled, steam launch, funded on 08 Jan 1896 and built that same year to provide inshore support work with the larger *USLHT Madrono*. Operated solely within the San Francisco Bay, serving until 1907.

MAYFLOWER, 1897

Name	Builder	Contracted	Launched	Commissioned	Disposition
Mayflower	Bath Iron Works Bath, ME	23 Jan 1897	1897	Nov 1897	Decom 08 Oct 1945 Sold 08 Oct 1945

Cost
  $72,000 (contract)
  $74,872.07 (actual)

Hull
  Displacement (tons) 668 (full) / 572 (std) / 392 (light)   Steel Hull
  Dimensions   164' (loa) / 155' (lwl) x 30' x 11'10" (9'0" max / 8'6" mean / 8'1" light draft)

Machinery
  Main Engines   2 Steeple compound inverted reciprocating steam   IHP 650
  Main Boilers   2 Almy watertube   Coal fired
  Propulsion   Twin propellers

Complement
  4 officers, 19 men (1909)
  5 officers, 22 men (1915)
  5 officers, 24 men (1924)
  7 officers, 25 men (1937)

Design
  Built as a Bay and Sound Tender. Considered a half-sister to *Mangrove*.

Appropriation for $37,500 authorized on 11 Jun 1896 for a tender for the Second LHD, with a second appropriation for $37,500 on 04 Jun 1897 to complete. Although built as the *Mayflower*, it was immediately taken over by the USN on 27 Apr 1898 for service during the Spanish-American War, and commissioned as *USS Suwanee*, and serving until 23 Sep 1898. It was cited by the Navy for "Conspicuous Service." Returned to the LHS in Dec 1898, it was placed into service as *USLHT Mayflower* and assigned to the Second LHD in Boston. In 1924, it was relieved by the new *USLHT Lotus* in the Second LHD, then was transferred to the Fifth LHD. In Dec 1939, it was decommissioned and transferred to the Maritime Training Service in Boston, but was recommissioned as a Tender in the Coast Guard as *USCGC Mayflower* (WAGL-236) in Jul 1940 and relocated to Norfolk, VA. On 15 Aug 1943, its name was changed to *USCGC Hydrangea*, to avoid a naming conflict with another naval vessel called *USS Mayflower*. Upon decommissioning in 1945, it was transferred to the Maritime Commission for final disposal.

USLHT Mayflower, the only vessel in the Lighthouse Service to have three different names while in federal service, 1897. *U.S. Coast Guard*

USLHT Mangrove, 1897. *U.S. Coast Guard*

MANGROVE, 1897

Name	Builder	Contracted	Launched	Commissioned	Disposition
Mangrove	Crescent Shipyard Elizabethport, NJ	14 Jan 1897	NA	01 Dec 1897	Decom 22 Aug 1946 Sold 06 May 1947

Cost
  $72,000 (contract)
  $74,997.63 (actual)

Hull
  Displacement (tons)   821 (full) / 682 (std) / 572 (light)   Steel Hull, Wood Decks
  Dimensions   164' (loa) / 155' (lbp) x 30' x 11'10" (8'6" max / 8'0" mean / 7'0" light draft)

Machinery
  Main Engines   2 compound inverted reciprocating steam   SHP 650 IHP 550
  Main Boilers   2 Page & Burton watertube   Coal fired
  Propulsion   Twin propellers, cast iron, 4 blade, 7'0" diam.
                  Hydraulic hoisting winch

Complement
  2 officers, 29 men (1897)
  6 officers, 22 men (1910-15)
  7 officers, 24 men (1922-24)

Design
   Built of composite construction with a steel hull and wood decking, to be used as a Lighthouse Cargo Tender. Similar in design and considered a half-sister of *USLHT Mayflower*.

Funds were appropriated on 11 Jun 1896 for $37,500 for a tender for the Seventh and Eighth LHDs, and additional funds on 04 Jun 1897 for $37,500 to be completed and relieve *USLHT Laurel*. It was completed in 1897 and assigned to the Seventh LHD at Key West. *USLHT Mangrove* brought back the surviving wounded to Key West from the exploded *USS Maine* in Havana harbor. Later it also brought back guns salvaged off the *Maine* and American civilians leaving Cuba at the start of the Spanish-American War. *USLHT Mangrove* served with the USN (10 Apr-18 Aug 1898) in the Spanish-American War and cited by the Navy for "Conspicuous Service," operating out of Key West, FL. In Oct 1909, while still at Key West, it assisted *USRC Forward* which had been stranded by a hurricane. By 1922, it had been reassigned to Charleston, SC, in the Sixth LHD where it remained for the rest of its career. With the onset of WWII, it was designated WAGL-232 in Jan 1942 when all tenders were assigned hull designations and numbers for the first time.

PINK, 1898

Name	Builder	Contracted	Launched	Commissioned	Disposition
Pink		NA	NA	1898	Decom <1923

Cost
  $2,290

Hull
  Displacement (tons)   unknown   Wood Hull
  Dimensions   30' x 7' x 6' (3'6" mean draft)

Machinery
  Main Engines   Gasoline internal combustion   BHP 18
  Propulsion   Single propeller

Complement
  No regular crew assigned

Originally built as a launch for *USLHT Armeria*. When *Armeria* moved to Alaska in 1907, *USLHT Pink* remained behind and operated as an independent harbor launch in the Third LHD. In 1911, it was relocated to the Eighth LHD.

NFR

IRIS, 1899

Name	Builder	Built	Purchased	Commissioned	Disposition
Iris	Neafie & Levy Philadelphia, PA	1897	1899	18 Dec 1899	Decom Sold 21 Jun 1934

Cost
  $84,406.76 (purchase price)

Hull
  Displacement (tons)   606 (full) / 519 (std) / 428 (light)   Steel Hull
  Dimensions   153'(loa)/141'8"(lwl) x 30'1" x 13'4" (9'6" max / 8'7" light draft)

Machinery
  Main Engine   Steam   IHP 800
  Main Boiler   Coal fired
  Propulsion   Single propeller

Complement
  5 officers, 16 men (1907)
  5 officers, 18 men (1910)
  5 officers, 21 men (1924)

Design
  Built as the private vessel *SS Plymouth* in 1897 for the Winthrop Steamship Co.

An appropriation was authorized for $85,000 on 03 Mar 1899 to build a new tender for the Third LHD. However, due to urgent needs, it was decided to purchase rather than buy, with an estimated cost of $77,500 plus an additonal $6,500 to outfit. Purchased and commissioned as *USLHT Iris* in 1899, it was used as an Engineering Tender in the Fourth LHD, and operated out of Philadelphia for most of its career. Replaced by *USLHT Lilac*, the old *Iris* was sold in 1934 into private hands, and used as the private freighter *Big Chief*. At the start of WWII, it served as U.S. Army Large Tug *Big Chief*. It was later acquired by the Navy on 05 May 1943 as *USS Big Chief* (IX-101) until after WWII. It was then sold and re-engined with a 450 HP diesel, becoming the private vessel *B.O. Colonna*, operating as a fishing vessel until scrapped in 1973.

USLHT Iris, 1899.   *National Archives*

AGUACATE, 1901

Name	Builder	Aquired	Launched	Commissioned	Disposition
Aguacate		29 Oct 1901	NA	Oct 1901	Decom Dec 1901

A small 38-foot sloop, a U.S. Army war prize from the Spanish-American War, turned over to the LHS on 29 Oct 1901 and commissioned as *USLHT Aguacate* (original name retained), serving in Puerto Rico. Severe damaged in a storm on 05 Dec 1901, made this the tender with the shortest life span in USLHS history: 38 days!!
NFR

JUNIPER, 1903

Name	Builder	Contracted	Launched	Commissioned	Disposition
Juniper	Spedden Shipbuilding Co. Baltimore, MD	25 Aug 1902	1902	1903	Decom 01 Nov 1932 Sold 22 Dec 1932

Cost
   $27,300 (contract)
   $29,425.20 (actual)

Hull
   Displacement (tons)   146 (max) / 125 (mean) / 108 (light)   Steel Hull
   Dimensions   95'4"(loa) / 90'11" (lbp) x 18'2" x 8'1" (5'6" max / 4'6" light draft)

Machinery
   Main Engines   2 inclined cylindrical inverted direct acting steam   IHP 290 BHP 300
   Main Boiler   1 Roberts water tube   Coal fired
   Propulsion   Twin Propellers, cast iron, 4 blade, 3'3" diam.

Complement
   2 officers, 4 men (1907-11)
   2 officers, 5 men (1915)
   4 officers, 8 men (1924-25)
   4 officers, 9 men (1930)

Design
   Built as a Inland/Harbor Tender, to replace *USLHT Bramble*.

Authorized and funded by appropriations 06 Jun 1900 ($20,000) and 28 Jun 1902 ($12,000), the keel was laid in 1902 and it completed in 1903. It was assigned to the Fifth LHD at Baltimore as an Inspection Tender, replacing the old *USLHT Bramble*. New boilers were installed in 1920. Sold in 1932 into private hands, it was rebuilt as the freighter *SS Juniper*, operating out of Norfolk, VA. Later, it served as the tanker *Aubrey L. Hudgins* until 1979.

USLHT Juniper, 1924.

LILAC, 1903

Name	Builder	Contracted	Launched	Commissioned	Disposition
Lilac		NA	1903	1903	Decom NA

A small steam launch put into service on the lower Mississippi River in 1903 as *USLHT Lilac*. After 1904, no further records. It is unknown whether the launch was placed out of service, or the name was removed to avoid a naming conflict with a larger *USLHT Lilac*, which served from 1892 to 1924.

NFR

OLEANDER, 1903

Name	Builder	Contracted	Launched	Commissioned	Disposition
Oleander	Iowa Iron Works Dubuque, IA	03 Mar 1901	1902	23 Jan 1903	Decom 23 Apr 1928 Trans to War Dept 1928

Cost
   $56,000 (contract)
   $60,000 (actual)

Hull
   Displacement (tons)[F.W.]   548 (full) / 463 (std) / 344 (light)   Steel Hull & Deck, Wood upperworks
   Dimensions   188'6" (loa) / 165'(lbp) x 34' x 7'
   (4'6" max / 3'8" light draft)

Machinery
   Main Engines   2 Baldwin-Vulclain horizontal compound steam   IHP 600
   Main Boilers   2 Hopkinds combined tubular and water tube   Coal fired
   Propulsion   Stern paddle wheel (22' diam, 21' wide)
   Twin rudders
   Steam winch

Complement
   6 officers, 23 men (1907)
   6 officers, 18 men (1910)
   4 officers, 17 men (1922)

Design
   Built as a River Tender, with a steel hull and wood superstructure, to replace *USLHT Joseph Henry*.

Authorized and funds appropriated ($30,000) on 06 Jun 1900 as a replacement for *USLHT Joseph Henry*, and completed in 1903. Served on the upper Mississippi River, primarily out of St. Louis. Transferred to the War Department (Army) in 1928, and replaced by *USLHT Willow*.

NFR

USLHT Oleander, 1904.

National Archives

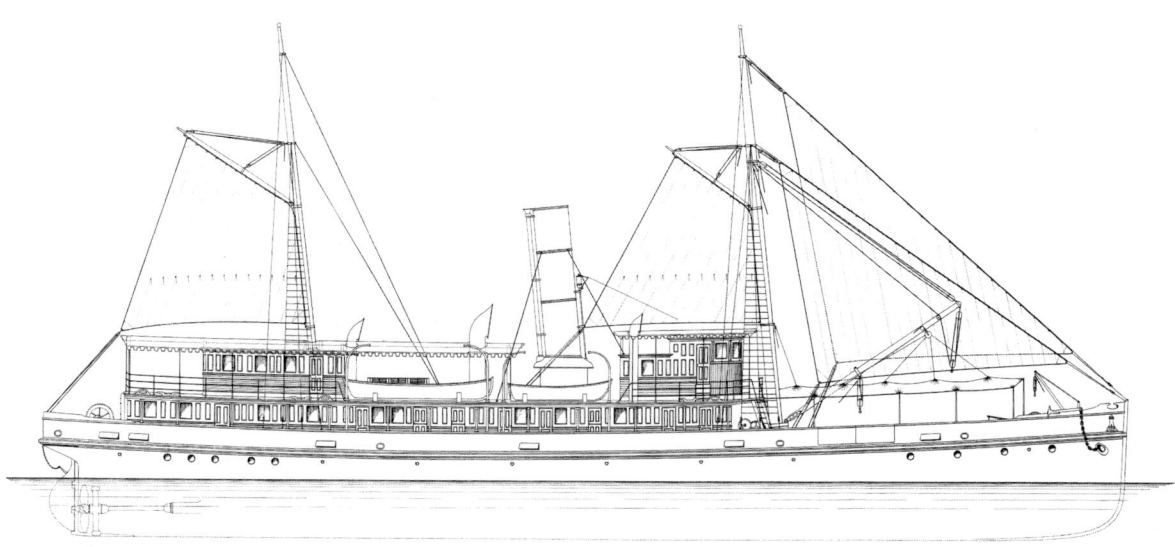

Plan for *USLHT Larkspur*, 1900. — National Archives

LARKSPUR, 1903

Name	Builder	Contracted	Launched	Commissioned	Disposition
Larkspur		01 Apr 1901	NA	24 Feb 1903	Decom 10 Jan 1946
	Port Richmond, NY				Sold 19 Feb 1946

Cost
  $123,258.77

Hull
  Displacement (tons) 888 (max) / 738 (std), 685 (light) Steel Hull
  Dimensions 169'2"(loa) / 162'(lbp) x 30' x 14'1"
  (10'6" max / 9'10" mean / 9'01" light draft)

Machinery
  Main Engines 2 vertical inverted compound fore & aft express steam   IHP 750
  Main Boilers 2 watertube express (gunboat type)   Coal fired
  Propulsion Twin propellers, cast iron, 4 blade, 7'6" diam.

Complement
  2 officers, 27 men (1903)
  5 officers, 22 men (1910)
  6 officers, 22 men (1911-15)
  6 officers, 24 men (1917)
  7 officers, 25 men (1925)

Design
  Built as a Bay and Sound Tender with a steel hull and composite superstructure and forward derrick.

Planned in 1900 with an appropriation on 06 Jun 1900 for $62,500 for a new tender for the Third LHD, with an additional $62,500 appropriated on 03 Mar 1901 to complete. Contracted in 1901, *USLHT Larkspur* was completed in 1903 and assigned as an Inspection Tender in the Third LHD at Staten Island, NY. On 26 Feb 1909, it assisted *USRC Mohawk* which was aground on rocks near Hell Gate in New York harbor. New boilers and machinery were installed at a cost of $84,778 in 1916-1917. In Jun 1933, it was laid up for three years. Then it was rebuilt in 1938 and converted from coal to oil burning, then transferred to the Eighth LHD at Mobile, AL, where it was recommissioned in Apr 1939. Designated WAGL-226 at the start of WWII.

USLHT Heather, 1903.
Columbia River Maritime Museum

HEATHER, 1903

Name	Builder	Contracted	Launched	Commissioned	Disposition
Heather	Moran Shipbuilding Seattle, WA	06 Jun 1900	1902	10 Jun 1903	Decom 06 Sep 1940 Trans War Dept 06 Sep 1940

Cost
   $118,567.58

Hull
   Displacement (tons)   831 (max) / 731 (mean) / 631 (light)   Composite Hull
   Dimensions   178'6" (loa) / 170' (lwl) / 165' (lbp) x 28'6" x 14'11"
   (11'6" max / 9'6" mean draft)

Machinery
   Main Engine   1 vertical condensing fore & aft compound steam   IHP 685 SHP 750
   Main Boilers   2 Scotch type   Coal fired
   Propulsion   Single Propeller, cast iron, 9'6" diam.

Complement
   5 officers, 19 men (1907)
   6 officers, 20 men (1910)
   7 officers, 20 men (1924)

Design
   Built as a seagoing or Coastwise Tender, with a composite hull (steel and wood).

Authorized by an appropriation of $100,000 on 03 Mar 1899 for a tender for the Thirteenth LHD, and a supplemental appropriation of $20,000 on 06 Jun 1900 to complete. Contracted in 1900, completion was delayed due to a labor strike to the builder and it wasn't completed until 16 Mar 1903. Assigned to the Thirteenth LHD in Seattle, WA. Re-engined with a single 685 HP diesel engine in the late 1930s. Became *USCGC Heather* on 01 Sep 1939 when the LHS became part of the Coast Guard. On 03 Sep 1940 *Heather* was loaned to the War Department (U.S. Army). Three days later on 06 Sep 1940, the transfer was made permanent and it became Army ship *Heather* (FS-534). The new *USCGC Fir* assumed the duties of the old *Heather*. After WWII, the old *Heather* was sold foreign and converted to an oil burner. It was reportedly operating as a freighter off the China coast in the 1950s.

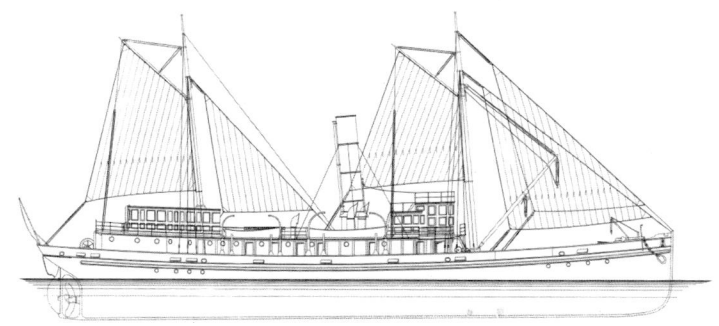

This plan for *USLHT Heather,* dated 1899, shows that although steam was the primary propulsion, a sail plan was still part of the design.

National Archives

USLHT Sumac, c. 1934. *National Archives*

SUMAC, 1903

Name	Builder	Contracted	Launched	Commissioned	Disposition
Sumac	Burlee Dry Dock Co. Port Richmond, NY	27 May 1901	NA	21 Jun 1903	Decom Jul 1937 Sold 1937

Cost
    $111,310 (contract)
    $114,992.27 (actual)

Hull
    Displacement (tons)[F.W.]   875 (full) / 675 (std) / 600 (light)   Mild Steel Hull
    Dimensions   168'10"(loa) / 160'(lbp) x 30' x 14'11"
    (11'9" max / 8'10" light draft)

Machinery
    Main Engines   2 vertical inverted fore & aft compound steam   IHP 700
    Main Boilers   2 Scotch type   Coal fired
    Propulsion   Twin Propellers, cast iron, 4 blade, 7'6" diam.
    Steam windlass/winch

Complement
    6 officers, 18 men (1907)
    6 officers, 21 men (1910)
    6 officers, 22 men (1911-15)
    5 officers, 23 men (1918)
    6 officers, 23 men (1925)

Design
    Built exclusively for service in the Great Lakes.

Authorized on 03 Mar 1899 for $85,000, but by 25 Jun 1900 there were no takers to build due to potential cost of construction. A new appropriation was authorized on 03 Mar 1901 for $115,000, a contract was accepted and its keel was laid in 1901 and was completed in 1903. *USLHT Sumac* was assigned to the Ninth LHD at Milwaukee as an Inspector's Tender. In 1925, it was assigned to the Twelfth LHD as a Bay and Sound Tender. After decommissioning, it was replaced by *USLHT Hollyhock*. The old tender was then sold to Canadian owners, and it became the tug *Oscar Lehtinen* and used to tow log rafts. It was scrapped in 1957.

USLHT Hyacinth, 1904. *National Archives*

HYACINTH, 1903

Name	Builder	Contracted	Launched	Commissioned	Disposition
Hyacinth	Jenks Shipbuilding Co. Port Huron, MI	22 Jul 1901	26 Jul 1902	26 Jun 1903	Decom 15 Nov 1945 Sold 19 Oct 1946

Cost
  $107,560.45 (contract)
  $115,000 (actual)

Hull
  Displacement (tons) [F.W.]   950 (max) / 914 (full) / 718 (mean) / 493 (light)   Steel Hull
  Dimensions   160'6" (loa) / 150'8" (lwl) x 28' x 14' (11'6" max / 7'0" light draft)

Machinery
  Main Engine   1 compound fore & aft express steam   SHP 878 IHP 768
  Main Boilers   2 Scotch type   Coal fired
  Propulsion   Single Propeller, cast iron, 4 blade, 10'0" diam.

Complement
  5 officers, 18 men (1907)
  5 officers, 19 men (1911-15)
  5 officers, 20 men (1917)
  6 officers, 20 men (1922-25)

Design
  Composite construction with a steel hull and wood deck/superstucture.

Proposed in 1899 and authorized on 06 Jun 1900 by an appropriation of $50,000 for a new construction tender for the Ninth LHD. Bids were opened on 10 Jul 1901 and the contract let. The keel was laid on 18 Oct 1901. Additional appropriations for $65,000 were authorized on 28 Jun 1902, and it was completed in 1903. *USLHT Hyacinth* was assigned to the Ninth LHD at Milwaukee on Lake Michigan as an Engineering Tender where it spent its entire career. Converted from coal to oil fired steam in the mid-1930s.

USLHT Ivy, 1904. *U.S. Coast Guard*

MAGNOLIA class, 1904

Name	Builder	Contracted	Launched	Commissioned	Disposition
Magnolia	Baltimore Shipbuilding & Dry Dock, Baltimore, OH	1902	Oct 1903	05 May 1904	Sunk 25 Aug 1945
Ivy	Baltimore Shipbuilding & Dry Dock, Baltimore, OH	1902	08 Nov 1903	09 May 1904	Decom 06 Nov 1940, Sold 25 Apr 1941

Cost
  $124,873.60 (Magnolia)
  $123,860.46 (Ivy)

Hull
  Displacement (tons) 877 (full) / 736 (std) / 550 (light)   Steel Hull
  Dimensions   173' (loa) / 165' (lwl/lbp) x 30'5" x 13'1"
                       (9'6" max / 8'5" mean draft)

Machinery
  Main Engines   2 compound surface condensing steam   IHP 750 SHP 700
  Main Boilers   2 Page & Burton watertube   Coal fired
  Propulsion   Twin Propellers

Complement
  5 officers, 22 men (1907-17)
  7 officers, 25 men (1924)

CORRECTION--page 79

The tenders MAGNOLIA and IVY were built at the Baltimore Shipbuilding & Dry Dock of Baltimore, Maryland ... not Ohio

Magnolia
Appropriation of $125,000 authorized on 03 Mar 1901 for a tender for the Eighth LHD. Assigned as an Inspection Tender in the Eighth LHD at Mobile, AL, and occasionally at New Orleans, for its entire career. Converted from coal to oil burning in the 1934. On 25 Aug 1945 off Mobile, AL, *USCGC Magnolia* (WAGL-231) was rammed amidships by the new C-3 cargo ship *SS Marguerite LeHand* which was on its maiden voyage. *Magnolia* sank in two minutes, with the loss of one life and 49 survivors. That crew was assigned to the new *USCGC Salvia* (WAGL-400), which then assumed the duties of the old *Magnolia* at Mobile Bay.

Ivy
Authorized by an appropriation on 03 Mar 1901 of $85,000 for a tender for the Seventh LHD. Upon completion, it was homeported at Key West, FL, in the Seventh LHD, serving the Seventh and Eighth LHDs as an Engineering Tender. In Apr 1914, it was relieved by *USLHT Myrtle* and transferred to the Fifth LHD at Portsmouth, VA. The steam plant was converted from coal to oil burning in Mar 1930. It became *USCGC Ivy* when the LHS merged into the Coast Guard on 01 Sep 1939. It was decommissioned and sold before the onset of WWII.

USLHT Crocus, working on a lighted buoy, 1905. U.S. Coast Guard

CROCUS, 1905

Name	Builder	Contracted	Launched	Commissioned	Disposition
Crocus	Townsend-Downey Co. Shooters Islands, Richmond, NY	18 Aug 1902	1903	26 Jul 1905	Decom 13 Jul 1946 Sold Jul 1946

Cost
  $113,900 (contract)
  $119,718.44 (actual)

Hull
  Displacement (tons)[F.W.]   1035 (max) / 910 (full) / 626 (std)   Steel Hull, wood superstructure
  Dimensions   164'7" (loa)/154'6"(lbp) x 29' x 13'6"
               (12'3" max / 9'0" mean draft)

Machinery
  Main Engines   2 vertical inverted compound reciprocating steam   IHP 700 SHP 720
  Main Boilers   2 Scotch (gunboat type)   Coal fired
  Propulsion   Twin cast iron propellers, 7'8" diam.
                 Steam derrick

Complement
  5 officers, 20 men (1908)
  6 officers, 22 men (1911)
  5 officers, 23 men (1923)
  6 officers, 23 men (1930)

Design
  Built with a steel hull and composite (steel and wood) superstructure.

$120,000 was appropriated by Congress on 03 Mar 1901 for an Inspector's Tender for the Tenth LHD, and the ship's construction was contracted the following year. It replaced the old *USLHT Haze*, and took her crew. Upon commissioning in 1905, it was assigned to the Tenth LHD, serving out of Buffalo, NY. In 1932, it was converted to oil-fired boilers. By the late 1930s its homeport had been changed to Detroit. In Jan 1942, *USCGC Crocus* was designatd WAGL-210 and served during WWII out of Toledo, OH.

USLHT Aspen with its crew, 1906.   *National Archives*

ASPEN, 1906

Name	Builder	Contracted	Launched	Commissioned	Disposition
Aspen	Craig Shipbuilding Co. Toledo, OH	1904	1905	08 May 1906	Decom 25 Jan 1947 Sold 26 Jan 1948

Cost
  $70,572.50

Hull
  Displacement (tons)[F.W.]   415 (full) / 353 (std) / 276 (std)   Steel Hull
  Dimensions   125'9"(loa) / 117'8"(lwl/lbp) x 25' x 11'10"
                              (9'6" max / 8'3" mean / 7'3" light draft)

Machinery
  Main Engines   1 compound reciprocating steam   IHP 440 SHP 424
  Main Boilers   1 cylindrical Scotch type   Coal fired
  Propulsion   Single propeller

Complement
  4 officers, 8 men (1908)
  4 officers, 11 men (1911)
  4 officers, 10 men (1915-25)
  4 officers, 14 men (1937)

Design
  Built as a Bay and Sound tender.

After many years of unanswered requests for a "patrol steamer" for the Saint Mary's River in the Great Lakes, an appropriation of $4,000 was authorized for a tender. However, the funds were insufficient and no action was taken towards construction until $75,000 was authorized on 03 Mar 1903. Upon completion, it was assigned to the Eleventh LHD at Detroit, MI. A new boiler was installed in 1932. When the Coast Guard assigned hull numbers to all its newly acquired Buoy Tenders in Jan 1942, *USCGC Aspen* was designated WAGL-204. For the duration and after WWII, it was homeported at Sault Ste. Marie.

After it was decommissioned in 1947, it was sold into private hands in 1948. The hull was last spotted near Grand Haven, MI, in 1962, in storage for possible conversion and use.

USLHT Yerba Buena harbor launch in San Francisco Bay. The Bay Bridge is under construction in the background.

U.S. Coast Guard

YERBA BUENA, 1907

Name	Builder	Contracted	Built	Commissioned	Disposition
Yerba Buena		NA	1906	1907	Decom 1933
					Sold Dec 1933

Cost
  $4,241

Hull
  Displacement (tons) 14   Wood Hull
  Dimensions   42' x 10' x 6' (4'2" max draft)

Machinery
  Main Engines   Internal combustion, gasoline   BHP 45
  Propulsion   Single propeller

Complement
  No officers, 2 men (1910)
  No permanent crew (1930-33)

Design
  Built as a harbor launch to tend aids in the San Francisco Bay, and ferry workers from San Francisco and Oakland to Yerba Buena Island in the middle of San Francisco Bay, where the Lighthouse Depot was located. *USLHT Yerba Buena* was placed out of service before the new San Francisco-Oakland Bay Bridge was completed, connecting San Francisco to Oakland via Yerba Buena Island.

CLOVER, 1907

Name	Builder	Contracted	Launched	Commissioned	Disposition
Clover		NA	NA	NA	Decom 1911

A small, steam launch, served in the Eleventh LHD. Was rebuilt in 1907, serving until 1911.

NFR

LOTUS, 1907

Name	Builder	Contracted	Launched	Commissioned	Disposition
Lotus		NA	NA	NA	Decom <1923

Hull
    Displacement (tons) unknown   Steel Hull
    Dimensions unknown

Machinery
    Main Engines steam
    Propulsion unknown

Complement
    No regular crew assigned.

A steam launch which served in the Eleventh LHD in 1907.

NFR

DANDELION, 1907

A proposed river tender authorized by special appropriation of $60,000 on 04 Mar 1907 for the Fifteenth LHD, but construction permanently deferred in 1908 due to funding limitations, and not built. On 27 Jul 1912, the funding authorization which was still pending was modified for the construction of a smaller tender for the Atlantic Coast, to be named *Laurel*.

See *Laurel* 1915 for details.

USLHT Sunflower, 1907. *Nautical Research Centre*

SUNFLOWER, 1907

Name	Builder	Contracted	Launched	Commissioned	Disposition
Sunflower	Wilmington, DE	14 Sep 1905	04 Aug 1906	23 Mar 1907	Decom 10 Jan 1946 Sold 19 Feb 1947

Cost
  $124,958.32

Hull
  Displacement (tons) 1246 (full) / 806 (std) / 727 (light) Steel Hull
  Dimensions 173'7"(loa) / 163'6" (lbp) x 32' x 15'6"
    (13'3" max / 12'2" mean / 9'8" light draft)

Machinery
  Main Engines 2 triple expansion steam SHP 900
  Main Boilers 2 Babcock & Wilcox watertube (Scotch) Coal fired
  Propulsion Twin propellers, 7'6" diam.
    Steam winch

Complement
  5 officers, 24 men (1907)
  6 officers, 23 men (1910)
  6 officers, 26 men (1917)
  7 officers, 27 men (1922)

Design
  Built as a Coastwise Tender, she was the first to use wire rope instead of manila.

Authorized by an appropriation of $50,000 on 28 Apr 1904 as an Inspection Tender for the Fourth LHD, an additional $75,000 was appropriated on 03 Mar 1905 to complete construction. It was reassigned from Philadelphia in the Fourth LHD to the Eighth LHD at New Orleans in Jan 1913 for the remainder of its career. Converted from coal burning to oil burning steam in the summer of 1931. Just before WWII, she was operating out of Galveston, TX. Designated WAGL-247 at the start of WWII.

MANZANITA class, 1908

Name	Builder	Keel Laid	Launched	Delivered	Disposition
Anemone	New York Shipbuilding Co. Camden, NJ	12 Nov 1907	13 Jun 1908	25 Jul 1908	Decom 01 Jul 1946 Trans to Phil. 01 Jul 1947
Cypress	New York Shipbuilding Co. Camden, NJ	15 Oct 1907	05 Nov 1908	21 Jul 1908	Decom 20 Aug 1946 Sold 18 Mar 1947
Hibiscus	New York Shipbuilding Co. Camden, NJ	07 Nov 1907	09 Jun 1908	15 Aug 1908	Decom 03 Sep 1946 Sold 26 Jun 1947
Kukui	New York Shipbuilding Co. Camden, NJ	28 Oct 1907	25 Apr 1908	1 Aug 1908	Decom 01 Feb 1947 Sold 08 Apr 1947
Manzanita	New York Shipbuilding Co. Camden, NJ	08 Oct 1907	04 Apr 1908	07 Jun 1908	Decom 29 Nov 1946 Sold 30 Apr 1947
Orchid	New York Shipbuilding Co. Camden, NJ	29 Oct 1907	12 May 1908	05 Aug 1908	Decom 01 Dec 1945 Trans to Phil. 01 Dec 1945
Sequoia	New York Shipbuilding Co. Camden, NJ	15 Oct 1907	04 Jun 1908	13 Aug 1908	Decom 01 Jul 1946 Trans to Phil. Jul 1947
Tulip	New York Shipbuilding Co. Camden, NJ	08 Aug 1907	16 Apr 1908	14 Jul 1908	Decom 01 Dec 1945 Trans Phil. Jul 1947

Cost
   $191,998.88 (Anemone) $211,816.97 (Manzanita)
   $191,633.34 (Cypress) $186,150.83 (Orchid)
   $184,642.59 (Hibiscus) $213,499.00 (Sequoia)
   $213,879.99 (Kukui) $191,658.26 (Tulip)

Hull
   Displacement (tons)   1081 (max) / 818 (mean) / 774 (light)   Steel Hull, Wood Deckhouses
   Dimensions   190'0"(loa) / 174'0" (lbp) / 173'4"(lwl) x 30'0" x 15'5½"
          (13'3" max / 11'8" mean draft)

Machinery
   Main Engines   2 triple expansion inverted direct acting steam   IHP 1000 SHP 1100
   Main Boilers   2 (Scotch type) (various makes)   Coal fired
   Propulsion   Twin propellers, bronze, 7'6" diam.
          Steel boom, 15-ton capy, steam windlass

Complement
   5 officers, 23 men (1909)   7 officers, 27 men (1924)
   6 officers, 22 men (1911)   7 officers, 29 men (1926)

Design
   As built, this was the first major class of tenders built to a standard design for the USLHS. Originally called the "Eight Tender" class, (eight of the class were built) it is more commonly identified by the lead ship as the "Manzanita" class. With engineering by the Navy Department, these Coastwise Tenders were authorized in 1904, and were all contracted for construction on 18 May 1907. And for the first time, all utilized steel booms instead of wood, and wire rope instead of manila line. These were also the largest tenders (except for the custom built *USLHT Cedar* in 1917) built for the service until 1996 when the Coast Guard's new 225-foot "Juniper" class Seagoing Buoy Tenders were built.

Anemone
Authorized and funded on 28 Apr 1904 for $50,000 and on 03 Mar 1905 for additional $90,000 as a tender for the Eleventh LHD. Assigned briefly to the Eleventh LHD at San Francisco after commissioning, *USLHT Anemone* was transferred to the Second LHD at Boston and Woods Hole, MA, around 1915, where it served for the rest of its career. Like its sisters, its steam plant was converted from coal-fired to oil-fired and new water tube boilers installed in the 1932. When all buoy tenders were assigned hull numbers at the start of WWII, *USCGC Anemone* was designated WAGL-202 (Buoy Tender). In Jul 1946 *USCGC Anemone* was decommissioned and with three sisters (*Orchid*, *Sequoia*, and *Tulip*) was transferred to the Philippine Government in Jul 1947.

Cypress
Authorized and funded on 28 Apr 1904 for $50,000 and on 03 Mar 1905 for additional $75,000 as a tender for the Sixth LHD. After completion, it replaced *USLHT Wistaria* at Charleston, SC, in the Sixth LHD where it remained for its entire career. *USLHT Cypress* served with the USN during WWI (1917-1919), in the Sixth Naval District. Radio "wireless" equipment was installed in 1916. It was converted from coal fired to oil fired steam plant in 1933. In Jan 1942, it was designated WAGL-211. After the end of WWII, it was sold in 1947, becoming the merchant ship *Drafin*.

Hibiscus

Originally assigned to the Seventh LHD, it was moved to the First LHD at Portland, ME, where it served well into WWII. Although not designed for the task, *USLHT Hibicus* was called upon for icebreaking duties on the Kennebec River as early as 1918. It was equipped with wireless (radio) equipment in 1919. It was converted from coal to oil, and new Scotch boilers installed in 1930. At the start of World War II, it was designated WAGL-218. In May 1942, *USCGC Hibiscus* (WAGL-218), now a Coast Guard Cutter, caught fire and was badly damaged and beached, but repaired and returned to service in Oct 1942. In the later part of the war, it serviced bouys and tended submarine nets at Argentia, Newfoundland. Sold after WWII, it became the SS HIBISCUS.

Kukui

It started its career in the Twelfth LHD, then served at Ketchikan, AK, with the Sixteenth LHD from 1914 to 1917, to fill in for the sunken *USLHT Armeria* and until a replacement could be built. It was then moved to the Nineteenth LHD at Honolulu in the Territory of Hawaii in 1917. Because of the distant duty, it became the first Lighthouse Tender to be equipped with a 'wireless' radio set. In 1926, it was converted from being coal fired to oil fired boilers. Immediately after the attack on Pearl Harbor, *USCGC Kukui* took custody of a downed Japanese pilot on one of the northern Hawaiian islands, thus taking one of the first Prisoners of War in the Pacific War. In Jan 1942, it was designated WAGL-225.

Manzanita

Lead ship of the class, it replaced the old *USLHT Manzanita*. In what might be the most unique convoy in history, three new Lighthouse Tenders (*Manzanita*, *Sequoia* and *Kukui*) plus three new Lightships, all destined for duties on the Pacific Coast, sailed together from New York to San Francisco, "round the horn." The steam plant

USLHT Anemone exhibits a "turtle-back" foc'sle. *National Archives*

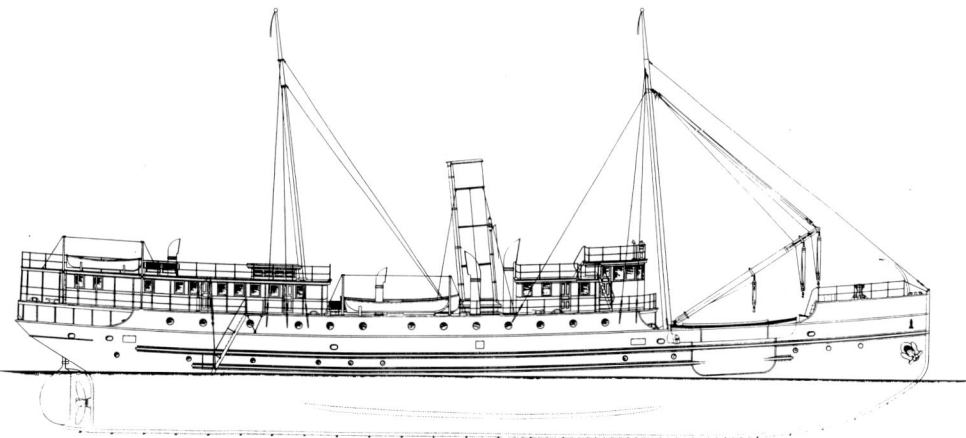

Plan for *USLHT Anemone*, 1906. *National Archives*

was changed from coal fired to oil fired in 1928. It was assigned to the old Seventeenth LHD and homeported out of Astoria and Portland, OR. At the start of WWII, it was designated WAGL-223. During WWII, it laid anti-submarine cables off Prince Rupert, British Columbia, and Dutch Harbor, AK. Like all its sister ships, it was disposed of after WWII.

Orchid

Appropriations on 03 Mar 1905 for $50,000 authorized a new tender for Long Island Sound in the Third LHD. Upon commissioning, it was assigned to the Third LHD for a brief period, to replace the aging *USLHT Cactus*. Around 1915, it was then reassigned to the Fifth LHD at Baltimore (1911-1924), then Portsmouth, VA, for the remainder of its career. Its steam plant was converted from coal to oil fired in the summer of 1932. The old Scotch boilers were also removed and replaced with new water tube boilers at a cost of $31,997. When the Coast Guard assigned classifications and hull numbers to all its tenders in Jan 1942, *USCGC Orchid* was designated WAGL-240. In 1945, it was decommissioned and transferred to the Philippine government, where it was used as a Survey Ship through the mid 1950s.

Sequoia

Assigned to the Twelfth LHD at San Francisco upon commissioning, it served there for the rest of its career. It was converted from coal to oil in Dec 1924. It was designated WAGL-243 (Buoy Tender) at the start of WWII. Sequoia was decommissioned with plans to transfer her to the Philippines in Jul 1946. Transferred in Oct 1946, she departed Philadelphia in Dec 1946 for the Philippines, becoming a Survey Ship (like its sisters *Orchid* and *Tulip*). It was retired in 1960.

Tulip

It spent its entire career assigned to the Third LHD, operating out of Staten Island, NY. In 1917, it was the first maritime test platform for an experimental device called a "radio compass," thus becoming the first ship in the United States to be equipped with the "radio compass" (now known as the 'radio direction finder'). The steam plant was changed from coal fired to oil fired in the summer of 1932. In Sep 1938, as a result of a hurricane that swept through the region, *USLHT Tulip* was run aground near New London, CT, on to the tracks of the New Haven RR. However, she was refloated and continued to serve as before. *USCGC Tulip* was designated WAGL-249 in Jan 1942. After decommissioning in Dec 1945, it was transferred to the Philippine government in Jul 1947, where it was used as a Survey Ship through the mid 1950s.

The *Manzanita Class*, also known as the "8-tender class," under construction at the New York Shipbuilding Co. yard, 1908.

U.S. Coast Guard

USLHT Two Myrtles at White Shoals, 1910. *Dossin Great Lakes Museum*

After rehabilitation including new boilers, *Two Myrtles* was renamed *USLHT Clover*, 1913. *Dossin Great Lakes Museum*

TWO MYRTLES, 1908

Name	Builder	Built	Purchased	Commissioned	Disposition
Two Myrtles	Burger & Burger Manitowoc, WI	1899	1908	1908	Decom 1935 Sold 25 May 1935

Cost
  $5,700

Hull
  Displacement (tons)   [F.W.]   205 (max) / 163 (mean)   Wood Hull
  Dimension   (1908)   88' (loa) / 80'2" (lbp) x 22'10" x 7'1"
                                (6'4" max / 5'4" mean draft)
                       (1932)   93' (loa)

Machinery
  Main Engine   steam   IHP 140 BHP 100
  Main Boiler   Coal fired   High-pressure, non-condensing
  Propulsion   Single propeller

Complement
  2 officers, 5 men (1910-11)
  4 officers, 8 men (1915-25)

Design
  Built in 1899 as a private steamer, and named *Two Myrtles* for the wife and daughter of the first owner, both who were named Myrtle.

Purchased by the LHS in 1908 and commissioned as *USLHT Two Myrtles* (private name retained). It was assigned to the Eleventh LHD at Milwaukee in the Great Lakes as an Engineering Tender, then laid up in 1911. It was renamed *USLHT Clover* in 1912 and rebuilt, including receiving new boilers, at Manitowoc, WI, in 1913. It then continued to serve in the Great Lakes, first at Detroit, then at Sault Sainte Marie, working aids on the St. Mary's River. *USLHT Clover* was rebuilt again in 1932 and lengthened to 93-feet. Decommissioned and replaced by *USLHT Tamarack*, it was sold in 1935 and was utilized as the private freighter *SS Two Myrtles* until 1947 when it was abandoned by its owners due to old age.

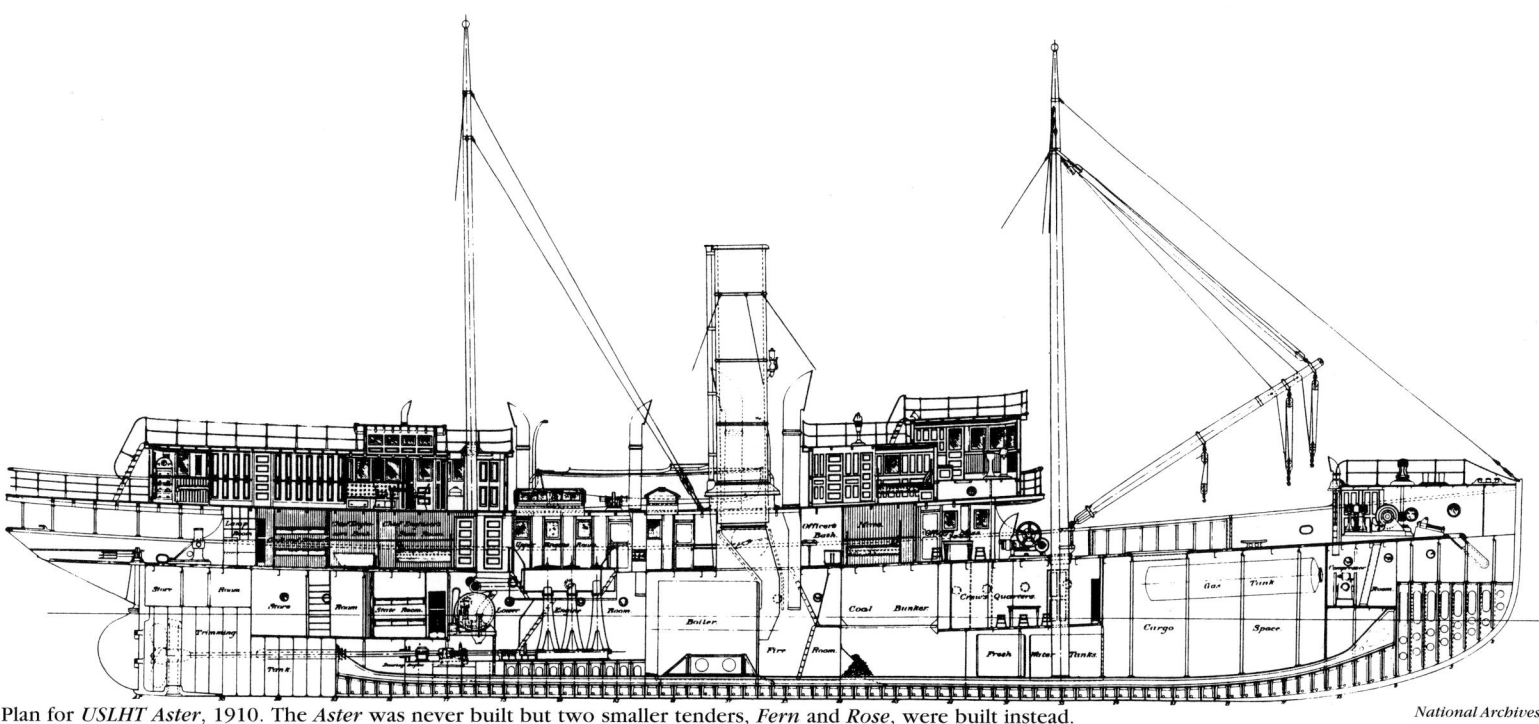

Plan for *USLHT Aster*, 1910. The *Aster* was never built but two smaller tenders, *Fern* and *Rose*, were built instead.

National Archives

ASTER, 1908

A proposed tender for the First LHD to replace the aging *USLHT Geranium* was authorized on 14 May 1908 with a $100,000 appropriation on 27 May 1908. A second appropriation was authorized for an additional $100,000 on 04 Mar 1909, for a total of $200,000 to build the new larger tender.
The design specifications were as follows:

Hull
    Displacement (tons)   870
    Dimensions   179' (loa) / 163'06" (lwl) x 32' (10' draft)

Machinery
    Main Engines   2 triple expansion inverted direct-acting steam
    Main Boilers   2 Scotch type   Coal fired
    Propulsion   Twin propellers, bronze, 7'6" diam.

However, construction was permanently deferred in 1910 due to funding limitations, and the tender was not built. On 27 Jul 1912, the authorization to build the new tender was modified, splitting the appropriation to fund two new smaller tenders. The two new tenders, *USLHT Fern* and *USLHT Rose*, were completed in 1915 and 1916 respectively.

PALMETTO, 1909

A proposed tender authorized by an initial appropriation of $30,000 on 04 Mar 1907, with an additional $30,000 appropriated on 27 May 1908, but proposals were not put out for bid until 1909. It was planned to be an 84-foot tender to be named *USLHT Palmetto*. Bids for a contract were opened on 28 Jun 1910, but were rejected. The reasons given dealt with the LHS having been just reorganized and the rearrangement of the use of the tenders already in service. Therefore, the project was deferred and the funding put on hold. A new contract for an improved design, renamed as *USLHT Laurel* in 1912, based on the original authorization was developed in 1913.

See *Laurel*, 1915 for details.

FORGETMENOT, 1910

Name	Builder	Contracted	Launched	Commissioned	Disposition
Forgetmenot	NA	1908	1910	1910	Decom 1933 Sold

Cost
$1,265.75

Hull
  Displacement (tons) unknown   Wood Hull
  Dimensions   41'(loa) / 40'(lwl) x 10' x 4' (2'6" mean draft)

Machinery
  Main Engines   Internal combustion, gasoline   BHP 24
  Propulsion   Single Propeller

Complement
  No officers, 3 men (1910-15)
  No regular crew (1930)

Design
  Built as a harbor launch, and used as a Buoy Boat.

Assigned to the Eleventh LHD as a Buoy Boat, with no regular crew.
                                                                NFR

MARGUERITE, 1910

Name	Builder	Contracted	Launched	Commissioned	Disposition
Marguerite		NA	NA	NA	Decom <1923

Hull
  Displacement (tons) unknown   Steel Hull
  Dimensions   35' x 6' x 3' (2'6" draft)

Machinery
  Main Engines   BHP 50
  Propulsion   Single propeller

Complement
  No regular crew assigned

A small harbor launch used as a Buoy Boat in the Fifteenth LHD.
                                                                NFR

CHAPTER III
With the Bureau of Lighthouses 1911-1939

The Lighthouse Board had been successful. The Lighthouse Service was now bigger and better than anyone had originally conceived. The tenders, while still built one at a time for a specific region or assignment, were generally of a standard design, and all steam powered. Tenders serviced aids to navigation on almost every navigatible water (coasts and rivers) of the United States and most of its territories (including Alaska, Puerto Rico, Hawaii, Guam and the Philippines).

The service was now operating 51 tenders (not including about 750 unmanned and unnamed launches under 50 feet in length) supporting 1,397 lighthouses and 2,256 lighted beacons, 63 lightships (32 self-propelled and 31 sail power only), 506 fog signals, 6,472 buoys (including 374 lighted buoys) and 3,698 assorted other minor aids (beacons and day marks). Obviously, the organization and its mission was continuing to grow.

Effective 01 July 1910, the entire Lighthouse Establishment was reorganized. Gone was the old Lighthouse Board, District Inspectors, and a bureaucracy that had grown too big with the maturation of the Service. In its place, a new Bureau of Lighthouses supervised by a single Commissioner, and a simplified administration with totally reorganized districts, each with a Lighthouse Inspector. Lighthouse Districts were realigned and renumbered, to better focus on the expanded workloads of the service.

The Lighthouse Service had proved during the Spanish-American War that it could serve successfully with the military. World War I would test the mantle of the Lighthouse Service even further. And as a result of that war, Army Mine Planters, not needed after the end of the war, were transferred to the Lighthouse Service and converted for use as Tenders. It was hoped that this type of vessel could be dual purpose: mine planters during war and Lighthouse Tenders during peacetime. The expense of conversion proved the theory impracticable.

The tenders themselves were now being built more as "general purpose," rather than being built for a specific location or as a replacement of an another tender. The working or tending of buoys was becoming a primary function, even though the ships remained classed as Lighthouse Tenders. New duties which would continue to grow in importance included Search and Rescue (SAR) and icebreaking, functions previous relegated only to the Revenue Cutter Service (soon to become the Coast Guard in 1915).

New standards were also put in place standardizing how tenders were to be painted. Black hulls, stacks and deck machinery, with white deckhouses, life rings and handrails. "Straw" (tan) deck fittings, and masts and booms from the deck to height of wake of smoke discharge from the funnel. The black hulls would hide any scuffs or rub marks of the buoys that might bounce off the hull while the buoy was being serviced. A small brass lighthouse still adorned each side of the bow of the tender, and the Lighthouse Service triangular pennant still flew from the mast.

In the past, tenders had been grouped according to a specific function (i.e., Engineering, Supply or Inspection Tenders). By the 1920s, tenders were being classed instead according to their capabilities and sizes. The largest tenders which could navigate and work aids on the open and coastal waters of the ocean were classed as Coastwise or Seagoing Tenders (type 'A'). Slightly smaller Tenders, usually working aids in the more sheltered waters along the coasts, and in the Great Lakes, were classed as the Lake or Bay Tenders (type 'B'). Smaller still, capable only of working the smallest of aids in the most sheltered waters were the Inside Waters Tenders (type 'C'). Another category were the River Tenders, those shallow draft flat bottomed Tenders specifically designed for work on the Mississippi, Missouri and Ohio Rivers and their tributaries. And a new class would be officially added in 1927, when 'harbor launches', those small craft (usually under 50-feet in length and unnamed) with no permanent crews assigned, would be officially designated as Buoy Boats (type 'D')

The Lighthouse Service, with its fleet, was now the largest, most modern and technologically advanced aids to navigation organization in the world.

USLHT Tulip and *Scotland Lightship*, 1920.   National Archives

USLHT Camellia, 1911. *U.S. Coast Guard*

CAMELLIA, 1911

Name	Builder	Keel Laid	Launched	Commissioned	Disposition
Camellia	Racine Boat Manuf. Co. Muskegon, MI	18 Oct 1909		13 July 1911	Decom 18 Aug 1947 Sold 29 Dec 1947

Cost
  $57,412

Hull
  Displacement (tons)   377 (max) / 276 (light)   Steel Hull, wood superstructure
  Dimensions   116'7"(loa) / 106'2"(lwl) x 24' x 10' (7'7" max / 5'10" mean draft)

Machinery
  Main Engines   2 triple expansion inverted direct-acting steam   IHP 280 SHP 440
  Main Boilers   2 water tube (Almy type)   Coal fired
  Propulsion   Twin Propellers, cast iron, 4'10' diam.
                   5 ton capy wood boom, steam winch

Complement
  4 officers, 12 men (1911-15)
  4 officers, 17 men (1917)
  4 officers, 18 men (1937)

Design
  Built as a shallow water Bay Tender for work on Lake Pontchartrain and Lake Borgne in the Eighth LHD.

Authorized 26 Feb 1907 and $60,000 appropriated for construction on 04 Mar 1907. It contracted in 1909 and commissioned as *USLHT Camellia* in 1911, assigned to Eighth LHD at New Orleans. On 04 Sep 1915, it was driven aground on the Mississippi River Delta, and refloated on 07 Oct with only minor damage. During WWI, it served first with the War Department, then with the USN (01 Jul 1917 - 01 Jul 1919) in the Eighth Naval District. The original steam engines were replaced with two Atlas Imperial diesel engines (220 SHP) in 1933. Designated WAGL-206 at the start of WWII. In 1947, it was decommissioned. In 1949, it was transferred to the government of the Dominican Republic and renamed *Capotillo* (FB-101) and designated as Survey Craft #1. Rebuilt in 1970, it was still in service through the mid 1980s.

WOODBINE, 1914

Name	Builder	Contracted	Launched	Commissioned	Disposition
Woodbine		1907	1913	01 Mar 1914	Decom 16 Apr 1933
	West New Brighton, NY				Sold 20 Oct 1933

Cost
$24,727.85

Hull
- Displacement (tons): 107 (full) / 85 (std) / 62 (light)   Wood Hull
- Dimensions: 95'01" (loa) / 85'11" (lwl) / 85'0"(lbp) x 16' x 7'0" (5'11" max / 5'02" mean / 4'5" light draft)

Machinery
- Main Engine: Corliss internal combustion kerosene   BHP 125
- Propulsion: Single propeller, 4'6" diam.
  Wood derrick, 3 ton capy

Complement
2 officers, 4 men (1914-1917)
2 officers, 6 men (1925-1930)

Design
A tender designed for working aids to navigation on inside waters. Originally designed with a triple expansion inverted direct acting steam engine with one oil-fired water tube boiler.

Initially authorized on 04 Mar 1907 with a $25,000 appropriation and planned for Lake Champlain in the Third LHD. Although contracted in 1907, excessive delays by the contractor which went bankrupt forced the government to take over the unfinished vessel on 22 Oct 1912. It was launched in early 1912 and moved to Baltimore for completion. To save expenses, it was powered by a gasoline engine. Commissioned as USLHT *Woodbine* in 1914, and initially assigned to Baltimore in the Fifth LHD. It was reassigned to Philadelphia in the Fourth LHD in 1915. In 1925, it was rebuilt and a steam engine [one triple expansion surface condensing engine with an oil-fired water tube (bent-tube type) boiler] installed at a cost of $32,847. It was then reassigned to the Fourth LHD for the remainder of its career. Decommissioned and sold in 1933, it was replaced by the new USLHT *Wistaria*. The old tender then became the freighter SS *Woodbine*, and operated until 1942.

USLHT *Woodbine* at Edgemoore, DE, 1915.   *Collection, P. Hornberger*

LAUREL, 1915

Name	Builder	Contracted	Launched	Commissioned	Disposition
Laurel	Speddin Ship Bldg. Baltimore, MD	09 Sep 1913	24 Jun 1914	21 May 1915	Decom 06 Oct 1930 Sold 24 Mar 1931

Cost
  $41,000 (contract)
  $55,522.15 (actual)

Hull
  Displacement (tons) 299 (full) / 218 (mean)   Wood Hull, steel bulkheads
  Dimensions   104'6"(loa) / 99'7"(lwl) / 95'6"(lbp) x 22' x 9' (6'10" max / 6'01" mean draft)

Machinery
  Main Engine   1 triple expansion inverted direct acting steam   IHP 160
  Main Boiler   1 water tube (Almy type)   Coal fired
  Propulsion   Single propeller, cast iron, 5'8" diam.
                 Wood boom, steam hoist

Complement
  4 officers, 8 men (1915)
  4 officers, 11 men (1917)
  4 officers, 12 men (1924-25)

Design
  Built as a Bay and Sound Tender, to work the inland waters of the Central Atlantic Coast and Chesapeake Bay in the Fifth LHD.

Authorized by Congress in 1907, and contracted in 1909 for construction of an 84-foot tender to be named *Palmetto*. However, funding for construction was deferred in 1912 due to reorganization of the LHS. A new contract for an improved design, based on the original authorization, was let in 1913 and the keel laid on 31 Oct 1913. The ship was completed and commissioned as *USLHT Laurel* and was assigned to the Fifth LHD at Baltimore where it served its entire career. The name Palmetto was then issued to another new tender contracted in 1915. On 08 Jan 1924, *USLHT Laurel* assisted in refloating the grounded Coast Guard Cutter *Apache*. When decommissioned in 1930, it was replaced by *USLHT Linden*. It was then sold for $2,165, and became the freighter *Lake George*, operating until 1948 when finally abandoned due to old age.

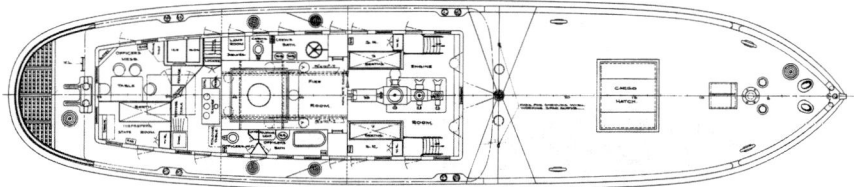

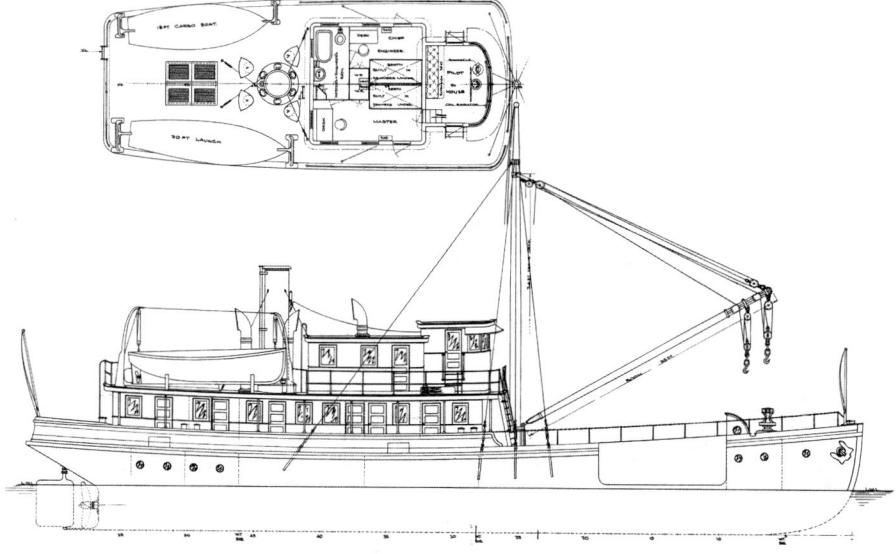

Plan for the improved design of *USLHT Laurel*, 1915.

National Archives

USLHT Fern, 1915. *U.S. Lighthouse Society*

FERN, 1915

Name	Builder	Contracted	Launched	Commissioned	Disposition
Fern	Hall Brothers SB Co. Winslow, WA	17 Apr 1914	06 Feb 1915	25 Jun 1915	Decom 1934 Sold 19 Sep 1934

Cost
  $62,100

Hull
  Displacement (tons)   317 max / 253 mean / 245 light
Wood Hull
  Dimensions   112'0" (loa) / 104'0" (lwl) / 98'5" (lbp) x 22' x 10' (8'6" max / 7'1" light draft)

Machinery
  Main Engine   1 triple expansion vertical inverted steam
IHP 300
  Main Boiler   1 water tube (Almy type)
Oil fired
  Propulsion   Single propeller, bronze, 6'4" diam. Wood derrick, steam winch

Complement
  4 officers, 8 men (1915-1917)
  5 officers, 12 men (1924-25)
  6 officers, 13 men (1930)

Design
  Built as a Bay and Sound Tender, specifically for the inland waters of the Southeastern Alaska panhandle.

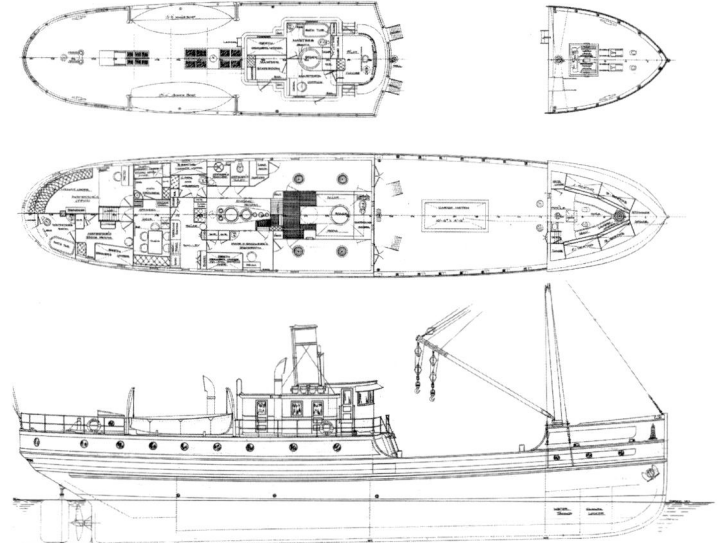

Plan for *USLHT Fern*, 1914. This was one of the smallest tenders assigned to Alaska. *National Archives*

Authorized for construction on 27 Jun 1912 from funds appropriated on 04 Mar 1909. Keel was laid on 11 Jun 1914. Assigned to the Sixteenth LHD at Ketchikan, AK. Decommissioned and sold in 1934, replaced by *USLHT Hemlock*. In 1938, the U.S. Army acquired the former tender, had it reengined with a 300 HP diesel, and commissioned it as the *S.D. Mason* (FS-551), using it for freight and supply duties. After the war, it was sold and became the private freight boat *M/V Fern*, out of Seward, AK. By the 1960s it was being used as *F/V Northern I*, with no further record after 1981.

USLHT Rose, 1923. Although this was the third vessel to carry the name *Rose*, it was the first *Rose* built specifically for the LHS.

National Archives

ROSE, 1916

Name	Builder	Contracted	Launched	Commissioned	Disposition
Rose	Anderson Steamboat Co. Seattle, WA	06 Nov 1914	19 Feb 1916	08 Aug 1916	Decom 15 Oct 1947 Sold 14 Jun 1948

Cost
  $87,950 (contract)
  $92,135 (actual)

Hull
  Displacement (tons)   567 (full) / 427 (std) / 395 (light)   Steel Hull, upper houses wood
  Dimensions   [1916]   127'9" (loa) / 119' (lbp)
               [1936]   137'9" (loa) x 24'6" x 11' (9'4" max / 7'0" light draft)

Machinery
  Main Engines   2 triple expansion, inverted, direct-acting steam   SHP 330
  Main Boilers   2 water tube (Almy type)   Oil fired
  Propulsion   2 4-blade propellers, cast iron, 5'6" diam.
                 Wood mast and boom, 8-ton capy, steam hoist

Complement
  4 officers, 16 men (1916)
  5 officers, 16 men (1924-25)

Design
  Built as a small Harbor & Inland Waters Tender for duty on the Oregon and Washington coast.

Although funding of $100,000 was authorized on 27 May 1908 as *USLHT Aster*, its name was not changed to *USLHT Rose* until 1912 and construction started until 1914. Upon completion, it was assigned to the Seventeenth LHD and operated out of Astoria and Portland, OR. Rebuilt and lengthened ten feet just forward of the deckhouse in 1936 at Anderson Marine in Seattle. Designated WAGL-242 in Jan 1942 when all buoy tenders were assigned hull numbers for the first time. After it was sold, it became the private vessel *Rose*. Still later, working for Canadian owners, it was renamed *Northern Express*.

PALMETTO, 1917

Name	Builder	Contracted	Launched	Commissioned	Disposition
Palmetto	Merrill-Stevens Dry Dock & Repair Jacksonville, FL	27 Sep 1915	30 Jun 1916	19 Mar 1917	Decom 23 May 1958 Sold 13 Apr 1959

Cost
  $28,975 (contract)
  $27,687.20 (actual)

Hull
  Displacement (tons)   168 max / 156 mean   Steel Hull, Wood Deck & Superstructure
  Dimensions   90' (loa) / 80'6" (lbp) x 22' x 7'6"
                        (4'0" mean / 3'9" light draft)

Machinery
  Main Engines   2 four-cylinder internal combustion gas engines   BHP 150
  Propulsion   Twin 3 blade propellers, bronze, 38" diam.
                        Wood derrick, 8-ton capy, gas engine hoist

Complement
  3 officers, 8 men (1917-1925)
  4 officers, 8 men (1924)

Design
  Originally planned as a shallow water tender in the Fifteenth LHD to replace *USLHT Snowdrop*. Classed as small Bay Tender, with a steel hull, wood deck and superstructure, and a pile driver.

  Authorized under an appropriation of $30,000 on 27 May 1908. Replanned as a shallow water tender for the Sixth LHD on 12 Jul 1912, with the keel laid on 03 Sep 1915. Assigned to the Sixth LHD at Charleston, SC, after commissioning where it spent its entire career. In 1930, the engines were replaced with two Superior diesels, rated at 350 BHP. *USCGC Palmetto* was designated WAGL-265 in Jan 1942. Upon its decommissioning in 1958, it was replaced by *USCGC Azalea*, and sold, becoming the private *M/V Palmetto*, operating until 1973.

USLHT Dandelion, 1917. *National Archives*

DANDELION, 1917

Name	Builder	Built	Purchased	Commissioned	Disposition
Dandelion	Weyerhauser & Deukanan Rock Island, IL	1893	02 Mar 1917	06 Apr 1917	Decom 1926 Sold 27 Oct 1927

Cost
   $23,173.90 (purchase price)

Hull
   Displacement (tons)   302 (max) / 246 (mean) / 232 (light)   Wood Hull, Oak frames
   Dimensions   140'0"(lbp) x 31'0" x 4'5" (3'3" max / 2'7" light draft)   Fir planking

Machinery
   Main Engine   1 horizontal single cylinder steam   IHP 503
   Main Boilers   3 horizontal water tube (Mississippi River type)   Coal fired
   Propulsion   Stern paddle wheel, wood, 19' diam., 18' wide

Complement
   4 officers, 13 men (1917)
   4 officers, 15 men (1925)

Wood boom, steam winch

Design
   Built as the private river boat *F. Weyerhauser* for the famous lumber company in St. Paul, MN, and used as a log pusher on the Mississippi River.

An appropriation dated 04 Mar 1907, of $60,000, with authorization granted on 27 May 1908, proposed building a shallow water tender for the Upper Mississippi and Illinois rivers in the Fifteenth LHD. This proposed side-wheel tender was to be 150 feet long, 26' beam, with a draft of 30" loaded, propelled by two independent oscillating compound marine steam engines with two water tube boilers. However, the project was put on hold due to other urgent matters. The private river boat *F. Weyerhauser* was purchased from the Rock Island Steamboat Co. in 1917. It had sixteen staterooms and berthing for thirty people, and had been recently rebuilt by its owners in 1915. It was commissioned by the LHS as *USLHT Dandelion* in 1917 for use as a River Tender. It operated out of Rock Island, IL, servicing aids to navigation on the upper Mississippi River. Laid up in 1926 and sold the following year. It then became the river towboat *SS Dandelion*, but was abandoned in 1931 due to old age. The old tender was replaced by *USLHT Wakerobin*.

USLHT Cedar, 1931. *National Archives*

CEDAR, 1917

Name	Builder	Contracted	Launched	Commissioned	Disposition
Cedar	Craig Shipbuilding Co. Long Beach, CA	04 May 1915	27 Dec 1916	30 Jun 1917	Decom 29 Jun 1950 Sold 27 Jun 1955

Cost
 $234,000 (contract)
 $248,188.88 (actual)

Hull
 Displacement (tons) 1970 (full) / 1890 mean / 1245 light   Steel Hull, Wood superstructure
 Dimensions   200'8"(loa) / 188' (lbp) x 36'6" x 18'6" (13'6" max / 9'6" light draft)
                      Double Bottom

Machinery
 Main Engine   1 Triple expansion reciprocating vertical inverted steam   IHP 1455
 Main Boilers   2 3-burner furnace marine boilers (Scotch type)   Oil fired
 Propulsion   Single Propeller, cast steel, 11'6" diam.   SHP 1200
                Steel mast, wood boom, steam hoist, steel wire-rope, 20 ton capy

Complement
 7 officers, 22 men (1917)
 8 officers, 26 men (1924-1930)

Design
  Designed and built specifically for service in Alaskan waters, to replace the sunken *USLHT Armeria*. It was the largest Lighthouse Tender ever built for the service, equipped with a double bottom, and it was the first tender specifically designed to be radio equipped.

Authorized on 15 Jan 1915, and funded by a special Appropriations Act for $250,000 on 25 Jan 1915. *USLHT Cedar* was assigned to the Sixteenth LHD and based out of Ketchikan, AK. During WWI, it served (Aug 1917-Jul 1919) with the U.S. Navy in the Thirteenth Naval District. At the start of WWII, it was designated WAGL-207 (Buoy Tender). After WWII, its homeport became Kodiak, AK.

The private tow boat *Avalon* was formerly *USLHT Birch*, 1917.

National Archives

BIRCH, 1917

Name	Builder	Contracted	Launched	Commissioned	Disposition
Birch	NA	NA	NA	1917	Decom 1930
	Erie, PA				Sold 08 Sep 1932

Cost
  unknown

Hull
  Displacement (tons)   13 (full) / 8 (net)   Steel Hull
  Dimensions   40'(loa) / 34'10"(lbp) x 13'7" x 5'6"

Machinery
  Main Engines   Steam   BHP 35
  Propulsion   Single Screw

Complement
  No assigned regular crew (1930)

Design
  Built as a small Harbor Tender.

Used as a Buoy Boat in the Tenth LHD at Buffalo, NY, with no regularly assigned crew. Declared beyond economical repair in 1929, it was decommissioned the following year and replaced by *USLHT Cherry*. It was then sold in 1932, becoming the private tow boat *Avalon*, operating until 1942 when abandoned due to old age.

NFR

PINE, 1918

Name	Builder	Contracted	Launched	Commissioned	Disposition
Pine	Nyack Shipbuilding, Nyack, NY	22 Jun 1918	1918	11 Nov 1918	Decom 1939

Cost
  $ 9,500 (contract)
  $16,187 (actual)

Hull
  Displacement (tons) 56   Wood Hull
  Dimensions   61'(lbp) X 15' x 5'8" (4'4" mean draft)

Machinery
  Main Engine   Internal combustion gasoline   BHP 50
  Propulsion   Single 3-bladed propeller, bronze, 36" diam.
                 Wood boom on 'A' frame, gas engine hoist

Complement
  2 officers, 3 men (1919-1925)

Design
  Built as an Inside Waters Tender for the inlets of New Jersey.

Built with general funds appropriated in 1918 and keel laid on 27 Jun 1918. Assigned to the Third LHD, it served out of Thompkinsville (Staten Island), NY, and Atlantic City, NJ.

POINSETTIA, 1919

Name	Builder	Built	Transferred	Commissioned	Disposition
Poinsettia		1915	1917 (USN)	1917 (USN)	
	Miami, FL		04 Jun 1919 (LHS)	1919 (LHS)	Burned 27 Dec 1928

Cost
  $6,500

Hull
  Displacement (tons)   50 (max) / 31 (mean) / 27 (light)   Wood Hull
  Dimensions   50'(loa) / 48'(lwl) / 44'7"(lbp) x 16' x 6' (2'9" max / 2'5" light draft)

Machinery
  Main Engine   Internal combustion gasoline   BHP 50
  Propulsion   Single Propeller

Complement
  2 officers, 3 men (1922-1925)

Design
  Built as the private passenger boat *Niagara* in 1915. Purchased by the USN in 1917 for use as a Section Patrol boat *USS Niagara* (SP-263).

Transferred to the LHS on 04 Jun 1919 and commissioned as *USLHT Poinsettia*, as assigned to the Seventh LHD at Key West. Destroyed by an explosion and fire on 27 Dec 1928. *USLHT Poinciana* was built to replace it.

USS Niagara (SP-263) was used by the U.S. Navy as a section patrol boat before it was purchased by the LHS and renamed *Poinsettia*.

National Archives

USLHT Poinsettia at Key West, FL, 1928.

National Archives

USLHT Cosmos, 1925. *National Archives*

COSMOS, 1919

Name	Builder	Built	Purchased	Commissioned	Disposition
Cosmos		1909	1917 (USN)	04 Jun 1917 (USN)	Decom 1936
	City Island, NY		31 May 1919 (LHS)	1919 (LHS)	Sold 24 Jun 1936

Hull
  Displacement (tons)   61 (max) / 57 (light)   Wood Hull
  Dimensions   75' (loa) / 66'8" (lbp) x 15'2" x 6' (4' max / 3'9" light draft)

Machinery
  Main Engines   Internal combustion, gasoline   BHP 80 IHP 100
  Propulsion   Twin propellers

Complement
  1 officer, 4 men (1919)
  2 officers, 3 men (1924)

Design
  Built in 1909 as the private yacht *Elmasada*.

Acquired by the Navy in 1917 for use during WWI as a coastal Section Patrol vessel *USS Elmasada* (SP-109). Struck from the Navy roles on 20 May 1919, and transferred to the LHS in the Eight LHD at New Orleans on 31 May 1919. Commissioned as *USLHT Cosmos*, it was assigned the Eighth LHD at New Orleans and used as an Inland Tender. After it was decommissioned, it was replaced by *USLHT Jasmine*. It then became the private tow boat *Elmasada*, operating until 1950.

USLHT Elm, 1919. *U.S. Coast Guard*

ELM, 1919

Name	Builder	Contracted	Launched	Commissioned	Disposition
Elm	Rice Brothers East Boothbay, ME	13 Jan 1917	05 Jun 1918	18 Jul 1919	Laid up 01 Jul 1932 Sold 14 Aug 1934

Cost
  $93,638: $29,400 for hull, $64,238 for machinery

Hull
  Displacement (tons)   318 mean / 259 light   Wood Hull
  Dimensions   101' x 30' x 9' (6'9" mean / 5'6" light draft)

Machinery
  Main Engine   1 3 cyl internal combustion, kerosene engine   BHP 150
  Propulsion   Single 4-bladed propeller, cast iron, 5'6" diam.
                         Twin wood booms, steam hoist

Complement
  2 officers, 4 men (1919-24)
  2 officers, 8 men (1922)
  2 officers, 4 men (1925-1930)

Design
  Built as a Working Power Derrick Barge for aids to navigation on the Hudson River.

Authorized for construction in 1916 with $100,000 appropriated on 01 Jul 1916. Contracted in 1917, construction was started on 13 Jan 1917. On 10 Jul 1917, the partially completed tender burned completely while still in stocks under construction.

   Totally rebuilt and completed in 1919, it was commissioned as *USLHT Elm* and assigned to the Third LHD out of Staten Island, NY. In 1930 it was reassigned to the Eleventh LHD. Laid up in 1932 and sold in 1934. It then became the private vessel *Salvager*, being used as a dredge and a workboat. It was finally abandoned due to old age in 1949.

USLHT Shrub, 1929. — National Archives

SHRUB, 1920

Name	Builder	Built	Purchased	Commissioned	Disposition
Shrub	William G. Abbott SB	1912	1917 (USN)	20 Jun 1917 (USN)	Decom 01 Jul 1947
	Milford, DE		28 Oct 1919 (LHS)	31 Jul 1920 (LHS)	Sold 29 Dec 1947

Cost
  $42,000 (purchase price)

Hull
  Displacement (tons)   435 (max) / 362 (mean) / 214 (light)   Wood Hull
  Dimensions   107'(loa) / 100'(lbp) x 29' x 13' (6'9" max / 6'5" light draft)

Machinery
  Main Engine   1 compound reciprocating fore & aft steam   SHP 278 IHP 300
  Main Boiler   1 watertube, 150 psi
                 Coal fired
  Propulsion   Single Propeller

Complement
  2 officers, 13 men (1920-1922)
  3 officers, 12 men (1924)
  3 officers, 13 men (1937)

Design
  Built of wood as the private steam freighter in 1912, it was purchased by the S. Mansfield and Sons Company on 23 Jan 1913 and renamed *F. Mansfield & Sons*.

Originally built in 1912 as a private freighter, it was purchased by the USN and commissioned as the *USS F. Mansfield* (SP-691) in 1917. After WWI, it was acquired by the LHS on 28 Oct 1919, and rebuilt. Commissioned as *USLHT Shrub* in 1920, it served in the Second LHD out of Boston. On 06 Aug 1931, it ran aground on Black Rocks and sank in York Harbor, ME, but was raised on 13 Oct 1931, and repaired at Staten Island, NY, for $39,156, then restored to service in the Second LHD. At the start of WWII, *USCGC Shrub* was designated WAGL-244, continuing to serve in New England, out of Bristol, RI. After it was sold in 1947, it became the merchant vessel *Shrub*, operating until 1966.

USLHT Oak, 1921.
U.S. Coast Guard

OAK class, 1921

Name	Builder	Contracted	Launched	Commissioned	Disposition
Oak	Consolidated SB Corp. Morris Heights, NY	14 Jan 1920	18 Jun 1921	28 Dec 1921	Decom 06 Nov 1964 Trans Smithsonian 03 Mar 1967
Hawthorn	Consolidated SB Corp. Morris Heights, NY	14 Jan 1920	28 Jun 1921	31 Dec 1921	Decom 24 Jul 1964 Sold 29 Nov 1965

Cost
  $357,250 (contract, each)
  $378,510 (actual, Oak)
  $378,352 (actual, Hawthorn)

Hull
  Displacement (tons)   950 max, 875 mean, 800 light   Steel Hull
  Dimensions   160' (loa) / 149' (lbp) x 30' x 14' (10'6" max / 9'0" mean / 6'6" light draft)

Machinery
  Main Engine   1 triple-expansion fore and aft steam   IHP 700 / SHP 750 / BHP 875
  Main Boiler   1 three furnace (Scotch type)   Coal fired
  Propulsion   Single Propeller, cast iron, 8'4" diam.
                  Steel boom, 20 ton capy, steam winch

Complement
  4 officers 23 men (1922-24)

Design
  Built as a Bay and Sound tenders with a generous buoy deck. Both were authorized for construction in 1917 and funds appropriated by Congress in 1919.

Oak
Initial appropriation of $150,000 authorized for a proposed replacement of the aging *USLHT Gardenia* at New York. A larger $760,000 appropriation on 04 Nov 1919, authorized construction of both tenders. Assigned to the Third LHD, it was home ported out of Staten Island, NY. It was converted from coal to oil-burning boilers in 1934. In Jan 1942, *USCGC Oak* was designated WAGL-239. At the end of WWII, in May 1946, *USCCG Oak* was placed "in reserve" because of a shortage of personnel, but returned to active duty in Aug 1949. It was decommissioned in 1964, and replaced by the new *USCGC Red Beech* (WLM-686). The old hulk was transferred to the Smithsonian Institute in 1967 and her steam plant placed on exhibit in 1978.

Hawthorn
Built as a replacement for *USLHT Jessamine*, it also served in the Third LHD, primarily out of New London, CT. In 1934, it was converted from coal to oil-fired boilers. At the start of WWII, *USCGC Hawthorn* was designated WAGL-215.

ARMY STEAM LIGHTERS, 1922

Name	Builder	Built	Purchased	Commissioned	Disposition
Col. Hodgson	William J. Abbott	1915		1918 (USA)	Decom 1925
	Milford, DE		08 June 1920 (LHS)	1922 (LHS)	Trans to USCG 1925
Gen. George Gibson		NA		NA (USA)	Decom 1924
	Brooklyn, NY		08 June 1920 (LHS)	1922 (LHS)	Trans to USCG 1924

Cost
   $4,500 (purchase price, each)

Hull
   Displacement (tons)   172   Wood Hull
   Dimensions   115' (loa) / 100' (lwl) x 29' x 8'7"

Machinery
   Main Engines   steam   300 HP
   Main Boilers   Coal fired
   Propulsion   Single propeller

Design
   Used by the War Department (U.S. Army Quartermaster Corps) as steam lighter barges.

Colonel Hodgson
Built as the private streamer *George H. Johnson* in 1915. Acquired by the War Department in 1918, it was named *Colonel Fred G. Hodgson* and used as a steam lighter. Purchased by the LHS in 1920 and placed in service in 1922 as *USLHT Colonel Hodgson* (Army name retained) as a Supply Tender. Transferred to the USCG in 1925 and commissioned as *USCGC Colonel Hodgson*. It was sold into private hands in 1926, becoming the private lighter *Belleville*, in operation up to the start of WWII.

General George Gibson
Acquired from the U.S. Army by the LHS in 1920, and placed into service in 1922 as *USLHT General George Gibson* (Army name retained) and used as a Supply Tender. Transferred to the USCG in 1924. They sold it in 1927.

GENERAL LUDINGTON, 1922

Name	Builder	Built	Purchased	Commissioned	Disposition
General Ludington		NA	1922	1922 (LHS)	Decom 1922
					Sold to USCG 1925

Cost
   unknown

Hull
   Displacement (tons)   unknown
   Dimensions   unknown

Machinery
   Main Engines   Steam
   Main Boilers   Coal fired
   Propulsion   Propeller

Acquired from the Army in 1922? and placed in service as *USLHT General Ludington* (Army name retained) as a Supply Tender. Transferred to the USCG in 1925 and commissioned as *USCGC General Ludington*. It was sold in 1927.

BLUEBELL, 1922

Name	Builder	Contracted	Launched	Commissioned	Disposition
Bluebell	NA	NA	NA	NA	Decom NA
					Trans. 1936

Cost
  unknown

Hull
  Displacement (tons) unknown   Steel Hull
  Dimensions   42' (loa) / 35'5" (lbp) x 10'10" x 4'6"

Machinery
  Main Engines   Gasoline Engine   BHP 110
  Propulsion   Single Propeller

Complement
  No regularly assigned crew (1930)

Design
  Built as a shallow water Harbor Launch.

Dates unknown. Confirmed periods 1922-1936. Assigned to the Sixteenth LHD and used as a Buoy Boat. Transferred to the Department of Interior in 1936 and renamed *Institute II*. Sold into private hands in 1947 as the fishing vessel *Bluebell*, operating into the 1960s.

NFR

BUTTERCUP, 1922

Name	Builder	Contracted	Launched	Commissioned	Disposition
Buttercup	NA	NA	NA	NA	Decom NA

Hull
  Displacement (tons) unknown   Steel Hull
  Dimensions   25'

Machinery
  Main Engines   unknown
  Propulsion   unknown

Complement
  No regularly assigned crew (1922-1936)

Design
  Built as a small Harbor Tender.

Dates unknown. Assigned to the Eleventh LHD, operating out of Detroit, it was used as a Buoy Boat. Confirmed periods 1922-1936.

NFR

LEHUA, 1922

Name	Builder	Contracted	Launched	Commissioned	Disposition
Lehua		NA	NA	NA	Decom NA
	Honolulu, HI				Sold NA

Hull
   Displacement (tons) unknown   Steel Hull
   Dimensions 38' (lwl) / 30 (lbp)

Machinery
   Main Engines unknown
   Propulsion unknown

Complement
   No regular complement (1930)

Design
   Built as a shallow water Buoy Boat.

Dates unknown. Assigned to the Nineteenth LHD at Honolulu and used as a Buoy Boat. Confirmed periods 1922-1936.

                        NFR

PRIMROSE, 1922

Name	Builder	Contracted	Launched	Commissioned	Disposition
Primrose	NA	NA	NA	NA	Decom NA

Cost
   unknown

Hull
   Displacement (tons) unknown   Steel Hull
   Dimensions 43' (loa) / 31' (lbp)

Machinery
   Main Engines unknown
   Propulsion unknown

Complement
   No regularly assigned crew (1922-1936)

Design
   Built as a shallow water Harbor Tender.

Dates unknown. Assigned to the Tenth LHD and used as a Buoy Boat. Confirmed periods 1922-1936.

    NFR

USLHT Primrose, c. 1922.

National Archives

ASTER, 1922

Name	Builder	Contracted	Launched	Commissioned	Disposition
Aster	M. M. Flechas Pascagoula, MS	27 Apr 1921	16 Dec 1921	17 Jan 1922	Decom 24 Jan 1946 Sold 02 Oct 1946

Cost
  $14,400 (hull) + $5,249 (engine): $19,649 (bid total)
  $19,909.40 (actual)

Hull
  Displacement (tons)   109 (max) / 75 (mean) / 64 (light)   Wood Hull
  Dimensions   75'10" (loa) x 21'8" x 7'6" (5'7" max / 3'8" mean draft) 65' (lwl)

Machinery
  Main Engines   2 Standard Motor Co. 4 cyl. gasoline engines   BHP 70
  Propulsion   Twin 3-bladed propellers, bronze, 32" diam.
                  2 wood derricks, gas engine hoist

Complement
  2 officers, 5 men (1922)
  2 officers, 6 men (1925-1937)

Design
  Built as a small Bay Tender, for service in the Texas and Louisiana coastal waters. Constructed entirely of wood. It carried a detachable pile driver mounted on one side of the buoy deck.

Although authorized for construction with $20,000 appropriated in 01 Jul 1916, the contract for construction was let out for bid four times without any takers. It wasn't until after WWI had ended that the contract was finally signed. Assigned to Mobile, AL, upon commissioning and for most of its career. It also spent time at New Orleans, servicing aids in the Gulf of Mexico. It was re-engined with two Fairbanks-Morse diesels (rated at 90 BHP) in 1932. At the start of WWII, it was designated WAGL-269.

POPPY, 1923

Name	Builder	Built	Acquired	Commissioned	Disposition
Poppy	 Stamford, CT	1918	1918 (USA) 1922 (LHS)	1918 (USA) 1923 (LHS)	Decom 1938 Sold 1938?

Cost
  $20,989

Hull
  Displacement (tons)   53   Wood Hull
  Dimensions   61'0" x 12'10" x 6' (4'10" max draft)

Machinery
  Main Engines   diesel   BHP 65
  Propulsion   Single propeller

Complement
  2 officers, 3 men (1937)

Design
  Built in 1918 for the U.S. Army Quartermaster Corps and used as a harbor launch, designated Q-7.

Transferred to the LHS in 1922 and placed in service in 1923. Assigned to the Seventh LHD and used as a Buoy Boat with no regularly assigned crew. Served until 1938.

NFR

USLHT Speedwell. Note the rounded foc'sle, also known as a "Turtleback," designed to prevent buoys from hanging up on any corners.

National Archives

SPEEDWELL class, 1923

Name	Builder	Built	Acquired	Commissioned	Disposition
Speedwell (ex Col. John V. White)	Fabricated Shipbuilding & Coddington Engineering Co. Milwaukee, WI	1919	1922 (LHS)	1920 (USA) 23 Apr 1923 (LHS)	Decom 19 Jun 1947 Sold 30 Dec 1947
Spruce (ex Gen. Garland N. Whistler)	Fabricated Shipbuilding & Coddington Engineering Co. Milwaukee, WI	1919	1922 (LHS)	1920 (USA) 22 Dec 1923 (LHS)	Decom 28 Jun 1946 Sold 1947
Lotus (ex Col. Albert Todd)	Fabricated Shipbuilding & Coddington Engineering Co. Milwaukee, WI	1919	1922 (LHS)	1920 (USA) 1924 (LHS)	Decom 05 Nov 1946 Sold 11 Jun 1947
Ilex (ex Gen. Edmund Kirby)	Fabricated Shipbuilding & Coddington Engineering Co. Milwaukee, WI	1919	1922 (LHS)	1919 (USA) 1924 (LHS)	Decom 17 Apr 1947 Sold 14 Oct 1947
Acacia (ex Gen. John P. Story)	Fabricated Shipbuilding & Coddington Engineering Co. Milwaukee, WI	1919	1922 (LHS)	1919 (USA) 14 Apr 1927 (LHS)	Sunk 15 Mar 1942
Lupine (ex Gen. W. P. Randolph)	Fabricated Shipbuilding & Coddington Engineering Co. Milwaukee, WI	1918	1922 (LHS)	1919 (USA) 14 Apr 1927 (LHS)	Decom 07 Jan 1947 Sold 28 Nov 1947

USLHT Spruce, 1923. *National Archives*

SPEEDWELL class, 1923 (CONT.)

Cost
  $540,000 (each) to U.S. Army for construction
  None to USLHS to acquire

Cost of Alterations
  $48,371.50 (Speedwell and Spruce, each)
  $45,710.00 (Lotus)
  $44,000.00 (Ilex)
  $55,481.50 (Acacia and Lupine, each)

Hull
  Displacement (tons) 1130 max / 870 mean   Steel Hull
  Dimensions   172'6" (loa) x 32'0" x 17' (11'6" max / 10'10" mean / 9'0" light draft) 159'6" (lwl)

Machinery
  Main Engines   2 Allis Chalmers compound, inverted, reciprocating steam
  Main Boilers   2 Page & Burton watertube   Oil fired
  Propulsion   Twin propellers   SHP 1000 IHP 1040
                 Steel boom, 20 ton capy, steam hoist

Complement
  6 officers, 22 men (1924-25)
  7 officers, 20 men (1930)
  7 officers, 24 men (1937)

Design
  Originally built for the U.S. Army in 1918-1919 as Mineplanters, six of nine built were transferred to the USLHS at no cost in 1922. It was hoped that after conversion the vessels could be dual purpose: Mineplanters in case of war, and Lighthouse Tenders during peace time. However, the expense in converting them proved the theory impracticable and too expensive. All were modified and rebuilt as funds became available, then commissioned from 1923 to 1927 with new names.

USLHT Lupine at San Franciso, 1924. *Maritime Museum of Monterey*

SPEEDWELL class, 1923 (CONT.)

Acacia
Although acquired in 1922, renovation at Norfolk, VA, not completed until 1927. After commissioning, *USLHT Acacia* was assigned to the Ninth LHD at San Juan, Puerto Rico, replacing the *USLHT Columbine*. In Sep 1932, it was driven aground at Fajaro, Puerto Rico, in a hurricane, but was refloated. With the start of WWII, and now part of the Coast Guard, it was designated WAGL-200. On 15 Mar 1942, it was sunk by shell fire from German submarine U-161 off Haiti, 16°17'N63°44'W. It was the only tender lost in WWII due to enemy action, fortunately with no loss of life.

Ilex
Also acquired from the U.S. Army in 1922, in was one of the first to be reconditioned in 1923 and commissioned in 1924. Assigned to the First LHD and replacing *USLHT Zizania*, it served out of Portland, ME, for its entire career. It became a Coast Guard Cutter in 1939 when the LHS merged into the Coast Guard. And in 1942, it was designated WAGL-222. During the war, it served in the Gulf at Galveston, TX. In 1947, it was decommissioned and replaced by *USCGC Heather* (WAGL-331), another former Army mineplanter of a different class. Sold to Canadian owners, it caught fire and was beached and burned in 1948.

Lotus
Acquired in 1922 and renovated the following year, it was commissioned in 1924 as *USLHT Lotus*. Replacing *USLHT Mayflower* in the Second LHD, it was homeported in Boston until the start of WWII. It was then designated WAGL-229 (Buoy Tender), and served out of Puerto Rico and Norfolk, VA, during WWII.

Lupine
Like its sisters, it was transferred from the War Department (U.S. Army) in 1922, then kept in storage until funds were available for reconditioning. Rebuilt in 1926 and commissioned in 1927, it replaced the aging *USLHT Madrono* and was assigned to the Eighteenth LHD (San Francisco) until the start of WWII. In Jan 1942, it was designated WAGL-230 and continued to serve out of San Francisco for the duration of WWII. Decommissioned in 1947, it was sold to the Philippine government, where it was used as a Survey Ship through the mid 1980s.

Speedwell
First of the class to be rebuilt after acquisition from the Army in 1922, it was refurbished and commissioned in 1923. Homeported out of Baltimore prior to WWII. At the start of the war, it was designated WAGL-245 and moved to the Fifth LHD at Portsmouth, VA.

Spruce
Purchased in 1922, it was commissioned in 1923 after renovation. It was stationed in the Third LHD at Staten Island, NY, replacing *USLHT Myrtle*. It stayed there until the start of WWII. Designated WAGL-246, it was reassigned to San Juan, Puerto Rico. It was decommissioned in late 1946 and sold in 1947. The Coast Guard almost immediately commissioned a former Army 177-foot Freight and Supply ship, to be used as a Cargo Ship to support LORAN stations, keeping the same name and hull number: *USCGC Spruce* (WAK-246) (which has caused immense and continued frustration and confusion amongst historians tracking either of these vessels).

PYXIE, 1923

Name	Builder	Built	Acquired	Commissioned	Disposition
Pyxie		1909		1910 (USA)	
	Quincy, MA		1922 (LHS)	1923 (LHS)	Returned to Army 1923

Cost
   $58,000 to U.S. Army for construction
   None to USLHS to acquire

Hull
   Displacement (tons) 163   Steel Hull
   Dimensions   89'0"(lwl) x 22'0" x 10'3" (8'6")

Machinery
   Main Engines   steam
   Main Boilers   Coal fired
   Propulsion   Single propeller

Complement
   unknown

Design
   Built for the War Department (U.S. Army) Artillary Corps as the Small Mine Planter *General R.B. Ayres* in 1909, then used by the Army Quartermaster Corps as a tug.

Transferred to the USLHS in Jan 1922 at no cost. With renovations, it was commissioned in 1923 as *USLHT Pyxie*, and used as a towboat in the Third LHD. However, it was considered unsuitable and was returned to the War Department in late 1923. The Army then transferred it to the U.S. Public Health Service at New York where it was used as the boarding tug *Henry Carter*. It was renamed *H.R. Carter* in 1933 and continued operating until 1939.
   Another similar (but not identical) Army vessel, *Captain A.M. Wetherill*, was also received at the same time as the *General R.B. Ayres* (nee *USLHT Pyxie*). However, it was not placed into service. It also was considered unsuitable, and was returned to the War Department without being used, when *Pyxie* was returned.

SUNDEW, 1924

Name	Builder	Built	Acquired	Commissioned	Disposition
Sundew		1919		1919 (USA)	Decom 1939
	Rocky River, OH		1922 (LHS)	1924 (LHS)	Sold 1941

Cost
   $115,800 (reconditioning)

Hull
   Displacement (tons) 710 max / 580 light   Wood Hull
   Dimensions   101'(loa) / 98'(lwl) x 24' x 13' (11'0" max / 9'2" light draft)

Machinery
   Main Engines   steam   SHP 325
   Main Boilers   Coal fired
   Propulsion   Single Propeller

Complement
   2 officers, 8 men (1922)

Design
   Built in 1919 as U.S. Army Junior Mineplanter *Captain Edwin C. Long*.

Built in 1919 for the War Department, and transferred at no cost to USLHS in Jan 1922 and commissioned as *USLHT Sundew* in 1924. Assigned to the Seventh LHD at Key West through 1930, then transferred to the Tenth LHD on Lake Ontario. It was replaced by the new *USLHT Maple* in 1939.

USLHT Greenbriar. — National Archives

GREENBRIER, 1924

Name	Builder	Contracted	Launched	Commissioned	Disposition
Greenbrier	Charles Ward Engineering Works Charleston, WV	15 Aug 1922	NA	20 Jun 1924	Decom 19 Sep 1947 Sold 19 Apr 1948

Cost
  $128,000 (contract)
  $131,900 (actual)

Hull
  Displacement (tons) 440 max / 385 mean / 302 light   Steel Hull, composite superstructure
  Dimensions   164'6" (loa) / 140'0" (lbp) x 32'6" x 5' (4' max / 3'4" light draft)

Machinery
  Main Engines   2 horizontal non-condensing steam   SHP 500   IHP 350
  Main Boilers   3 horizontal flue fire tube (Mississippi type)   Coal fired
  Propulsion   Stern paddle wheel, staggered bucket, 20' diam, 19' wide

Complement
  2 officers, 13 men (1924-1925)
  4 officers, 15 men (1937)

Design
  Built as a typical river boat tender, to replace *USLHT Goldenrod* on the Ohio River in the Fourteenth LHD. Steel hull with superstructure of steel and wood.

Originally authorized on 12 Jun 1917 with $150,000 for a tender for the Third LHD, the project was reappropriated on 05 Jun 1920 and 04 Mar 1921 for this River Tender. Funding was limited so the contract wasn't let until 1922, with the keel laid on 19 Sep 1922. Replacing *USLHT Goldenrod*, it served most of its career servicing the Ohio and Kanawha rivers, homeported out of Cincinnati, OH. Designated WAGL-214 at the the start of WWII. After it was sold, it became the private river boat *Mississippi*, operating until 1975.

ALDER, 1924

Name	Builder	Built	Purchased	In Service	Disposition
Alder	NA	1917	Mar 1924	1924	Decom 11 Dec 1947
					Sold 14 Jun 1948

Cost
  NA

Hull
  Displacement (tons)   80   Wood Hull
  Dimensions   72' (loa) / 64'02" (lbp) x 16' (7'6" max draft)

Machinery
  Main Engines   1 Atlas Imperial diesel   SHP 110
  Propulsion   Single Propeller

Complement
  no permanent crew (1930)
  0 officers, 13 men   (1942)
  0 officers, 9 men   (1945)

Design
  Constructed in 1917 for commercial service, it was purchased by the LHS in 1924.

Placed into service as an unmanned Harbor Launch and berthed at LHS Base at Ketchikan in the Sixteenth LHD. *USLHT Alder* exploded and sank in Jun 1929, but was raised and rebuilt, and placed back in service in 1930. It was designated WAGL-216 in Jan 1942. Decommissioned and sold after the war, it became the fishing vessel *Acme* in 1949. In 1960, it changed owners again, becoming the log tugboat *Lummi* out of Everett, WA. It sank at sea on 15 Nov 1960 at 27-30N 115W.

THISTLE, 1927

Name	Builder	Built	Acquired	Commissioned	Disposition
Thistle		1907	1908? (USA)		Decom
	Newburgh, NY		1922 (LHS)	1927 (LHS)	Sold 04 Apr 1934

Cost
  unknown

Hull
  Displacement (tons)   128   Steel Hull
  Dimensions   59' x 20' x 10'

Machinery
  Main Engines   Steam
  Main Boilers   Coal fired
  Propulsion   Single Propeller

Complement
  No permanent crew attached. (1930-34)

Design
  Built by the War Department (U.S. Army) as a Auxiliary Steamer in 1907. Acquired from the War Department by the LHS in 1922, and commissioned in 1927 as *USLHT Thistle*. Employed as an unmanned harbor launch out of Detroit in the Eleventh LHD. It was replaced by *USLHT Dahlia*.

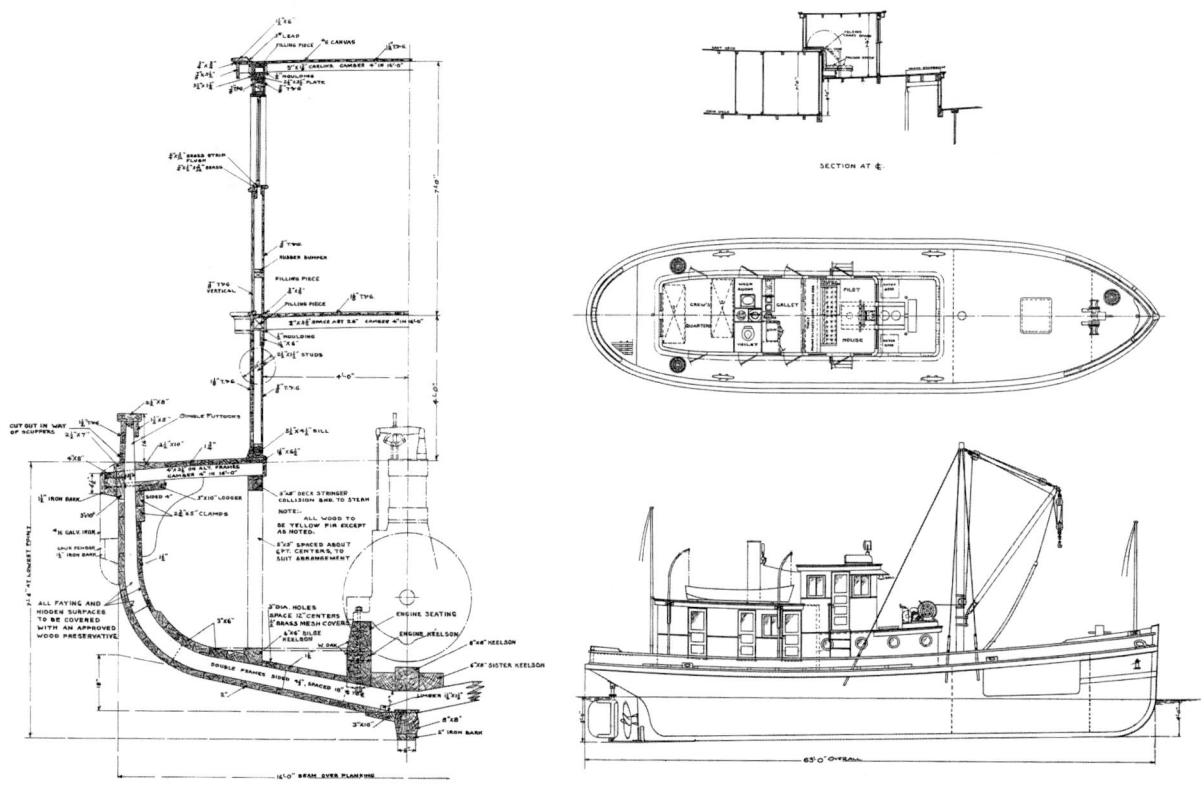

Plan for USLHT Larch, 1925.
National Archives

LARCH, 1926

Name	Builder	Contracted	Launched	Commissioned	Disposition
Larch	St. Helens Ship Co. St. Helens, OR	25 Sep 1925	NA	26 Jun 1926	Decom 28 Oct 1935 Sold 05 Nov 1935

Cost
  $23,430 (contract)
  $25,500 (actual)

Hull
  Displacement (tons) 79 full / 70 mean   Wood Hull
  Dimensions   63'(loa) / 59'6"(lwl) X 16'1" X 7' (6'6" max draft)

Machinery
  Main Engines   4 cyl. Washington Diesel engine   BHP 100   SHP 160
  Propulsion   Single propeller
                  Wood boom, 2½ ton copy, electric winch

Complement
  2 officer, 2 men (1930)

Design
  Built as a small Harbor Tender for the Columbia River. Authorized for construction on 27 Feb 1925. Assigned to the Seventeenth LHD. Transferred to the Federal Emergency Relief Administration (Oregon Division) in 1934. It was replaced by USLHT Rhododendron. Returned to the LHS, it was decommissioned on 28 Oct 1935. It was sold one week later, becoming the private tow boat Loyal, operating in the Puget Sound. In 1945, it was purchased by Foss Tug & Barge, reengined with a 250 SHP Enterprise diesel and renamed Elaine Foss, operating until 1967 when laid up. It was then sold, becoming the private vessel Trinity I, operating in the inland waters of Alaska until running aground near Lincoln Rocks in Clarence Straits on 06 Feb 1972. The next day, it sank in over forty fathoms of water.

USLHS 38-foot Buoy Boat, 1928.

U.S. Coast Guard

38-FOOT BUOY BOAT, 1927

Designed in 1927 in the Third LHD, to be used as an auxiliary vessel in support of the larger tenders, and officially designated as a "Buoy Boat"

Hull
   Wood Hull
   Dimensions   38'0" (loa) x 11' x 4'7½"

Machinery
   Gasoline engine   27 HP
   Wood boom, 1 ton capy, gas engine hoist

Complement
   No permanent crew assigned

A three compartment boat, the forward compartment held the power hoisting winch, with the mast/boom at the aft end of the forward compartment. The aft section contained the propulsion machinery, while the mid section was used for handling cargo and aids.
   No names were assigned, but this was generally accepted as a standard design. Many were made and used in the First, Second, Third and Nineteenth LHDs.
   This is the first time the official designation "BUOY BOAT" was utilized. Until now, "Harbor Launch" had been the generic term for small craft used by the LHS.

USLHT Wakerobin, 1927. This grand old lady was the last stern wheel Lighthouse Tender built for the LHS. It served on the Lower Mississippi River.

National Archives

WAKEROBIN, 1927

Name	Builder	Contracted	Launched	Commissioned	Disposition
Wakerobin	Dravo Construction Co. Neville Island, Pittsburgh, PA	09 Oct 1925	1926	15 Apr 1927	Decom 20 Apr 1955 Trans USACOE 1955

Cost
$187,000 (contract)
$187,500 (actual)

Hull

Displacement (tons)	622 (full) / 575 (mean)	Steel Hull/Deck	Wood Superstructure
Dimensions	182'(loa) / 129'8"(lbp) x 43' x 5' (4'02" max draft)		

Machinery

Main Engines	2 horizontal non-condensing steam	550 SHP 620 IHP
Main Boilers	2 Babcock & Wilcox sectional header Oil fired	
Propulsion	Stern Paddle wheel, staggered buckets, wood, 11'4" diameter Steam winch	

Complement
5 officers 18 men (1930)
1 officer, 1 warrant, 34 men (1947)

Built as a River Tender for service on the upper Mississippi River, to replace *USLHT Dandelion*. This was the last stern-wheel tender built for the USLHS, authorized for construction on 27 Feb 1925. After commissioning in 1927, it was assigned to the Thirteenth LHD at Rock Island, IL, then reassigned to the Fifteenth LHD until the start of WWII. Then assigned to Keokuk, IA, in the Ninth LHD working the lower Mississippi River. Designated WAGL-251 (Buoy Tender) in Jan 1942. After WWII, *USCGC Wakerobin* was homeported at Memphis, TN. It was loaned to the U.S. Army Corps of Engineers in 1949, replaced by *USCGC White Pine*. *Wakerobin* was permanently transferred to the Army in 1955. Later placed out of service by the Army the tender remained moored on the Ohio River below Cincinnati. In the early 1980s, the vessel was purchased with the intent to convert it into a restaurant, but a survey showed her integrity was gone. Laid up in 1992, she became the *USS Nightmare* an annual haunted ship event in Cincinnati. She was last reported to be serving as a similar project in the Pittsburg, PA area.

USLHT Willow. *Nautical Research Centre*

WILLOW, 1927

Name	Builder	Contracted	Launched	Commissioned	Disposition
Willow	Dubuque Boat & Boiler Co. Dubuque, IA	03 Jun 1924	26 Jul 1926	04 Oct 1927	Decom 01 Mar 1945 Trans USACOE 1945

Cost
   $327,000 (contract)
   $348,732 (actual)

Hull
   Displacement (tons)   [F.W.] 1070 max   Steel Hull
   Dimensions   200' x 65'(over guards) x 8' (6'6" max / 5'6" mean draft)

Machinery
   Main Engines   2 noncondensing steam   SHP 600 IHP 800
   Main Boilers   6 western river type, 225 psi   Oil Fired Propulsion
   Independent wood-side paddle wheels, 2 light derrick masts

Complement
   6 officers, 15 men (1930)

Design
   Designed for service on the lower Mississippi River, to replace *Oleander*. An initial appropriation of $240,000 was authorized on 05 Jan 1923, with an additional $100,000 appropriation approved on 28 May 1924. The last side-wheel tender in service. It was homeported out of Memphis, TN, in the Fifteenth LHD. It was one of the first federal vessels to demonstrate that a racially integrated crew could work together. Designated WAGL-253 at the start of WWII. On 15 Dec 1944, it collided with USN LST-841, but only suffered nominal damage.
   Decommissioned in 1945, it was immediately transferred to the USACOE, retaining the name *Willow*. The machinery was removed and it was used for berthing German P.O.W.s at the end of WWII. Sold by the Army in 1962 into private hands, it eventually was moved to Belgium and renovated in 1990. As of 1999 it was on display in London, England, as an example of "a typical American river showboat."

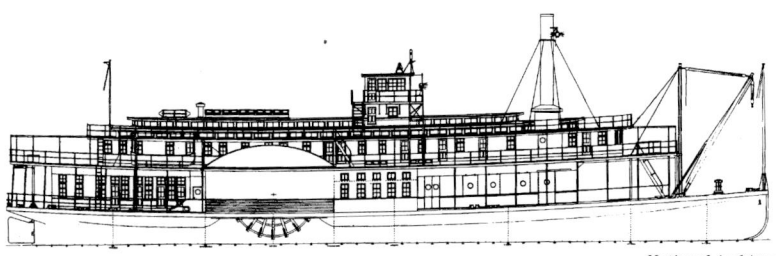

Plan for *USLHT Willow*, dated 1924. *National Archives*

BEECH, 1928

Name	Builder	Contracted	Launched	Commissioned	Disposition
Beech	Southern Shipyard Corp. Newport News, VA	16 Aug 1926	1927	Jan 1928	Decom 23 Jan 1963 Sold 28 Aug 1964

Cost
  $127,561 (contract)
  $133,306 (actual)

Hull
  Displacement (tons)   255 (max) / 220 (mean)   Steel Hull
  Dimensions   101-03' (loa) / 96' (lbp) / 92' (lwl) x 23' x 8'6" (7'3" max draft)

Machinery
  Main Engine   Triple expansion steam   BHP 200
  Main Boiler   water tube almy   Coal fired
  Propulsion   Single propeller, cast iron, 4 bladed
                  'A' frame derrick, boom capy 10 tons, electric winch

Complement
  3 officers, 8 men   (1930)
  2 warrants, 11 men (1959)

Design
  A Bay and Sound Tender, for use on Lake Champlain, to replace *USLHT Daisy*. Built entirely of steel except for a wood boat deck.

Assigned to the Third LHD at Staten Island, NY, *USLHT Beech* was originally built with a steam plant, which was replaced with a direct line 300 BHP Cooper-Bessemer diesel engine in 1940. Designated WAGL-205 in 1942. Decommissioned in 1963 and sold the following year, it was refurbished as a private vessel in 1968 and named *Catalyst*, manned and operated by Humboldt State University in Northern California. It sank in late 1975.

USLHT Althea, 1930. *National Archives*

ALTHEA class, 1930

Name	Builder	Contracted	Launched	Commissioned	Disposition
Althea	New London Ship & Engine Groton, CT	01 Dec 1928	24 Feb 1930	30 Apr 1930	Decom 10 Nov 1962 Sold 26 Nov 1963
Poinciana	Electric Boat Co. Groton, CT	17 Jun 1929	07 Jun 1930	08 Jul 1930	Decom 17 Aug 1962 Sold 26 Nov 1962

Cost
  $80,892 (Althea): $50,950 (hull bid) $61,234 (hull) + $19,658 (govt. purchased machinery)
  $82,743 (Poinciana): $63,700 (hull) + $19,043 (govt. purchased machinery)

Hull
  Displacement (tons) 120 (full) / 108 (mean)   Steel Hull
  Dimensions   80'9' x 19' x 6' (3'7" mean draft)

Machinery
  Main Engines   2 Cummins 4-cyl, 4 cycle diesels (55 HP)   SHP 100
  Propulsion   Twin 4-blade propellers, 33" diam.
                 Steel boom, 2 ton capy, electric hoist

Complement
  2 officers, 6 men (1930-1937)

Design
  Built as Bay and Sound Tenders.

Althea
Built to replace *USLHT Water Lily*, *USLHT Althea* was assigned to the Sixth LHD at Fort Pierce, FL. At the start of WWII, when all buoy tenders were assigned hull numbers, *USCGC Althea* was designated WAGL-223. After WWII, it served out of Fort Pierce, FL. After it was sold, it became *M/V Little Red*, operating until 1973.

Poinciana
Assigned to the Seventh LHD, it was a replacement for the wrecked *USLHT Poinsettia* at Key West, FL. In Jan 1942, it was designated WAGL-266 and operated out of Miami, FL. After its sale, it became the private vessel *Red's Baby*, operating until 1973.

USLHT Violet, 1930.

VIOLET class, 1930

Name	Builder	Contracted	Launched	Commissioned	Disposition
Violet	Manitowoc Shipbuilding Manitowoc, WI	06 Sep 1929	21 Aug 1930	21 Aug 1930	Decom 02 Jan 1962 Sold 08 Mar 1963
Lilac	Pusey & Jones Co. Wilmington, DE	16 Aug 1932	26 May 1933	1933	Decom 03 Feb 1972 Donated 06 Jun 1972
Mistletoe	Pusey & Jones Co. Wilmington, DE	1938	1938	15 Sep 1939	Decom 15 Aug 1968 Sold 14 Aug 1969

VIOLET class, 1930 (CONT.)

Cost
   Violet: $214,500 (bid), $337,745 (actual)
   Lilac: $225,000 (bid), $330,840 (actual)
   Mistletoe: $378,800 (actual)

Hull
   Displacement (tons)   1012 (full) / 799 (mean) / 770 (light)   Steel Hull
   Dimensions   173'4" (loa) / 163'9" (lbp) x 32' x 13' (10'6" max / 8'6" mean / 5'8" light draft) 171'0"(lwl)

Machinery
   Main Engines   2 triple expansion vertical inverted steam (each 500 HP)
   Main Boilers   2 Babcock & Wilcox watertube   Oil fired
   Propulsion   Two propellers, 4 bladed, 7'5" diam.   SHP 800
                              Steel boom, 20 ton capy, steam hoist

Complement
   7 officers, 23 men (1930)
   6 officers, 20 men (1937)
   2 officers, 2 warrants, 34 men (1961)

Design
   Built as Coastwise Tenders for the LHS and classed by the Coast Guard as Coastal Bouy Tenders.

Lilac
Originally contracted on 13 Apr 1931 to be built by Hampton Roads Shipbuilding of Portsmouth, VA, for $334,900 with the planned name *USLHT Azalea*. However, a lower contract bid was accepted from Pusey & Jones on 16 Aug 1931 with the new name *USLHT Lilac*. Its keel was laid on 15 Nov 1932 and she was launched as *USLHT Lilac* on 26 May 1933. Built as a replacement for *USLHT Iris*, it was assigned to Edgemoor, DE, in the Fourth LHD, working the Delaware River and Bay. Designated WAGL-227 at the start of WWII. Redesignated as WLM-227 in 1965. When decommissioned in 1972, it was the last steam driven buoy tender in the service. It was donated to the Harry Lundeberg Seafarers International Union seamanship school in Maryland. The union sold it about 1988, and as of 1999, it remains up for bid near Richmond, VA.

Mistletoe
Last of the class to be built, *USCGC Mistletoe* was designated WAGL-237 in 1942 and served out of Portsmouth, VA. It also was redesignated as a Coastal Buoy Tender (WLM-237) in 1965 when the Coast Guard overhauled the hull designation system for tenders.

Violet
Lead ship of the class, it was built to replace *USLHT Holly*. It was assigned to the Fifth LHD at Baltimore, and serviced AtoN on the Chesapeake Bay for its entire career.

USLHT Mistletoe, 1939.

National Archives

LINDEN class, 1931

Name	Builder	Contracted	Launched	Commissioned	Disposition
Linden	Merrill Stevens Shipbldg. Jacksonville, FL	26 Sep 1930	07 Mar 1931	22 Jul 1931	Decom 29 May 1969 Sold 22 May 1970
Columbine	Moore Dry Dock Co. Oakland, CA	19 Jan 1931	23 Jul 1931	21 Oct 1931	Decom 08 Oct 1965 Sold 29 Jun 1967
Wistaria	Union Dry Dock, Inc. Staten Island, NY	21 Jul 1932	03 Feb 1933	Mar 1933	Decom 07 Oct 1966 Sold 06 Dec 1968

Cost
    Linden: $169,110 (bid), $176,462 (actual)
    Columbine: $179,434 (bid), $192,076 (actual)
    Wistaria: $129,900 (bid)

Hull
    Displacement (tons)   400 (full) / 323 (mean)   Steel Hull
    Dimensions   121'4" (loa) / 114'8" (lwl) / 111'8" (lbp) x 25'0" x 9' (8'0" max / 6'8" mean draft)

Machinery
    Main Engines   1 electric motor by two G.E. generators from 2 Winton diesels; 150 HP each
    Propulsion   Single, 4 blade propeller, 4'10" diam.   SHP 240
    Steel boom   10 ton capy with electric hoist

Complement
    4 officers, 12 men (1932)
    4 officers, 13 men (1937)
    2 officers, 2 warrants, 34 men (1961)

Design
    Built as Bay and Sound Tenders. *USLHT Linden* was the first U.S. tender with Diesel-Electric drive.

Columbine
Assigned to San Francisco Bay in the Eighteenth LHD after commissioning. Designated WAGL-208 (Buoy Tender) at the start of WWII. During the war, was assigned to the San Francisco Bay region. Redesignated WLI-208 (Inland Buoy Tender) in Jan 1965 when the Coast Guard adopted a new hull designation system for its buoy tenders.

Linden
Built to replace *USLHT Laurel*, its keel was laid in Sep 1930. This was the first tender in the United States to have Diesel-Electric drive. Commissioned as *USLHT Linden*, it assigned to Portsmouth, VA, in the Fifth LHD when completed, replacing *USLHT Laurel*, and working the Chesapeake Bay. Designated WAGL-228 in Jan 1942. The lifting gear for the boom was replaced with an 8-ton air hoist system. Later, *Linden* it was sold, becoming the freighter *M/V Venture*, operating into the 1980s.

Wistaria
Last of the class built, it was a planned replacement for *USLHT Woodbine*, but was assigned to the Fifth LHD in Baltimore. After merging into the Coast Guard, and with the start of WWII, it was designated WAGL-254. On 01 Jan 1965, it was redesignated WLM-254 (Coastal Buoy Tender).

USLHT Wistaria as a Coast Guard Cutter in the late 1950s.   Collection, P. Hornberger

USLHT Locust became *USCGC Locust* in 1939 when the Lighthouse Service merged into the Coast Guard.

U.S. Coast Guard

LOCUST, 1931

Name	Builder	Built	Acquired	Commissioned	Disposition
Locust		1895	1931	1931 Sold	Decom 1954

Cost
  unknown

Hull
  Displacement (tons) unknown   Iron Hull
  Dimensions   72'

Machinery
  Main Engines   Steam
  Propulsion   Single Propeller

Design
  Built as a private ferry launch *Dart* in 1895.

Acquired by the Lighthouse Service in 1931 and commissioned as *USLHT Locust*. Used as a Buoy Boat in the Eighteenth LHD without a permanent crew assigned. Became *USCGC Locust* (CG-72013-D) when the LHS merged into the Coast Guard in 1939. Decommissioned in 1954, and replaced by *USCGC Bayberry*.

USLHT Cherry, 1932. Even in the harsh conditions of winter snow and ice, buoys had to be tended.

National Archives

CHERRY, 1932

Name	Builder	Contracted	Launched	Commissioned	Disposition
Cherry	Leathem D. Smith Dock Co. Sturgeon Bay, WI	02 Jan 1931	NA	19 May 1932	Decom 01 Dec 1964 Sold 20 May 1965

Cost
   $84,900 (hull) + $24,117.33 (govt. purchased machinery): $109,017.33 (total)

Hull
   Displacement (tons)   254 (max) / 202 (mean) [F.W.]   Steel Hull
   Dimensions   86'3" (loa) / 77'0" (lbp) x 23'6" x 11' (9'6" max / 7'9" mean draft)

Machinery
   Main Engine   1 Winton diesel to one electric motor   BHP 300
   Propulsion   Single Propeller, 4-bladed, 5'6" diam.
              Steel derrick, 7½ ton capy, electric hoist

Complement
   No regular crew assigned (1932)
   2 officers, 5 men   (1937)
   0 officers, 10 men (1958)

Design
   Built as a Bay and Sound Tender to replace *USLHT Birch*.

Assigned to the Tenth LHD at Buffalo, NY, after commissioning, working Lake Erie and the Niagara River. Designated WAGL-258 (Buoy Tender) in Jan 1942. Engine replaced in Jul 1950 with 500 HP GM diesel. From 1959 to 1964, *USCGC Cherry* was assigned to Sault Ste. Marie. On 01 Jan 1965, when the Coast Guard changed its hull designation system, *USCGC Cherry* was redesignated as a Construction Tender (WLIC-258). Decommissioned and transferred (with *USCGC Dahlia*) to the government of Surinam in 1965.

USLHT Myrtle.
U.S. Coast Guard

MYRTLE, 1932

Name	Builder	Contracted	Launched	Commissioned	Disposition
Myrtle	Dubuque Boat & Boiler Works Dubuque, IA	15 Feb 1932	30 Sep 1932	1932	Decom 08 Feb 1963 Sold 19 May 1964

Cost
  $95,000 (contract)
  $89,743 (actual)

Hull
  Displacement (tons)   186 (max) / 180 (mean)   Steel Hull
  Dimensions   92'8" x 23' x 7' (4'10" max / 4'6" mean draft)

Machinery
  Main Engines   2 Cummins diesels   BHP 250
  Propulsion   Twin Propellers   SHP 220
                  Steel boom, 3 ton capy, gas engine hoist

Complement
  2 officers, 6 men (1937)

Design
  Built as a Bay and Sound Tender, and planned to replace *USLHT Azalea*.

Assigned to the Eighth LHD at Galveston, TX, after commissioning. Designated WAGL-263 in Jan 1942. *USCGC Myrtle* spent its last year of service at Corpus Christi, TX, prior to decommissioning. Sold in 1864, it became the *M/V Sea Inspector*, but only operated for two more years.

USLHT Hickory. *U.S. Coast Guard*

HICKORY, 1933

Name	Builder	Contracted	Launched	Commissioned	Disposition
Hickory	Bath Iron Works Bath, ME	13 Apr 1932	09 Feb 1933	Mar 1933	Decom 10 Jan 1967 Sold 28 Apr 1969

Cost
   $152,480 (bid)

Hull
   Displacement (tons)   400 (1939)
   Dimensions   131'4" (loa) / 121'4" (lbp) x 24'6" x 12' (9'6" max draft)

Machinery
   Main Engine   1 triple exmpansion steam   BHP 500
   Main Boiler   1 Babcock & Wilcox watertube   oil fired
   Propulsion   Single propellor
                      Steel boom, 10 ton capy, steam hoist

Complement
   4 officers, 16 men (1937)
   1 warrant, 22 men (1962)

Design
   Built as a Coastwise Tender to replace *USLHT Pansy*.

Assigned to the Third LHD to tend AtoN in the New York Bay and Long Island Sound. Homeported at Staten Island, NY. Designated WAGL-219 at the start of WWII. Redesignated WLI-219 (Inland Tender) in 1965. It was sold in 1969 becoming the private vessel *Hickory*, operating in the 1980s.

USLHT Arbutus underway in Delaware River, 1933.
Collection, P. Hornberger

ARBUTUS, 1933

Name	Builder	Contracted	Launched	Commissioned	Disposition
Arbutus	Pusey & Jones Wilmington, DE	21 Jul 1932	25 Mar 1933	1933	Decom 27 Mar 1967 Sold 24 Mar 1969

Cost
 $250,000 (contract)
 $239,800 (actual)

Hull
Displacement (tons)	997 (max) / 960 (mean) / 770 (light)	Steel Hull
Dimensions	174'7" x 33' x 14'6" (12'3" max draft)	

Machinery
Main Engines	2 triple expansion reciprocating steam	SHP 1000
Main Boilers	2 Foster-Wheeler watertube oil fired	
Propulsion	Twin propellers	
	Boom capy, 20 tons, steam hoist	

Complement
 7 officers, 21 men (1937)

Design
 Planned as a Coastwise Tender, to replace *USLHT Ilex*.

Assigned to the Second LHD after completion, relieving *USLHT Azalea*. Designated WAGL-203 at the start of WWII, serving out of Woods Hole, MA. After WWII, *USCGC Arbutus* was reassigned to Staten Island, NY. Reclassed as a Coastal Buoy Tender (WLM-203) in 1965. In Jul 1966, *Arbutus* ran aground in Long Island Sound, but was refloated with no damage. Sold two years after decommissioning in 1967, eventually becoming a treasure diving platform and salvage ship out of Key West, FL.

USLHT Dahlia, 1933.
U.S. Coast Guard

DAHLIA, 1933

Name	Builder	Contracted	Launched	Commissioned	Disposition
Dahlia	Great Lakes Engineering Works River Rouge, MI	25 Feb 1933	15 Jun 1933	Aug 1933	Decom 09 Oct 1964 Sold 20 May 1965

Cost
   $66,566 (contract)
   $69,789 (actual)

Hull
   Displacement (tons)   160 [1933]
                             175 [1945]   Steel Hull
   Dimensions   81'2" (loa) / 72'0" (lbp) x 20' x 9' (7'0" max draft)

Machinery
   Main Engines   1 Winton diesel   BHP 235 SHP 500
   Propulsion   Single Propeller
   Boom capy 5 tons, electric hoist

Complement
   3 officers, 4 men (1937)
   0 officers, 10 men (1945)

Design
   Built as a Bay and Sound Tender, to replace *ULSHT Thistle*.

USLHT Dahlia was assigned to the Eleventh LHD in Detroit after commissioning replacing *USLHT Thistle*. Designated WAGL-288 at the start of WWII. Remained at Detroit, MI, during the war working the Detroit River and Lake St. Clair. It was reengined with a single 500 HP GM diesel engine after the war. After decommissioning, it was sold (with the former tender *Cherry*) to the government of Surinam on 20 May 1965.

USLHT Hemlock at Seattle, Washington, 1934. — National Archives

HEMLOCK, 1934

Name	Builder	Contracted	Launched	Commissioned	Disposition
Hemlock	Berg Shipbuilding Co. Seattle, WA	12 Jan 1933	20 Jan 1934	1934	Decom 17 Jun 1958 Sold 02 Aug 1961

Cost
  $228,480.60 (contract)
  $238,542.00 (actual)

Hull
  Displacement (tons)   1005 (max) / 960 (full) / 770 (mean)   Steel Hull
  Dimensions   174'6" (loa) / 163'6" (lbp) x 32' x 14'6" (13'3" max/12'7" mean draft)

Machinery
  Main Engines   2 triple-expansion steam   BHP 1000
  Main Boilers   2 Foster-Wheeler watertube   oil-fired
  Propulsion   Twin Propeller

Complement
  7 officers, 26 men (1937)
  2 officers, 4 warrants, 41 men (1957)

Design
  Built as a Coastwise Tender specifically for duty in Alaska waters. Equipped with a double bottom, and larger fuel and water tanks than normally found on similar tenders. Built to replace *USLHT Fern*.

Assigned to Sixteenth LHD after commissioning. Designated WAGL-217 at the start of WWII. Spent its entire career in Alaskan waters, primarily operating out of Ketchikan. After it was sold, it became the private vessel *Hemlock*. Later yet, its engines were removed and it was converted into a barge and continued to be used in Alaska into the 1980s.

USLHT Tamarack, 1934.
National Archives

TAMARACK, 1934

Name	Builder	Contracted	Launched	Commissioned	Disposition
Tamarack	Manitowoc Shipbuilding Manitowoc, WI	11 Dec 1933	1934	Nov 1934	Decom 27 Oct 1970 Sold 02 Aug 1971

Cost
  $233,917

Hull
  Displacement (tons)   400 (full) / 290 (light)   Steel Hull
  Dimensions   124'4"(loa) / 111'8"(lbp) x 30'3" x 10' (7'6" max draft)

Machinery
  Main Engines   1 Winton diesel   BHP 450 SHP 520
  Propulsion   Single Propeller
                  Boom capy, 10 tons, electric hoist

Complement
  4 officers, 10 men (1937)
  1 warrant, 19 men (1966)

Design
  Built as a Bay and Sound tender for service on the Saint Mary's River to replace *USLHT Clover*.

Assigned to the Eleventh LHD after commissioning as *USLHT Tamarack*, then to the Ninth Coast Guard District at Manitowoc, WI, during WWII. *USCGC Tamarack* was designated WAGL-248 (Buoy Tender) at the start of WWII in Jan 1942. After WWII it was stationed at Sault Ste. Marie. It was reclassed as WLI-248 (Inland Buoy Tender) in 1965.

USLHT Rhododenrdron immediately after launching, 1935.

U.S. Coast Guard

RHODODENDRON, 1935

Name	Builder	Contracted	Launched	Commissioned	Disposition
Rhododendron	Commercial Iron Works Portland, OR	23 Jul 1934	16 Mar 1935	12 Apr 1935 Donated 20 Aug 1958	Decom 20 Aug 1958

Cost
   $67,723

Hull
   Displacement (tons)   140 (max) / 114 (mean)   Steel Hull
   Dimensions   80'6"' X 20' X 5'11" (4' 2" max draft)

Machinery
   Main Engines   2 Imperial diesels   BHP/SHP 240
   Propulsion   Twin Propellers
                   Boom capy, 1½ tons, electric hoist

Complement
   2 officers, 5 men (1937)

Design
   Built as a Bay and Sound Tender, to replace *USLHT Larch*.

Contracted in 1934 and commissioned in 1935, it was assigned to the Seventeenth LHD on the Columbia River. Designated WAGL-267 in Jan 1942, it served out of Vancouver, WA (near Portland). From 1949 to 1958, its homeport was changed to Seattle, WA. After decommissioning in 1958, it was donated to the State of Washington Department of Civil Defense. They sold it on 20 Apr 1959, and it became the merchant ship *Kandu*. It sank in Alaska on 25 Nov 1966.

JASMINE class, 1935

Name	Builder	Contacted	Launched	Commissioned	Disposition
Jasmine	Dravo Constructing Company Neville Island, Pittsburgh, PA	1934	26 Mar 1935	May 1935	Decom 18 Jan 1965 Sold 19 May 1966
Bluebonnet	Dubuque Boat & Boiler Works Dubuque, IA	1938	1939	04 Nov 1939	Decom 18 Jan 1965 Sold 19 May 1966

Cost
   Bluebonnet: $132,500 (Contract)
   Jasmine: $114,850 (Actual)

Hull
   Displacement (tons)   184 (1935)   Steel Hull, Composite Superstructure
   Dimensions   91'4"(loa) / 82'0"(lbp) x 23' x 8'3" (5'3" max draft)

Machinery
   Main Engines   2 Cooper-Bessemer, 6 cyl, 4-cycle diesels   BHP 440 (Bluebonnet)
                           2 General Motors diesels   BHP 295 (Jasmine)
   Propulsion   Twin Propellers
                         Steel boom, 2½ ton capy, electric hoist

Complement
   2 officer, 6 men (1937)

   0 officers, 11 men (1958)

Design
Built as Bay and Sound Tenders for the LHS, and designated as Buoy Tenders in the Coast Guard. Both were classed as Inland Buoy Tenders (WLI) in 1965.

Bluebonnet
Assigned to Eighth LHD and operating out of Galveston, TX, after commissioning and through its entire career. After being incorporated into the Coast Guard, and with the start of WWII, *USCGC Bluebonnet* was designated WAGL-257 in Jan 1942. In Jan 1965, it was redesignated WLI-257 (Inland Tender). After it was sold, it became the fishing vessel *Tiffany*.

Jasmine
Keel laid 26 Dec 1934. Assigned to the Eighth LHD, *USLHT Jasmine* was homeport its entire career at New Orleans, it replaced *USLHT Cosmos*. Designated WAGL-261 at the start of WWII, and redesignated WLI-261 in 1965. After it was sold, it became the private vessel *P.E. Romanzoff*. In 1973, it was renamed the *Cape Romanzoff* and continued to operate into the 1980s.

Launching *USLHT Jasmine*, 1935.

National Archives

USLHT Walnut at Oakland, CA, during builder's trials, 1939.

U.S. Coast Guard

HOLLYHOCK class, 1937

Name	Builder	Contracted	Launched	Commissioned	Disposition
Hollyhock	Defoe Boat & Motor Works Bay City, MI	Mar 1936	24 Mar 1937	07 Aug 1937	Decom 31 Mar 1982 Sold 31 Mar 1982
Walnut	Moore Dry Dock Company Oakland, CA	17 Aug 1938	1939	27 Jun 1939	Decom 1 Jul 1982 Trans to Honduras Jul 1982
Fir	Moore Dry Dock Company Oakland, CA	17 Aug 1938	22 Mar 1939	01 Oct 1940	Decom 01 Oct 1991

Cost
  $347,800 (Hollyhock)
  $389,746 (Walnut and Fir, each)

Hull
  Displacement (tons) 885 (max) / 825 (mean)   Steel Hull
  Dimensions 174'10" (loa) / 163'6" (lbp) x 32' (11'3" max / 10'7" mean draft)

Machinery
  Main Engines 2 triple expansion horizontal steam   SHP 1000
  Main Boilers 2 Babcock & Wilcox watertube   Oil fired
  Propulsion Twin propellers
  Steel Boom, 20 ton capy, hydraulic hoist

Complement
  4 officers, 1 warrant, 69 men (1945)
  4 officers, 2 warrants, 35 enlisted (1991)

Design
    Designed as coastwise (type 'A') tenders for the LHS. After consolidation into the Coast Guard in 1939, and with the onset of WWII, all were designated as Coast Guard Tender class Cutters (WAGL) in Jan 1942. All were reengined to twin diesels with reduction gear (1350 SHP) in the early 1950s. When the Coast Guard developed its own hull classification system in 1965, all were designated as Coastal Tenders (WLM).

Fir during Builder's sea trials in San Francisco Bay, 1940. Although the ship is clearly marked on the bow with a lighthouse of the Old Lighthouse Service, fifteen months had passed since the LHS merged into the Coast Guard. Officially, this is USCGC *Fir*.

Columbia River Maritime Museum

Fir

Contracted by the LHS and keel laid on 07 Jan 1939, but completed after the LHS merged into the Coast Guard in 1939. Thus, this was the last Lighthouse Tender built. It was commissioned in 1940 as *USCGC Fir* (WAGL-212) and assigned to duty tending aids in Puget Sound, relieving the old *USLHT Heather*. It was reengined from steam to diesel in 1951, with twin 1350 HP Fairbanks-Morse diesels, using reduction gears. Except for a brief period in 1982 at Long Beach, it served its entire career operating out of Seattle, WA. Redesignated WLM-212 (Coastal Buoy Tender) in 1965. In 1982, a hydraulic boom system replaced the old electrically powered system. Decommissioned in 1991, this was the last Lighthouse Tender in service. After decommissioning, it remained in Seattle for many years, where efforts were being made to preserve the ship as a floating museum. However, the efforts failed, and the hull was transferred to MARAD in 1997 and placed in storage for final disposition.

Hollyhock

Keel laid 13 Apr 1936. The lead ship of this class, it was built to replace the aging *USLHT Sumac*, and was assigned to duty in the Twelfth LHD at Milwaukee, WI. Designated WAGL-220 at the start of WWII. Converted from steam to diesel in the mid 1950s.

USCGC Hollyhock served in Detroit, MI, from 1959 to 1962 and in Miami, FL, from 1962 until decommissioned in 1982. It had been redesignated WLM-220 in 1965. After decommissioning, it was sold, eventually becoming the *Good News Mission Ship*. It was later sunk as an artificial reef off Pompano Beach, FL, in 1990.

Walnut

Keel laid 05 Dec 1938. Planned for the Eleventh LHD as a replacement for the old *USLHT Marigold* at Cleveland, servicing aids in Lake Huron and Lake Superior. In Jun 1941, it was reassigned to tend AtoN in the Territory of Hawaii, and was designated WAGL-252 in Jan 1942. Re-engined in Willamette Iron & Steel, Portland, OR, from steam to two diesel engines through reduction gear (1350 SHP) in 1958. In Jan 1965, redesignated WLM-252 (Coastal Buoy Tender). In Sep 1965 it was involved in a collision with *M/V American Leader*, but no major damage was sustained. It was assigned to Miami, FL, from 1954 to 1967 and then San Pedro, CA, until decommissioned in 1982. After decommissioning, *Walnut* was transferred in Jul 1982 to the government of Honduras and renamed *Yojoa* (FNH-252). Refitted by that government in 1989, *Yajoa* remains in service into the late 1990s.

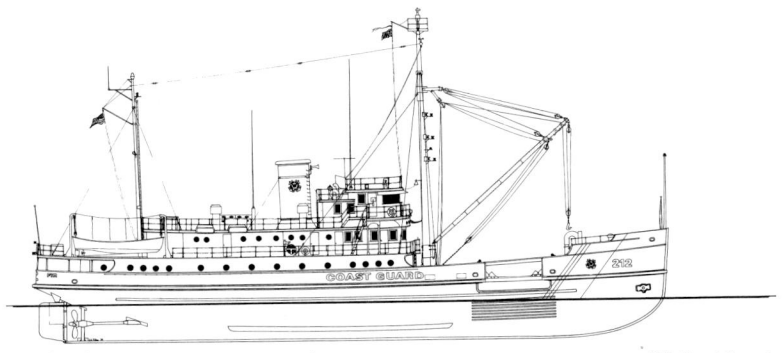

Plan for *USCG Tender Fir*, 1940.

U.S. Coast Guard

USLHT Goldenrod just after launch, 1939.   *U.S. Coast Guard*

GOLDENROD class, 1938

Name	Builder	Contracted	Launched	Commissioned	Disposition
Goldenrod	Dubuque Boat & Boiler Works Dubuque, IA	21 Jun 1937	1938	02 Jun 1938	Decom 26 May 1973 Trans 26 Sep 1973
Poplar	Dubuque Boat & Boiler Works Dubuque, IA	1938	1938	1939	Decom 17 Jun 1973 Trans 26 Sep 1973

Cost
  $115,375 (Goldenrod)
  $123,200 (Poplar)

Hull
  Displacement (tons) 193 (max) / 170 (mean)   Steel Hull
  Dimensions   103'6" (loa) / 99'7" (lbp) x 24'0" x 5'9" (4'2" max / 3'6" mean draft)

Machinery
  Main Engines   2 Fairbanks-Morse diesels (150 HP each) through red gear   BHP/SHP 400
  Propulsion   Twin propellers
                 Steel boom, 2½-ton capy, electric hoist, two spuds

Complement
  1 officer, 14 men (1945)
  1 warrant, 16 men (1964)

Design
  River Tenders with propellers mounted in tunnels for shallow water Mississippi and Missouri river operations. These were the prototypes for the later 114-foot "Dogwood" class River Tenders built by the Coast Guard in 1940. They were all steel except for the wood pilot house. Both were reengined in 1960. After decommissioning, both were transferred to the National Science Foundation in 1973 for further disposition.

Goldenrod
Assigned to duty tending aids in the upper Missouri River, homeported at Kansas City, MO. Designated WAGL-213 in Jan 1942. From 1950 to 1962, *USCGC Goldenrod* operated out of Peoria, IL, then from Keokuk, IA, until 1973. Redesignated as WLR-213 (River Tender) in 1965. After decommissioning, *Goldenrod* and sister *Poplar* with both transferred to the National Science Foundation on 26 Sep 1973 for final disposition.

Poplar
Assigned to duty out of St. Louis, MO, tending aids on the lower Missouri and Illinois rivers. Designated WAGL-241 at the start of WWII. Redesignated WLR-241 in 1965. Its homeport was changed to Sewickley, PA, in 1963. It had the same fate as *Goldenrod*.

USLHT Elm. *U.S. Coast Guard*

ELM, 1939

Name	Builder	Contracted	Launched	Commissioned	Disposition
Elm	Defoe Boat & Motor Works Bay City, MI	1938	1938	01 Apr 1939	Decom 30 Jul 1969 Donated 23 Oct 1970

Cost
   $77,177 (contract)

Hull
   Displacement (tons)   75 (max) / 69 (mean)   Steel Hull
   Dimensions   72'4" (loa) / 70'0" (lbp) x 17'6" (4'8" max / 3'8" mean draft)

Machinery
   Main Engines   2 Winton diesels (each 150 HP)   BHP/SHP 330
   Propulsion   Twin propellors
                   Steel boom, 3 ton capy, electric hoist

Complement
   1 officer, 27 men (1945)
   1 warrant, 16 men (1964)

Design
   Designed as a Bay and Sound Tender for the shallow rivers and inland waters of New Jersey.

Assigned to Atlantic City, NJ, it was designated WAGL-260 at the start of WWII. Re-engined in 1960. Redesignated WLR-72260 (River Tender) in 1965 when the Coast Guard overhauled its hull designation system. Vessels under 100 feet in length were assigned a five-digit hull number; the first two numbers denoting the length, and last three the sequence number. Donated to a private organization in 1970, they sold it on 19 Jul 1972.

USLHT Zinnia. Collection, P. Hornberger

ZINNIA class, 1939

Name	Builder	Contracted	Launched	Commissioned	Disposition
Zinnia	John H. Mathis Co. Camden, NJ	15 Apr 1938	04 Feb 1939	1939	Decom 14 Jan 1972 Trans 01 Mar 1972
Narcissus	John H. Mathis Co. Camden, NJ	15 Apr 1938	04 Feb 1939	1939	Decom Jan 1971 Trans 05 May 1971

Cost
   $220,023 (each)

Hull
   Displacement (tons)   355 (max) / 342 (mean)   Steel Hull
   Dimensions   122'2" x 27' (7'0" max / 6'6" mean draft)

Machinery
   Main Engines   2 Superior diesels with reduction gear   BHP 340 IHP 400
   Propulsion   Twin propellers   SHP 430
                  Steel boom, 10 ton capy, electric hoist

Complement
   3 officers, 40 men (1945)

Design
   Built as Bay and Sound Tenders, these were the first tenders to be extensively welded.

ZINNIA class, 1939 (CONT.)

Narcissus
Assigned to the Seventh LHD at Key West, FL, for duty. Reassigned to Portsmouth, VA, for the rest of its career and designated WAGL-238 at the start of WWII. On 01 Jul 1961, while moored, *USCGC Narcissus* was involved in a collision with the *M/V World Challenge*, which resulted in moderate topside damage. Redesignated WLI-238 (Inland Tender) in 1965. After decommissioning in 1971, transferred to the government of Guyana. Renamed the *SS Maripa*, it served until 1994 when laid up and deemed unserviceable.

Zinnia
Assigned to Edgemoor, DE, for AtoN duty, it was designated WAGL-255 in 1942. After WWII, it was reassigned to Gloucester City, NJ, for the next twenty years. *USCGC Zinnia* was redesignated WLI-255 (Inland Buoy Tender) in 1965. In 1967, it was reassigned to New York City for two years, then to New Orleans. After decommissioning, it was transferred to the U.S. Air Force on 01 Mar 1972.

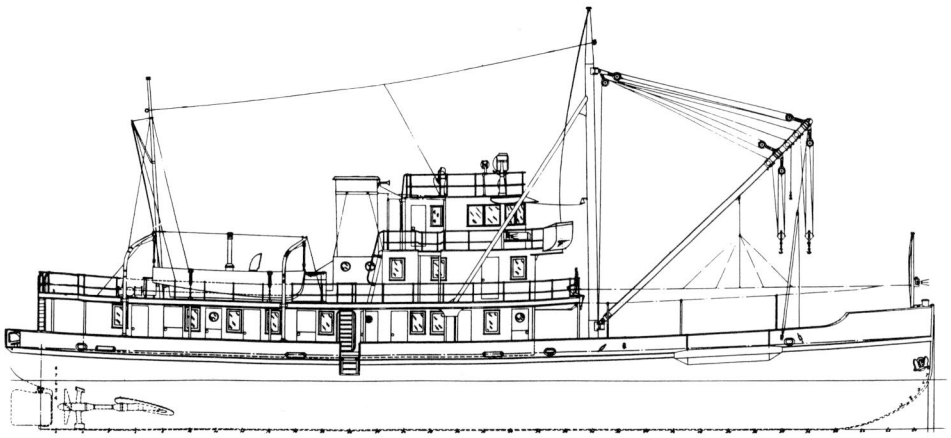

Plan for *USCGC Narcissus*, 1941.   *U.S. Coast Guard*

USCGC Narcissus.   *U.S. Coast Guard*

USCGC Maple was designated WAGL-234 at the start of WWII.

U.S. Coast Guard

MAPLE, 1939

Name	Builder	Contracted	Launched	Commissioned	Disposition
Maple	Marine Iron & Shipbuilding Duluth, MN	15 Apr 1938	29 Apr 1939	Jun 1939	Decom 01 Jun 1973 Trans 08 Aug 1973

Cost
$190,000

Hull
Displacement (tons)   342 (1938)   Steel Hull
Dimensions   122'3" (loa) / 113'9" (lbp) x 27' x 7' max (draft)(1938)

Machinery
Main Engines   2 Superior diesels   BHP 430   IHP 400
Propulsion   Twin propellors   SHP 460
               Steel boom, 10 ton capy, electric hoist

Complement
1 officer, 27 men (1945)
1 warrant, 19 men (1962)

Design
  Designed as a Bay and Sound Tender. Although specifications are similar to the Zinnia class tenders, *USLHT Maple* is distinctly different in profile and not of the same class or construction. *Maple* has a rounded forecastle where the *Zinnia*'s foc'sle is open. *Zinnia* has an open main deck along the superstructure from the foc'sle to the stern and *Maple* does not.

Contracted for construction on 15 Apr 1938, and completed just over a year later. *USLHT Maple* was assigned to the Tenth LHD on the Great Lakes upon completion, replacing the old *USLHT Sundew*. *USCGC Maple* was designated WAGL-234 at the start of WWII. In the early 1960s, it was reengined with two 800 HP GM diesels. Redesignated WLI-234 (Inland Tender) in 1965 when the Coast Guard adopted a new hull designation system. After decommissioning, it was transferred to the U.S. Navy who then gave it to the E.P.A. and renamed it *Roger R. Simons*. It operated out of Milwaukee as a research vessel, monitoring pollution on the Great Lakes until 1995 when it was placed out of service. It is now in private hands and moored at St. Ignace, MI, with plans to become a floating museum.

Tender *Le Claire* before it was renamed *Cottonwood*, 1938.

National Archives

COTTONWOOD, 1939

Name	Builder	Built	Purchased	Commissioned	Disposition
Cottonwood		1915		1915 (War Dept)	Decom 25 May 1946
	Grafton, IL		17 May 1938 (LHS)	1939 (LHS)	Sold 01 May 1947

Cost
 $44,238 construction
 $ 7,500 acquisition by LHS
 $ 2,500 conversion

Hull
 Displacement (tons)   243 (full)   Steel Hull
 Dimensions   151' x 34'8" x 4'5" max (1915)

Machinery
 Main Engines   2 tandem compound steam   SHP 320
 Main Boilers   1 Foster-Wheeler Express Coal Fired
 Propulsion   Stern Paddlewheel

Complement
 2 officers, 1 warrant, 33 men (1945)

Design
 A steel-hulled stern wheel river tender.

Originally built for the U.S. Army Corps of Engineers as the River Tug *Le Claire* (sometimes listed as *Le Clair*), it was acquired by the LHS on 17 May 1938 and converted for use as a River Tender, commissioned as *USLHT Cottonwood* in 1939 and stationed at Chattanooga, TN. It was employed in the Tennessee River for tending AtoN. *USCGC Cottonwood* was designated WAGL-209 in Jan 1942.

An identical sister ship, Army River Tug *Minneapolis*, was acquired by the Coast Guard in 1940 (after the LHS had already merged into the Coast Guard) and became the *USCGC Azalea* (WAGL-262).

BIRCH, 1939

Name	Builder	Contracted	Launched	Commissioned	Disposition
Birch	General Ship & Engine Works Boston, MA		1939	1939	Decom 24 Feb 1963 Sold 30 Jul 1964

Cost
  $74,000

Hull
  Displacement (tons)   137 (max) / 76 (light)   Steel Hull
  Dimensions   72'4" x 18'   (3'8" max draft)

Machinery
  Main Engines   2 Winton diesels   BHP 300
  Propulsion   Twin propellors   SHP 330
                 Steel boom, 2 ton capy, electric hoist

Complement
  0 officers, 9 men

Designed as a Bay and Sound Tender, it was commissioned in the Coast Guard and assigned to duty at St. Petersburg, FL, where it stayed its entire career. At the start of WWII, it was designated WAGL-256.

JUNIPER, 1940

Name	Builder	Contracted	Launched	Commissioned	Disposition
Juniper	John H. Mathis Co. Camden, NJ	21 Jul 1939	18 May 1940	01 Oct 1940	Decom 15 Jul 1975 Sold Dec 1975

Cost
  $396,464 (contract)

Hull
  Displacement (tons) 794 (max) / 720 (mean)   Steel Hull
  Dimensions   177'0" x 32'0" (8'7" max draft)

Machinery
  Main Engines   Diesel-Electric (two diesels engines 550 HP each) to two generators to two electric motors (450 HP each)
  Propulsion   Twin Propellers   SHP 900
                  Steel boom, 20-ton capy, electric hoist

Complement
  1 officer, 3 warrants, 34 men (1945)

This was planned as the lead ship of a three ship group. Completed and commissioned as *USCGC Juniper* (WAGL-224), its design was the prototype for the many 180-foot tenders built during WWII (many which are still in service into the mid 1990s). However, with war imminent, plans were deferred to build any further ocean going tenders without the Coast Guard's multi-purpose capability, specifically to include Search and Rescue and icebreaking missions. *USCGC Juniper* was redesignated WLM-224 (Coastal Buoy Tender) on 01 Jan 1965. Decommissioned in 1975, it was sold later that same year and its name struck from the roles in Oct 1978.

" ... and the last shall be first."

Many allege that *Juniper* was the last tender begun for the LHS before its merger into the United States Coast Guard on 01 Jul 1939. It was designed by the LHS, as were at least half a dozen others commissioned in the early 1940s. However, since the contract bid for construction was not opened until 21 Jul 1939 (three weeks after the LHS merged into the Coast Guard on 01 Jul 1939), this actually makes *USCGC Juniper* the first tender built by the Coast Guard!
The 'title' of the Last Tender of the LHS belongs to *Fir* (third and final of the Hollyhock class).

EPILOG

Into the Coast Guard

When President Roosevelt's Reorganization Plan #11 was implemented in July 1939, the United States Lighthouse Service had 64 tenders, 39 lightships (all self propelled, 30 regular + 9 reliefs), and 5,355 personnel (4,119 full time; 1,156 part time), all responsible for maintaining over 508 lighthouses, 1,764 fog signals and beacons, 15,675 buoys (including 1,874 lighted buoys) and 12,137 other aids to navigation. When it merged with the U.S. Coast Guard on 01 July 1939, one month shy of the Lighthouse Service's 150th anniversary and just under a hundred years from when the first tender was acquired, it doubled the size of the Coast Guard and brought in an organizational structure which still impacts the service to this day. The heritage of the old Lighthouse Service is still present in all facets of the modern Coast Guard.

The old Lighthouse Service areas of responsibility and organization, known as Districts, are the basis for the Coast Guard's District numbering system and boundaries (established shortly after the merger). It was also the basis for the Naval District system established in 1903 which still continues to this day.

Many of the 30 old Lighthouse Service Depots became major Coast Guard Bases which are still in use today, mooring numerous types of cutters. And some of the old depots still perform the same functions as originally built; maintaining and supplying the tenders that work the aids.

The monthly Lighthouse Service Bulletins, established in 1912, to keep its employees aware of what was going on, continues to this day, first as the Coast Guard Bulletin, and then as the Commandant's Bulletin (now renamed Coast Guard Magazine), still providing information and news monthly to all its service members.

Most important are the tenders themselves. Still almost fifty percent of the entire Coast Guard fleet, these tenders continue to do the jobs they were built for. With the merger into the Coast Guard, the tenders gave up the famous triangular Lighthouse Service pennant for the vertically striped Coast Guard Ensign, and assumed the new title of Coast Guard Cutter. New roles required newer designs, to also include the ability to perform Search and Rescue, icebreaking, law enforcement and military missions. This also meant additional manning requirements, which is why crew sizes increased during and after World War II. To this day however, the paint schemes of the vessels and the aids to navigation missions remain unchanged. Also, the majority of the tenders are still named for plants, trees and shrubs.

With the merger in 1939, all sixty four of the Lighthouse Service Tenders (42 steam powered, 18 powered by diesel engines, and 4 with diesel-electric propulsion) became Coast Guard Cutters. Classed collectively as the Lighthouse Tender class, they continued to do their same jobs. However, with the onset of World War II, the Coast Guard and all its vessels became a working part of the Navy. Naval type hull classifications were assigned in January 1942. Thus evolved the tender hull designations which are known to all as "Coasties."

All manned tenders, regardless of size, kept the classification of Lighthouse Tender. Since the Navy had no such designation which would fit this category, they were designated as Miscellaneous Auxiliaries (or AG). The 'AG' was suffixed with an 'L' to indicate Lighthouse Tender, and prefixed with a 'W' to indicate it was a Coast Guard vessel. Thus the designation 'WAGL' was born. By 1943, the designation WAGL was renamed as "Buoy Tender" rather than the archaic term "Lighthouse Tender."

The remaining unmanned tenders, collectively known as Buoy Boats (type 'D' Lighthouse Service vessels), kept the 'D' designation with the Coast Guard 'W' prefix, thus becoming the WD Buoy Boat designation.

In 1965, the Coast Guard had realized that the all inclusive WAGL designation did nothing to clearly define the different types of Tenders it had in its fleet, so new more specific designations were created. The 'W' for Coast Guard, and the 'L' for tender would remain, then additional letters would be added to more clearly define what type of tender it was. What is interesting is that these newer hull classifications, with minor variations, are almost identical in breakdown to the old Lighthouse Service classifications of the 1920s:

Lighthouse Service	*(1920)*	*Coast Guard*	*(1942)*	*Coast Guard*	*(1965)*
Seagoing Tender	(type 'A')			Oceangoing Tender	WLB
Lake or Bay Tender	(type 'B')	"Tender" class	WAGL	Coastal Tender	WLM
Inside Waters Tender	(type 'C')			Inland Waters Tender	WLI
River Tender				River Tender	WLR
Buoy Boat	(type 'D')	Buoy Boat	WD		
Light Ship	(LV)	Light Ship	WAL	Light Vessel	WLV

The Tenders continue to be a major portion of the Coast Guard's fleet, even today. These tenders do everything the white cutters do (search and rescue, military readiness, icebreaking, law enforcement, etc.) plus their normal support of aids to navigation (often in places where the white cutters cannot or dare not to go). To many, they remain just "the black hull fleet," slow plodding vessels which usually don't travel very fast or far from shore, and are constantly doing dirty work. But to those who have served on a tender, there is a pride, a camaraderie and a sense of accomplishment of knowing you have helped put an aid on station and that it is "watching properly," protecting the waterways for all who navigate nearby. Often ignored, and not often cited for spectacular deeds or feats, these hard working black hulls and their crews are the unsung heroes of the sea.

The traditions of the old Lighthouse Service are still with us today in many ways, and will continue to be a point of pride to all who have served and are serving in the "Black Fleet," supporting and maintaining the best aids to navigation system in the world!

For further information on Coast Guard Buoy Tenders (all classes) after the 1939 merger of the Lighthouse Service into the United States Coast Guard, please refer to Robert Scheina's two books on Coast Guard Cutters and Craft.

Servicing a buoy. *U.S. Coast Guard*

APPENDIX A
Hired Vessels

Throughout the early history of the Lighthouse Service, vessels were often leased or chartered from private sources to take on various tasks. These "Hired Vessels," as the Annual Reports of the Lighthouse Service often called them, would usually be used at a specific location for a limited period of time to assist in the construction of a new lighthouse, or for hauling supplies to remote locations.

Prior to 1840 when the first Lighthouse Tender was purchased, the only way to support any operations afloat, was with the use of these "hired vessels." Often, local Pilot Boat Associations, Revenue Cutters, or other federal or state agencies would be contracted to provide labor for Lighthouse Service duties. And any time there was insufficient tenders available for any additional tasks, privately owned vessels would be chartered or hired to augment existing resources.

Sometimes, these chartered vessels would be manned and operated by Lighthouse Service personnel. When that occurred, the private vessels were often "commissioned" into the Lighthouse Service for the duration of their service. Those vessels would then be the sole responsibility of the Lighthouse Service, for its operation, maintenance and repair, until they were returned to their owners. Those "commissioned" chartered vessels are listed in the previous chapters.

However, at other times, vessels would be "hired," but retain their civilian crews. The pay of these civilian crews and costs relating to the operation and maintenance of the vessel would by carried by the owner and not the Lighthouse Service.

The vessels listed below are of this second category of "Hired Vessels." They are listed in alphabetical order, with the known (or approximate) dates they served, and any other additional information that might be known.

Hired Vessel	**Times of Service**	**Comments**
ALICE M. GILL	01 May-28 Nov 1900 01 Jul-09 Dec 1901 01 Jul-31 Oct 1902	A 140-foot (loa)/127-foot (lwl) 264-ton steam tug, built at Grand Haven in 1887. Served in Ninth LHD. Working on Lake Michigan. Working in the Milwaukee region.
ALLIANCE	1886-1891	A small steamer, chartered as a barracks ship and to move large granite blocks for the construction of St. George Reef Light off the northern California coast.
ARCADIA	01 Jul-20 Nov 1899	A wooden steam barge (length 118-foot, beam 26, depth 9, 146-tons, built in Milwaukee in 1888), for repairs in the Ninth LHD along the shores of Lake Michigan.
AUGUSTA	1852-05 Oct 1853	A small schooner, chartered and used as a Supply Tender. It alternated with *USLHT Eliza* in delivering supplies to the Atlantic coast lighthouses. The owner's brother sold *Eliza* to the LHS.
AUGUSTA	part of 1871	A small schooner (different than the *Augusta* chartered in 1852), for work in the Seventh LHD on the lighthouses in the Florida Keys, for $10/day, plus wages, and subsistence of the crew.
AXLE	part of 1902 Spring 1903	A schooner, working in the Eighth LHD at Mobile Bay, AL. A schooner, delivering materials in the Eighth LHD at Chandeleur light station, repairs of dock at depot, transport supplies for Oyster Bayou. Was discharged from contract as being unseaworthy.
CLEOPATRA	Mar-20 Aug 1900	A schooner, $3/day for four months, for construction in Tampa Bay.

Appendix A - Hired Vessels

Hired Vessel	Times of Service	Comments
DAWN	Jun 1904 one month 1905	A schooner used for one month only, delivering materials in the Seventh LHD. Deliver materials and build beacon in Florida, Seventh LHD.
DISCHOSE	02 Mar-30 Apr 1902	A 100-ton schooner, $13.33/day, at Puerto Rico, before any regular Lighthouse Tenders were assigned to the region.
DREAM	May 1862-Nov 1862	A small 92-foot, 80-ton topsail schooner, chartered at $300/month, replacing the old *USLHT Lamplighter* in the Eleventh LHD.
ELLEN C	Apr 1903-Jul 1904 one month 1905	Deliver materials and assist construction in Louisiana. Also for repairs and maintenance of lights along Florida Keys, and Gulf Coast regions. Construction of Sabine Light, TX, in Eighth LHD.
EXCEL	two months 1904	A schooner, in the Eighth LHD, for driving piles in Mobile Bay.
FEDERAL JACK	1812-01 Mar 1813	A 90-ton schooner, used to upgrade lighthouse lanterns on the East Coast. Seized on 01 Mar 1813 by the British frigate *Aeolus* during the War of 1812.
GARLAND	last half 1855	A small 113-ton schooner, chartered for $1,200/month, and used to transport construction materials for Farallon Island Light, outside San Francisco Bay.
GENERAL PIKE	1852	A small 47-ton pilot boat (draft 7'), used in Delaware Bay for placing buoys and supplying lights.
HENRIETTA SHARIT	two months 1900	A schooner, $5/day, to repair lights in Seventh LHD in Apalachicola Bay, FL.
HOMER	23 Jun-09 Dec 1902 20 Apr-01 Dec 1903 28 Apr-18 Jul 1904 13 Jun 1905	A 665-ton screw steamer, in the Thirteenth LHD, building Scotch Cap Light in Alaska. Construction of remote light stations in Alaska. Construction of remote light stations in Alaska. Construction in Alaska.
INDIA	02 May-14 Aug 1902	A 110-ton schooner for $13.33/day.
J. N. ELY	27 Apr-16 Jul 1867	A schooner, chartered for temporary service in the Fifth LHD.
JOHN JOHNSON	1887	Wood tug, working out of Buffalo, NY.
LEMON	Spring 1903	A schooner, to help build day beacons in Eighth LHD bayous of Louisiana.
LESTER	two months 1899	A schooner. In the Eighth LHD in Texas.
LIZZIE HAAS	Jun 1901 part of 1902	For work in Mobile Bay. For work in Mobile Bay.

Hired Vessel	**Times of Service**	**Comments**
LUCY H	part of 1905	A schooner, in the Seventh LHD, building and repairing beacons.
MARTHA	part of 1904	A schooner, in the Seventh LHD, assisting in building day markers/beacons in Tampa Bay and along the west coast of central Florida.
	part of 1905	Delivered materials in the Seventh LHD and assisted in repairing and painting numerous beacons.
MARY T	1903	A schooner, in the Seventh LHD, to deliver supplies to the lights in the Florida Keys.
	part of 1904	Delivery of materials and repairs to beacons in southern Florida.
	one month 1905	Construction of a new beacon in the Seventh LHD.
ME-ME	27 Mar-25 Aug 1838	A schooner, for survey work and delivering supplies and construction materials on the east side of Lake Michigan. This is the earliest known record of any "hired vessel."
MIAMI	1888	Wood "steam barge" (131 x 37 x 11), used in the Great Lakes.
MONAGHAN	Fall 1913	A steamer, hired for supply support in southeast Alaska.
NARRAGANSETT	01 Jun 1855-fall 1855	A small schooner, used to augment/supplement work of USLHT *Sunbeam* in the New York Harbor/Long Island Sound region. Note: This is a different vessel than the USLHT *Narragansett* of 1867.
NEW HAVEN	03 Oct-20 Oct 1888	$30/day in the Fifteenth LHD. A light draft stern wheeler used because the water level on the river was too low for USLHT *Goldenrod*.
SIDNEY	01 Dec 1893-13 Feb 1894	A schooner. $385/day.
	June-July 1903	Construction of aids in Mississippi River Delta.
	one month in 1904	Construction of a beacon light in Mississippi delta.
THREE BROTHERS	two months 1905	Repairs of Florida Reef Light in the Seventh LHD.
WANDERER	1900-20 Jun 1901	A schooner, used for one year in Mississippi River Delta.
	part of 1902	Working in Eighth LHD at Mobile Bay, AL.
	part of 1903	Deliver construction materials in Mobile Bay, and transport Eighth LHD Inspector on Mississippi Sound. Also delivered supplies to the Florida panhandle.
WILLIAM F. MARTIN	Jan 1869- 05 Apr 1869	A schooner, chartered in the Fifth LHD for $400/month.
	Jul-Nov 1869	Rechartered in the Fifth LHD at $10/day.

APPENDIX B
The Lighthouse Districts
U.S. Lighthouse Establishment Districts, 1838

From its conception in 1789 when it had only eight lighthouses, the Lighthouse Establishment had grown in less than 40 years to include 210 lighthouses and 28 lightships, plus some assorted primitive buoys. To make the most of existing resources and better support the establishment's mission, areas of responsibility were divided into "districts" with the organization of the Lighthouse Service. The first such organization of districts was authorized by Congress on 07 July 1838, creating six Atlantic and two Great Lakes districts. However, the exact definition of these boundaries has been lost, and can be only approximated.

Also, at this time, the districts were only named, not numbered, for the regions they covered.

The six Atlantic and two Great Lakes districts as enacted by Congress on 07 July 1838, were:

District	Area
Maine	Maine, New Hampshire
Massachusetts	Massachusetts, Rhode Island, Connecticut
New York	New York, New Jersey
Wilmington	Delaware, Maryland
Norfolk	Virginia, North Carolina
Charleston	South Carolina, Georgia, Florida, Gulf of Mexico
Lake Ontario	Lake Ontario
Northwestern Lakes	Lakes Erie, Huron, Michigan, Superior

Appendix B - The Lighthouse Districts 153

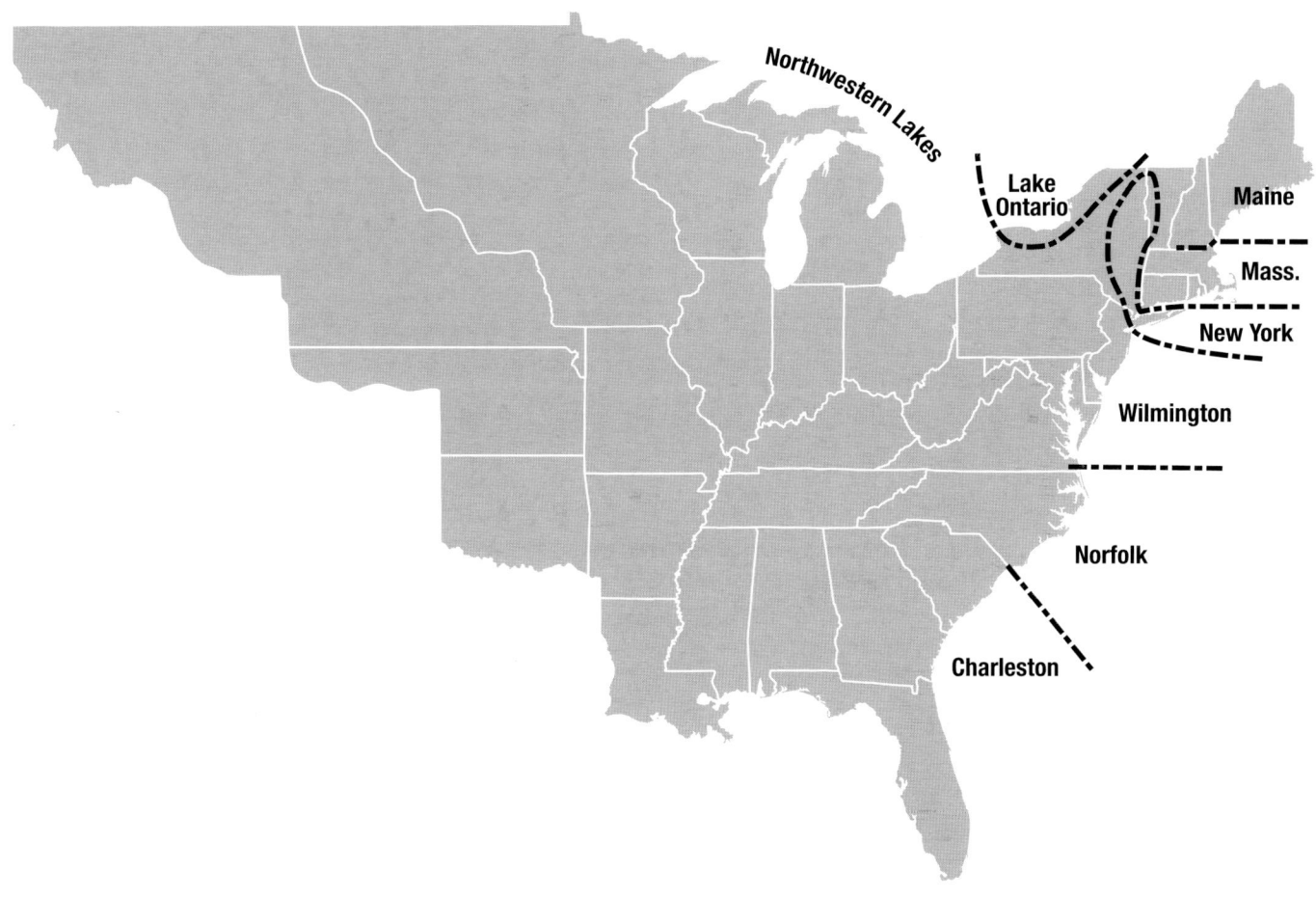

U.S. Lighthouse Establishment Districts, 1838

© D.R. Peterson 1999

U.S. Lighthouse Board Districts, 1852

By 1852, the United States had grown, reaching the West Coast, and the Lighthouse Service had grown as well. The Lighthouse Service was now responsible for over 297 major lights, 35 lightships, two lighthouse tenders, and over a thousand assorted buoys. The new Lighthouse Board had assumed control and reorganized into twelve regions called Lighthouse Districts (LHD) and the expanding role of the Service was redefined. Some of the new features included a separate district for the Gulf of Mexico and another for the Pacific Coast. Districts were numbered for the first time starting in the northeast and counting southward with a progression to the west. Each District was headed by a District Inspector, who was to be assisted by a District Engineer (both of whom would be officers in either the Navy or the Army).

This map shows the district boundaries that were established by the Lighthouse Board in 1852. Some significant changes were enacted by the Lighthouse Board before it relinquished control in 1910, as shown on the third map.

Lighthouse Districts enacted by the Lighthouse Board in 1852:

1. Maine, New Hampshire
2. Massachusetts
3. Rhode Island, Connecticut, New York, upper New Jersey to Squam Inlet, Lake Champlain, Hudson River
4. South of Squam Inlet New Jersey, Delaware, Delaware Bay and tributaries, north of Metomkin Inlet Virginia
5. South of Metomkin Inlet Virginia, Chesapeake Bay, Maryland, Albermarle Sound North Carolina (north of New River)
6. North Carolina (south of New River), South Carolina, Georgia, Florida (north of Cape Canaveral)
7. Florida (south of Cape Canaveral to Key West to Egmont Key)
8. Florida (west of St. Marks), Alabama, Louisiana (to Lake Pontchartrain)
9. Louisiana (mouth of Mississippi River), Texas
10. Lakes Ontario and Erie, St. Lawrence and Niagara rivers
11. Lakes St. Clair, Huron, Michigan, Superior
12. Entire Pacific Coast: California, Oregon, Washington

Appendix B - The Lighthouse Districts 155

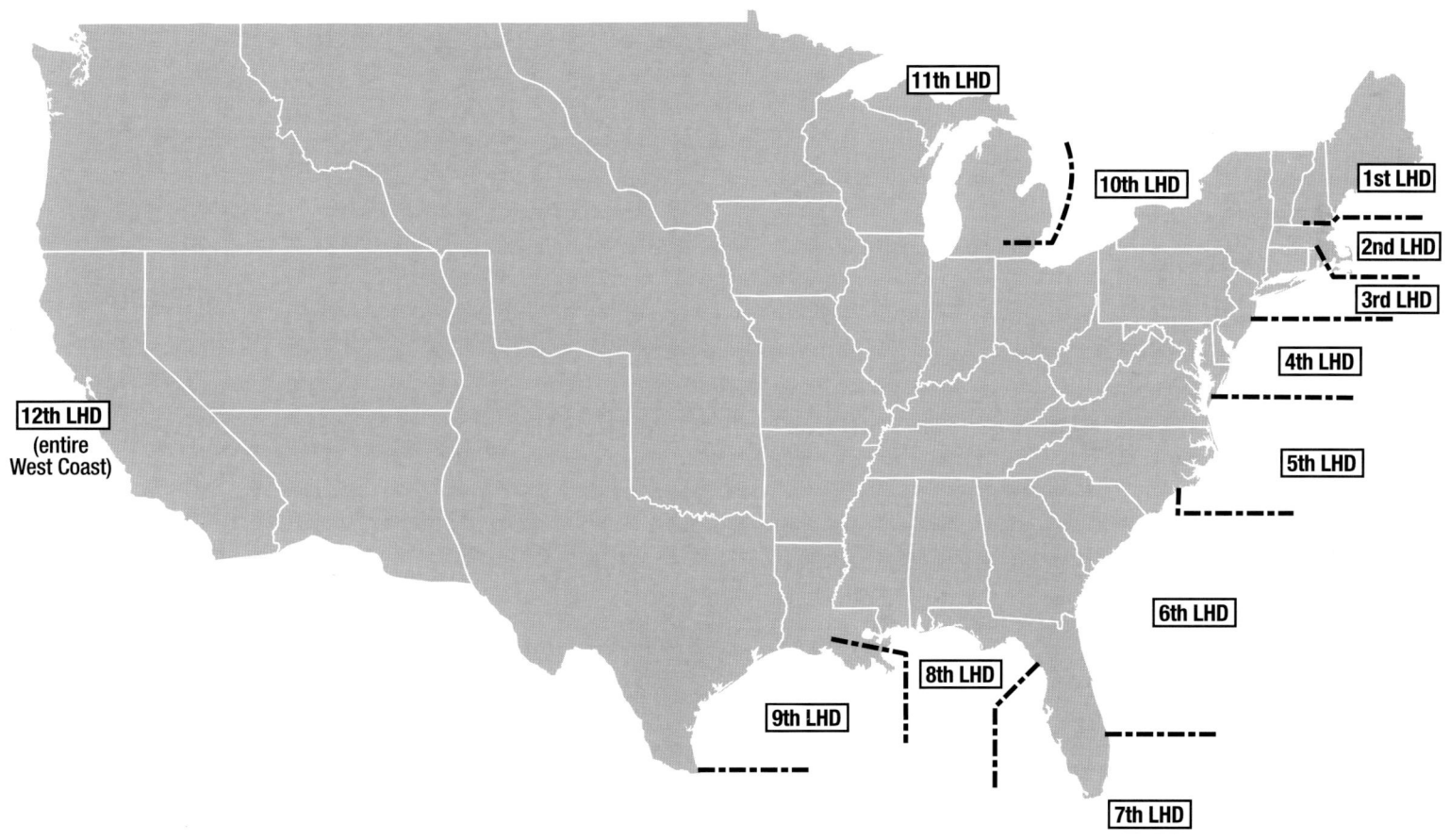

U.S. Lighthouse Board Districts, through 1910

During the next half century after the Lighthouse Board had established its twelve Lighthouse Districts (LHD), the responsibilities of the Service continued to expand.

First, with the enormous growth that was occurring on the west coast, the Twelfth LHD was divided, with Oregon and Washington becoming the new Thirteenth LHD. Then, to simplify responsibilities in the Gulf of Mexico, the old Eighth and Ninth LHDs (from the Florida panhandle to Texas, inclusive), were combined into a single District in 1867. One year later, when expanding responsibilities in the Great Lakes required splitting Lake Michigan from the Eleventh LHD, Lake Michigan assumed the title of the new Ninth LHD.

Growth was not the only factor in redesignating districts. A shift in responsibilities also played a part. Aids to Navigation was no longer the exclusive function of lighthouses and lightships. The Lighthouse Service now was also tasked with providing Day Markers (fixed smaller unmanned structures for navigation) and buoys to the rivers of the nation as a regular part of the inventory. To accommodate these expanded duties, two new districts were created in 1876. The Ohio River and its tributaries would be the new Fourteenth LHD, while the Mississippi and Missouri rivers would be the Fifteenth LHD. In 1887, the Fourteenth LHD would be further split, with the lower Mississippi (from Cairo, IL, to New Orleans) separated into a new Sixteenth District.

This expansion of Lighthouse Districts was not confined to the 48 states, but also included U.S. interests and responsibilities overseas. Puerto Rico was added to the Third LHD, because it could be supported from the Depot at Staten Island, New York. After the Spanish-American War in 1898, Cuba came under the responsibility of the Seventh LHD. The Territory of Alaska was put under the responsibility of the Thirteenth LHD in 1884, and the Territory of Hawaii became part of the Twelfth LHD in 1904.

The following map reflects the Lighthouse Districts through early 1910, in the final days of the Lighthouse Board, just before the Lighthouse Service was moved to the new Department of Commerce and reorganized.

As a further note of interest, the basic LHD boundaries and their numbering system used during this era were the basis for the Naval District system that was created in 1903. The U.S. Coast Guard, which absorbed the Lighthouse Service just before World War II, would adopt the Naval District numbering system for its own Coast Guard District system in 1942.

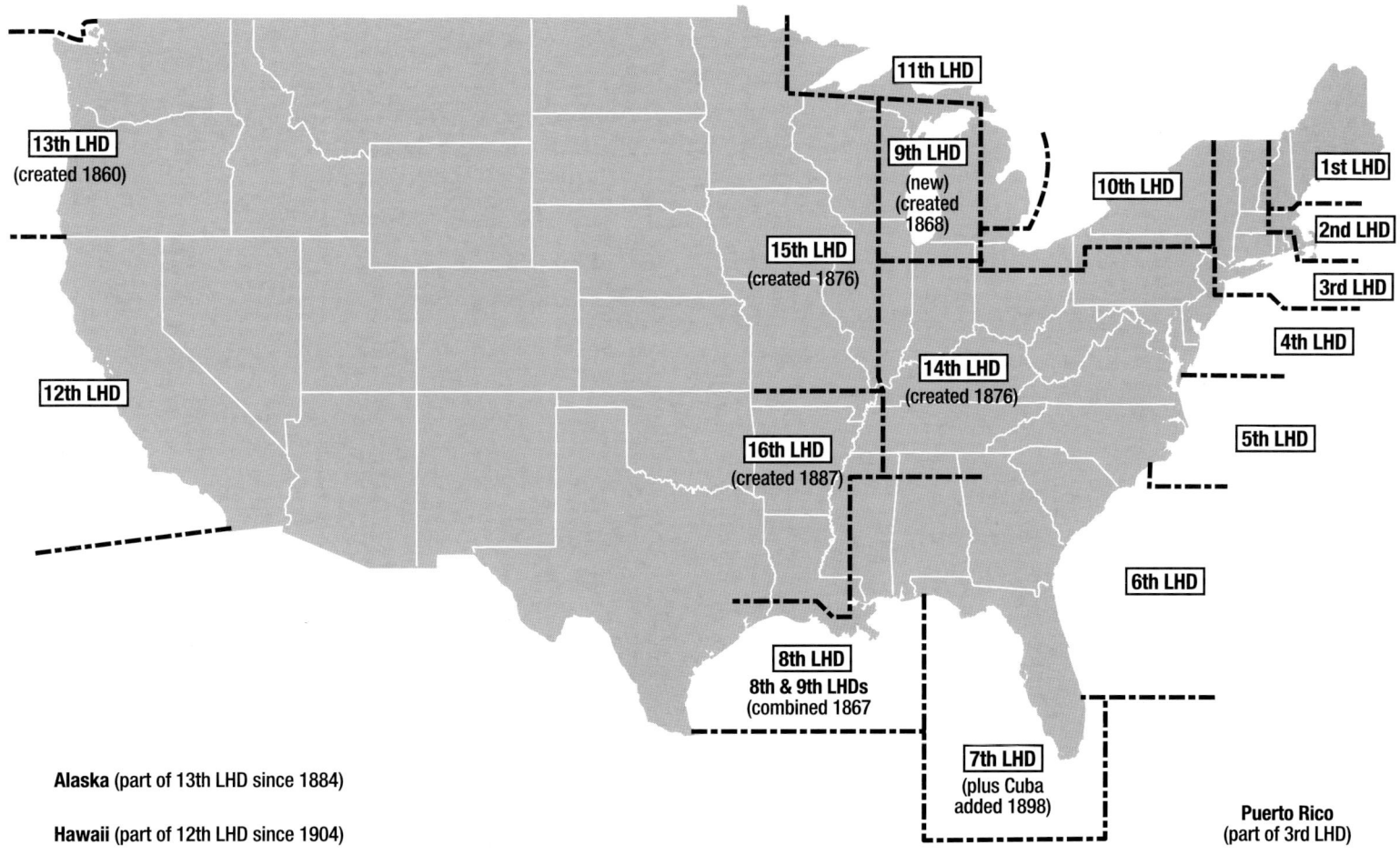

U.S. Bureau of Lighthouses Districts, 1910-1939

Now under the new Department of Commerce, the reorganized Bureau of Lighthouses had a simplified administration. A civilian Lighthouse Commissioner, with each District headed by a Superintendent, replaced the old Lighthouse Board on 01 July 1910. The Lighthouse Service had to oversee 1,397 major lights, 63 lightships, 51 lighthouse tenders, 457 fog signals, and more than 6,000 buoys.

A new district system with revised boundaries, reflected the ongoing expansion of the Service. Some of the Lighthouse Board districts were split and areas were further defined and renumbered leading to nineteen districts in total.

Again, the new districts would be numbered from north to south, starting on the East Coast and working west. New districts, split off from other districts, included: Puerto Rico (Ninth LHD), Alaska (Sixteenth LHD), and Hawaii (Nineteenth LHD). By 1915, the new Nineteenth LHD had expanded to include Midway, Guam, and American Samoa.

With only one major exception and a few minor administrative changes, these districts and boundaries would remain as they were until the Lighthouse Service merged into the United States Coast Guard in 1939. The only major changed to the Lighthouse Districts during this era would be the consolidation of the Thirteenth and Fourteenth LHDs into the Fifteenth LHD on 01 March 1933, with oversight of the entire river system of the Great Plains and Midwest.

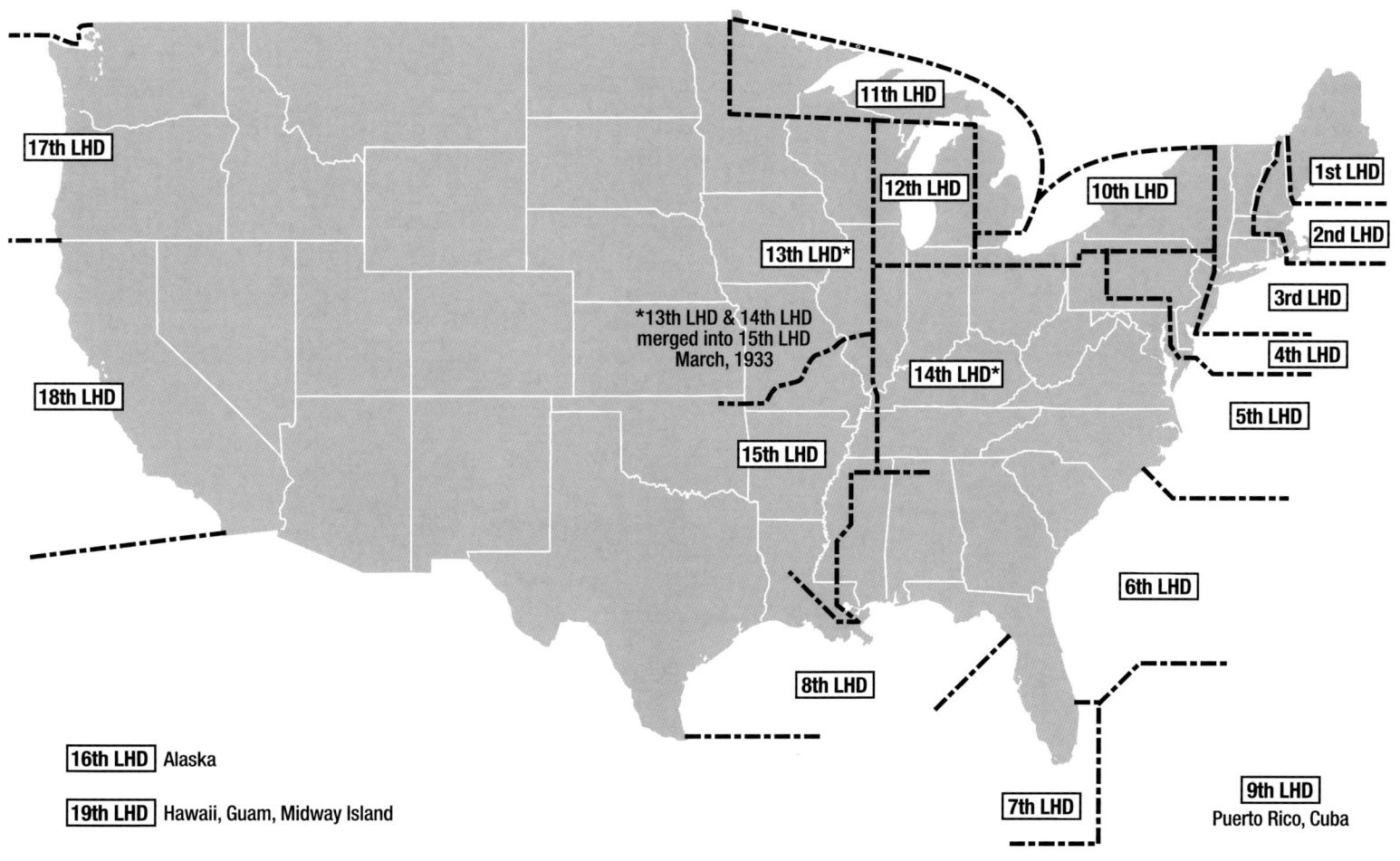

BIBLIOGRAPHY

Bloomfield, Howard V. L.
The Compact History of the United States Coast Guard
New York: Hawthorn Books, Inc., 1966

Bauer, K.J. & Roberts, Stephen S.
Register of Ships of the U.S.Navy 1775-1990
New York: Greenwood Press, 1991

Bradford, James C., editor
Captains of the Old Steam Navy: Makers of the American Naval Tradition, 1840-1880
Annapolis, MD: U.S. Naval Institute Press, 1986

Canney, Donald L.
U.S. Coast Guard and Revenue Cutters, 1790-1935
Annapolis, MD: U. S. Naval Institute Press, 1995

Cipra, David L.
Lighthouses, Lightships, and the Gulf of Mexico
Alexandria, VA: Cypress Communications, 1997

Cogar, William B.
Dictionary of Admirals of the U.S.Navy, Volume 1, 1862-1900
Annapolis MD: U.S. Naval Institute Press, 1989

Cowart, RADM Kenneth K., USCG
Development of Vessels Servicing Aids to Navigation for the U.S.Coast Guard Annual Report "TRANSACTIONS", vol. 66
New York: Society of Naval Architects and Marine Engineers, 1958

Dean, Love
The Lighthouses of Hawai'i
Honolulu, HI: University of Hawaii Press, 1991

Dowling, Edward J.
Lighthouse Tenders of the Great Lakes
Detroit, MI: Dossin Great Lakes Museum *Telescope*, 1962

Flint, Willard
Lightships of the United States Government
Washington, DC: U.S.Coast Guard, 1989

Greenwood, John Orvile
Name Sakes, 1930-1955
Cleveland, OH: Freshwater Press, 1986

Gibbs, James A.
Lighthouses of the Pacific
Atglen, PA: Schiffer Publishing Ltd, 1986

Gibbs, James A.
Oregon's Seacoast Lighthouses
Medford, OR: Webb Research Group, 1992

Gibbs, James A. Jr.
Sentinals of the North Pacific
Portland, OR: Binfords & Morts, 1955

Grover, David H.
U.S. Army Ships and Watercraft of World War II
Annapolis, MD: U.S. Naval Institute Press, 1987

Hall, Wes (Mid-Atlantic Technology & Environmental Research, Inc.)
Historical Context and Statement of Significance for USCG Buoy Tenders: 133-foot "White" class, 157-foot "Red" class, and 180-foot "Cactus, Mesquite, and Basswood" Classes
Washington, DC: U.S. Coast Guard (Office of Cutter Management), 1997

Hornberger, Patrick and Linda Turbyville
Forgotten Beacons: The Lost Lighthouses of the Chesapeake Bay
Annapolis, MD: Eastwind Publishing, 1997

Johnson, Allen and Dumas Malone
Dictionary of American Biography, 20 volumes + supplements
New York: Charles Scribner's Sons, 1930

Johnson, Robert Erwin
Guardians of the Sea
Annapolis, MD: U.S. Naval Institute Press, 1987

Kern, Florence
United States Revenue Cutters in the Civil War
Washington, DC: U.S. Coast Guard; 1990

Marshall, Amy K
A History of Buoys and Tenders, A Supplement to the Commandant's Bulletin
Washington, DC: U.S. Coast Guard; 1995

Miller, Francis T.
Photographic History of the Civil War
Springfield, MA: Patriot Publishing Co., 1911

Mitchell, Thorton W. and Arthur Dyer
List of Logs of USCG Vessels, 1790-1941 [NAVCG116]
Washington, DC: National Archives, 1944

Moebs, Thomas Truxton
Confederate States Research Guide
Williamsburg, VA: Moebs Publishing Co., 1991

Musgrove, H.E. "Pete"
U.S. Naval Ships Data - Volume 5: U.S. Coast Guard
Stoughton, WI: Nautical Books, 1978

Noble, Dennis L.
Lighthouses & Keepers: The U.S. Lighthouse Service and Its Legacy
Annapolis, MD: U.S. Naval Institute Press, 1997

Peterson, Douglas R.
Dictionary of Cutters and Tenders of the U.S. Coast Guard
(unpublished manuscript), 1998

Putnam, George R.
Lighthouses and Lightships of the United States
New York: Houghton Mifflin Company, 1917

Rutherford, Donald
The Guardian of St. George Reef: America's Costliest Lighthouse
Peekskill, NY: National Maritime Historical Society *Sea History*, Autumn 1992

Scheina, Robert L.
U.S. Coast Guard Cutters and Craft of World War II
Annapolis, MD: U.S. Naval Institute Press, 1982

Scheina, Robert L.
U.S. Coast Guard Cutters and Craft, 1946-1990
Annapolis, MD: U.S. Naval Institute Press, 1990

Shanks, Ralph, and Lisa Woo Shanks
Guardians of the Golden Gate
Petaluma, CA: Costaño Books, 1990

Silverstone, Paul H.
Warships of the Civil War Navies
Annapolis, MD: U.S. Naval Institute Press, 1989

Silverstone, Paul H.
U.S. Warships of World War II
Garden City, NJ: Doubleday & Co., 1965

Silverstone, Paul H.
U.S. Warships Since 1945
Annapolis, MD: U.S. Naval Institute Press, 1987

Smith, Horatio Davis, Captain Commandant, U.S.R.C.S.
Early History of the United States Revenue Marine Service
Bryn Mawr, PA: R.L. Polk Printing Co., 1932.

Smith, Thomas, Captain USLHS
Journal of the U.S. Lighthouse Schooner Sunbeam
handwritten ships log: 05 Aug 1853 to 30 Jun 1855
held by U.S. Lighthouse Society, San Francisco

Strobridge, Truman R.
Chronology of Aids to Navigation and the old Lighthouse Service Coast Guard Publication CG-458
Washington, DC: U.S. Coast Guard Public Affairs Office, 1980

Weiss, George
U.S. Lighthouse Service: Its History, Activities and Organization Service Monograph of the U.S. Government, No. 40
Baltimore, MD: John Hopkins Press, 1926
    (reprint): New Ays Press, 1974

White, Richard D. and Truman R. Strobridge
Nineteenth Century Lighthouse Tenders on the Great Lakes
Vermillion, OH: Great Lakes Historical Society *Inland Seas*, Summer 1975

Willoughby, Malcolm F.
U.S. Coast Guard in World War II
Annapolis, MD: United States Naval Institute Press, 1957

Ninth Coast Guard District Public Affairs Office
Guardians of the Eighth Sea: A History of the U.S. Coast Guard on the Great Lakes
Washington, DC: U.S. Coast Guard, 1976

Naval Historical Center, Department of the Navy
Dictionary of American Naval Fighting Ships [DANFS], 8 vols
Washington, DC: U. S. Government Printing Office, 1959-1981

Department of the Navy, Rush, Richard, et al, editors
Official Records of the Union and Confederate Navies of the War of the Rebellion, 31 volumes
Washington, DC: U.S. Government Printing Office, 1894-1922

U.S. Lighthouse Service
Journal of Tenders and Light Vessels, "Red Book"
Washington, DC: Lighthouse Service, hand-written journal, (~1875-1909)

U.S. Coast Guard, Office of Assistant Commandant
Record of Movements: Vessels of the United States Coast Guard, 2 vols.
Washington, DC: U.S. Coast Guard, 1933

U.S. Coast Guard
Historian's Office Files
Washington, DC

U.S. National Archives
Site Files Records Group 26
Washington, DC: U.S. Coast Guard (and predecessor services)

ANNUALS & PERIODICALS

Jane, Fred T. ed., et al
Jane's Fighting Ships (various editions, 1914 to present)
London: Sampson, Low and Marston & Co.
and New York: Jane's Publishing Inc.

U.S. Coast Guard
Register of Officers and Vessels of the U.S. Coast Guard
Washington, DC: GPO, 1939-1940

U.S. Coast Guard
Register of Cutters of the U.S. Coast Guard CG-197 / COMDTINST M5441.5 (series)
Washington, DC: GPO, 1942-1996

U.S. Department of the Treasury
List of Merchant Vessels of the United States,
Washington, DC: GPO, 1870-1938

U.S. Department of Commerce
Annual Reports of the Coast Survey
Washington, DC: GPO, 1847-1881

Secretary of the Treasury
Annual Report of the Secretary
Washington, DC: U.S. Department of the Treasury, 1977

Commandant, U.S. Coast Guard
Commandant's Bulletin
Washington, DC: U.S. Coast Guard, 1939-1996

Commandant, U.S. Coast Guard
Coast Guard Magazine
Washington, DC: U.S. Coast Guard, 1997-

Commissioner, U.S. Lighthouse Service
U.S.L.H.S. Bulletins
Washington, DC: U.S. Department of Commerce, 1912-1939

Lighthouse Board
U.S. Lighthouse Service Annual Reports
Washington DC: U.S. Department of the Treasury, 1853-1910

Commissioner, U.S. Lighthouse Service
U.S. Lighthouse Service Annual Reports
Washington DC: U.S. Department of Commerce, 1910-1937

Proceedings Magazine
Annapolis MD: U.S. Naval Institute

Naval History Magazine
Annapolis, MD: U.S. Naval Institute

The Keeper's Log
San Francisco, CA: U.S. Lighthouse Society

Lighthouse Digest
Wells, ME: Lighthouse Digest Inc.

American Neptune
Salem, MA: Peabody Museum of Salem, MA

Inland Seas
Vermillion, OH: Great Lakes Historical Society

National Geographic
Washington, DE: National Geographic Society

Telescope
Detroit, MI: Dossin Great Lakes Museum, Great Lakes Maritime Institute

The New York Times
New York, NY

Pacific Marine Review
San Francisco, CA

The author and Eastwind Publishing gratefully acknowledges the contributions of the following institutions and individuals for the loan of their photography and illustrations.

The National Archives - College Park, Maryland
The U. S. Coast Guard Historian's Office - Washington, DC
The Library of Congress - Washington, DC
The U. S. Naval Historical Center - Washington, DC
The Mariners' Museum - Newport News, Virginia
The Columbia River Maritime Museum - Astoria, Oregon
The Dossin Great Lakes Museum - Detroit, Michigan
Nautical Research Centre - Petaluma, California
The Maritime Museum of Monterey - Monterey, California
The U. S. Lighthouse Society - San Francisco, California
James A. Gibbs - Seattle, Washington
Patrick Hornberger - Trappe, Maryland

Publisher's Note:

While every effort has been made to present
a complete history of U.S. Lighthouse Service
tenders, the author and publisher recognize the
lack of detailed information on some of the very
early vessels. We welcome readers comments and
additional information on any of the
tenders shown in this book.

Please submit your comments to:

Patrick Hornberger
Eastwind Publishing
P.O. Box 1773
Annapolis, MD 21401

INDEX

- Names listed in capital letters are those of vessels commissioned as Lighthouse Tenders, and are listed in chronological order in the book.
- Names in lower case are of other ownership, such as Navy or privately owned vessels.
- All tenders are listed by the first (or original) name assigned.
- The year noted in parenthesis is the year of commissioning or when placed in service.
- Those vessels chartered or hired (used but not commissioned in the Lighthouse Service) are listed in Appendix A and are marked here with a diamond (◆).
- Tenders whose names were later repeated on newer vessels (after 1939) in the U.S. Coast Guard are marked with an asterisk (*).

Aaron Wilbur. See ARBUTUS (1871)
ACACIA (1927)* See SPEEDWELL class (1923)
Acme. See ALDER (1924)
ACTIVE (1843), 3
ACTIVE (1856)*, 11
A.D. Bache, USCSS. See BACHE (1869)
Adario, USS (YNT-25). See ZIZANIA (1888)
AGUACATE (1901), 73
AIKEN, GOVERNOR (1855), 8
ALANTHUS (1870). See VERBENA class (1870)
ALDER (1924)*, 117
ALERT (1855)*, 9
Alert, CSS. See Alert (1855)
Alfred Van Sant Voort.
    See VAN SANTVOORT (1857)
ALICE (1875), 40
Alice. See VAN SANTVOORT (1857)
Alice M. Gill (1900-1902)◆, 149
Alliance (1886-1891), 149
ALTHEA (1930), 123
ALTHEA class (1930), 123
AMARANTH (1892), 63
ANEMONE (1908). See MANZANITA class (1908)
Anna Deane. See DUPONT (1863)
ARBUTUS (1871), 33
ARBUTUS (1879), 46
ARBUTUS (1933)*, 131
Arcadia (1899)◆, 149
ARCTURUS (1872). See LYRA class (1872)
ARMERIA (1890), 60
Army Mine Planters. See SPEEDWELL class (1923)
ARUM (1893) launch, 65
ASPEN (1906)*, 81
ASTER (1908), 89
ASTER (1922)*, 111
ATLANTIC (1873), 38

Aubrey L. Hudgins. See JUNIPER (1903)
Augusta (1852)◆, 149
Augusta (1871)◆, 149
Avalon. See BIRCH (1917)
Ayres, General. See PYXIE (1923)
Axle (1902)◆, 149
AZALEA (1891), 61
AZALEA (1931)* See LILAC (1933)
AZALEA (1940)* See COTTONWOOD (1939)
B.O. Colonna. See IRIS (1899)
BACHE (1869), 2
BEECH (1928), 122
BELLE (1863), 17
Belle Stevens. See BELLE (1863)
BIBB (1864)*, 17
Big Chief. See IRIS (1899)
BIRCH (1917) launch, 101
BIRCH (1939), 145
BLUEBELL (1889) launch, 58
BLUEBELL (1922)* launch, 108
BLUEBONNET (1939). See JASMINE class (1935)
BOUQUET (1889), 57
BOWEN (1855), 9
BRAMBLE (1879)*, 45
Brandon. See BRAMBLE (1879)
BUCHANAN (1858), 15
Buoy Boats, 38-foot, unnamed (1927), 119
BUTTERCUP (1922) launch, 109
C.W. Thomas. See DANDELION (1872)
CACTUS (1865)*, 19
CAMELLIA (1911), 93
Cape Romanzoff. See JASMINE (1935)
Capt. A.M. Wetherill, USA (1923). See PYXIE (1923)
Capt. Edwin C. Long, USA. See SUNDEW (1924)
Capotillo. See CAMELLIA (1911)
Carter, Henry. See PYXIE (1923)

Catalyst. See BEECH (1928)
CEDAR (1917), 100
CHALLENGE (1856), 10
CHAOS (1865), 20
Charles H. Werner. See VIOLET (1871)
CHASE (1861)*, 16
CHERRY (1932), 128
Christiana. See AZALEA (1891)
Christmas Tree Island, FL. See WISTARIA (1882)
Clarence. See DAISY (1873)
Cleopatra (1900)◆, 149
CLOVER (1889), 58
CLOVER (1907) launch, 83
CLOVER (1912)* See TWO MYRTLES (1908)
Coast Survey. See U.S. Coast Survey
COBB, HOWELL (1857), 15
COEUR DE LEON (1860).
    See VAN SANTVOORT (1857)
Colonel Albert Todd, USA. See LOTUS (1924)
Colonel Charles Willard. See MADRONO (1885)
COLONEL HODGSON (1922), 108
Colonel John White, USA. See SPEEDWELL (1923)
COLUMBINE (1892). See LILAC class (1892)
COLUMBINE (1931)* See LINDEN class (1931)
Commodore. See IVY (1870)

Confederate States Ships (CSS):
    Alert. See ALERT (1855)
    Anna Deane. See DuPONT (1863)
    Helen. See HELEN (1858)
    King, William B. See WM. R. KING (1853)

Cora. See ARBUTUS (1871)
CORINNE (1868), 24
COSMOS (1919)*, 104
COTTONWOOD (1939), 144

CROCUS (1874), 39
CROCUS (1905), 80
Cynthia. See THISTLE (1890)
CYPRESS (1908)* See MANZANITA class (1908)
Daffodil, USS. See ARBUTUS (1871)
DAFFODIL (1890). See THISTLE (1890)
DAHLIA (1874), 39
DAHLIA (1933), 132
DAISY (1873), 38
DAISY (1895), 68
DANDELION (1872), 37
DANDELION (1907), 83
DANDELION (1917), 99
Dandy. See VERBENA (1870)
Daniel Kern. See MANZANITA (1880)
DARLING, GRACE (1883), 53
Dart. See LOCUST (1931)
Dawn (1904-1905)♦, 150
DELAWARE (1856), 10
Dischose (1902)♦, 150
Drafin. See CYPRESS (1908)
Dream (1862)♦, 150
DRIFT (1894), 67
DUPONT (1863), 17
Eight Tender Class. See MANZANITA class (1908)
Elaine Foss. See LARCH (1926)
ELIZA (1853), 6
ELIZABETH (1854), 6
Ellen C (1903-1905)♦, 150
ELM (1919), 105
ELM (1939)*, 140
Elma. See LILAC (1892)
Elmasada. See COSMOS (1919)
Ely, J.N. (1867)♦, 150
ESSAYONS (1855), 9
Excel (1904)♦, 150
F. Mansfield, USS. See SHRUB (1920)
F. Weyerhauser. See DANDELION (1917)
FAIRY (1854), 6
Federal Jack (1812)♦, 150
FERN (1871), 34

FERN (1915)*, 96
FIR (1940)* See HOLLYHOCK class (1937)
FIREFLY (1852), 3
First Commissioned Tender in LHS.
    See RUSH (1840)
First Pacific Coast Tender. See SHUBRICK (1857)
First Propeller driven Tender. See IRIS (1865)
First Propeller driven Tender in Great Lakes.
    See HAZE (1867)
First Radio equipped Tender. See KUKUI (1908)
First RDF equipped Tender. See TULIP (1908)
First Steam Tender. See SHUBRICK (1857)
First Stern Wheel Tender.
    See GOLDENROD (1888)
First Tender built for Coast Guard.
    See JUNIPER (1940)
First Tender built for Great Lakes.
    See DAHLIA (1874)
First Tender built for LHS. See SHUBRICK (1857)
First Tender built for rivers. See LILY (1875)
First Diesel-Electric drive Tender.
    See LINDEN (1931)
FLORIDA (1855). See BOWEN (1855)
Flora M. Hill. See DAHLIA (1874)
FORGETMENOT (1910) launch, 90
FRANKLIN PIERCE (1853), 5
G.L. Bowen. See BOWEN (1855)
GARDENIA (1888), 55
Garland (1855)♦, 150
General R.B. Ayres, USA. See PYXIE (1923)
GENERAL GEORGE GIBSON (1922), 108
General Edmund Kirby, USA. See ILEX (1924)
GENERAL LUDINGTON (1922), 108
General Pike (1852)♦, 150
GENERAL POE (1870), 30
GENERAL PUTNAM (1865), 18
General W.P. Randolph, USA. See LUPINE (1927)
General John P. Story, USA. See ACACIA (1927)
General Garland Whistler. See SPRUCE (1923)
Genevieve. See DAISY (1895)
George W. Beale. See GARDENIA (1888)

George M. Bibb, USRC. See BIBB (1964)
George H. Johnson. See COL. HODGSON (1922)
George E. Smoot. See MAGNOLIA (1871)
GEORGE STEERS (1854), 8
GERANIUM (1865), 21
GIBSON, GENERAL GEORGE (1922), 108
Gill, Alice M. (1900-1902)♦, 49
GOLDENROD (1888), 56
GOLDENROD (1938), 139
GOLDENROD class (1938), 139
Good News Mission Ship.
    See HOLLYHOCK (1937)
Gopher, USS. See FERN (1872)
GOVERNOR AIKEN (1855), 8
GRACE DARLING (1883), 53
GRANITE (1860), 16
GREENBRIER (1924)*, 116
GUTHRIE (1869), 24
H.H. Talman. See PHAROS (1854)
H.R. Carter. See PYXIE (1923)
Haas, Lizzie (1901-1902)♦, 150
HAWTHORN (1921). See OAK class (1921)
HAZE (1867), 23
HAZEL (1893) launch, 65
HEATHER (1903)*, 76
HELEN (1858), 15
HELIOTROPE (1865), 19
HEMLOCK (1934), 133
Henrietta Sharit (1900)♦, 150
HENRY, JOSEPH (1880), 47
Henry Carter (USPHS). See PYXIE (1923)
Henry Warrington. See WARRINGTON (1871)
HEROINE (1853), 5
HIBISCUS (1908). See MANZANITA class (1908)
HICKORY (1933), 130
HODGSON, COLONEL (1922), 108
HOLLY (1881), 49
HOLLY class (1881), 49
HOLLYHOCK (1937)*, 137
HOLLYHOCK class (1937)*, 137
Homer (1902-1905)♦, 150

HOWELL COBB (1857), 15
HYACINTH (1903), 78
Hydrangea, USCGC. See MAYFLOWER (1897)
I.N. Seymour, USS. See SEYMOUR (1867)
ILEX (1924). See SPEEDWELL class (1923)
India (1902)♦, 150
Institute II. See BLUEBELL (1922)
Irene. See MAGGIE (1868)
IRIS (1865), 20
IRIS (1899)*, 72
IVY (1870), 30
IVY (1881), 50
IVY (1904)* See MAGNOLIA class (1904)
J.N. Ely (1867)♦, 150
J.N. SEYMOUR (1867), 22
J.S. Ruby. See RUBY (1890)
JASMINE (1935), 136
JASMINE class (1935), 136
JASPER (1857). See FIREFLY (1852)
JESSAMINE (1881). See HOLLY class (1881)
John A. Dix. See GERANIUM (1865)
John Bolgiano. See HELIOTROPE (1865)
John Johnson (1887)♦, 150
JOHN RODGERS (1883), 52
Johnson, John (1887)♦, 150
Jonas Smith. See ARBUTUS (1871)
JOSEPH HENRY (1880), 47
JUNIPER (1903), 73
JUNIPER (1940)*, 146
Kandu. See RHODODENDRON (1935)
KING, WILLIAM R. (1853), 5
KUKUI (1908)* See MANZANITA class (1908)
LaBelle. See IVY (1881)
Lake George. See LAUREL (1915)
LAMPLIGHTER (1857). See CHALLENGE (1856)
LAMPLIGHTER (1874), 40
LARCH (1926), 118
Largest Tender built for LHS. See CEDAR (1917)
LARKSPUR (1903), 75
Last Sailing Tender built. See CLOVER (1889)
Last Sailing Tender in Service. See PHAROS (1873)

Last Sidewheel Tender. See WILLOW (1927)
Last Steam Driven Tender in service.
   See LILAC (1933)
Last Sternwheel Tender built.
   See WAKEROBIN (1927)
Last LHS Tender built. See FIR (1940)
Last LHS Tender in service. See FIR (1940)
LAUREL (1876), 42
LAUREL (1891) launch, 61
LAUREL (1915)*, 95
LEAL (1894) launch, 67
LeClaire, USA. See COTTONWOOD (1939)
LEHUA (1922) launch, 110
Lemon (1903)♦, 150
LENOX (1856), 10
Lester (1899)♦, 150
Lighthouse Districts. See Appendix B
Light Vessel #97. See DRIFT (1894)
LILAC (1892), 64
LILAC class (1892), 64
LILAC (1903) launch, 74
LILAC (1933). See VIOLET class (1930)
LILY (1875), 41
LINDEN (1931), 126
LINDEN class (1931), 126
Little Red. See ALTHEA (1930)
Lizzie Haas (1901-1902)♦, 150
LOCUST (1931), 127
Longest Length Lighthouse Tender.
   See ALICE (1875)
Longest Serving Lighthouse Tender.
   See MARIGOLD (1891)
LOOKOUT (1853), 4
Lookout. See ALERT (1855)
LOTUS (1880), 47
LOTUS (1907) launch, 83
LOTUS (1924). See SPEEDWELL class (1923)
Louisa. See PINK (1878)
Louisiana. See JOSEPH HENRY (1886)
Loyal. See LARCH (1926)
Lucy H (1905)♦, 151

LUDINGTON, GENERAL (1922), 108
Lummi. See ALDER (1924)
LUPINE (1927). See SPEEDWELL class (1923)
LYRA (1872), 37
LYRA class (1872), 37
MADRONO (1885), 54
MADRONO launch (1896), 70
MAGGIE (1868), 24
Maggie Baker. See HELIOTROPE (1865)
Magnolia. See SEYMOUR (1867)
MAGNOLIA (1871), 33
MAGNOLIA (1904)*, 79
MAGNOLIA class (1904), 79
Mahala Francis. See CORINNE (1868)
MANGROVE (1897), 71
Mansfield, USS. See SHRUB (1920)
MANZANITA (1880), 48
MANZANITA (1908), 85
MANZANITA class (1908), 85
MAPLE (1893), 66
MAPLE (1939)*, 143
MARGUERITE (1910) launch, 90
Marguerite LeLand. See MAGNOLIA (1904)
MARIE (1875) launch, 40
MARIGOLD (1891), 62
Maripa. See NARCISSUS (1939)
MARTHA (1862), 16
Martha (1904-1905)♦, 151
MARTHA WASHINGTON (1867), 23
Martha Washington. See VIOLET (1871)
Martin, William F. (1869)♦, 151
MARY (1870), 31
Mary T (1903-1905)♦, 151
Mayfair. See PANSY (1878)
MAYFLOWER (1897)*, 70
McClain. See MAPLE (1893)
Me-Me (1838)♦, 151
Merchant. See HAZE (1867)
Miami (1888)♦, 151
MIGNONETTE (1871).
   See NARRAGANSETT (1867)

MINNIE (1871), 33
MINOT (1857), 12
Mirror. See VIGILANT (1856)
Miss Mudhen II. See MARIGOLD (1891)
Mississippi. See GREENBRIER (1924)
MISTLETOE (1872), 35
MISTLETOE (1939). See VIOLET class (1930)
Monaghan (1913)◆, 150
MYRTLE (1872), 36
MYRTLE (1932), 129
NARCISSUS (1939). See ZINNIA class (1939)
Narragansett (1855)◆, 151
NARRAGANSETT (1867), 23
Navy Ships. See U.S. Navy
NETTLE (1879)*, 44
New Haven (1888)◆, 151
Niagara. See POINSETTIA (1919)
Nichols No. 6. See MAPLE (1893)
Nightmare,USS. See WAKEROBIN (1927)
NORTH WIND (1855)*, 8
Northern I. See FERN (1915)
Northern Express. See ROSE (1916)
NYMPHAEA. See GOLDENROD (1888)
OAK (1921)*, 107
OAK class (1921), 107
OLEANDER (1903)*, 74
Only WWII Tender Casualty. See ACACIA (1927)
On Time. See DAISY (1873)
ORCHID (1908). See MANZANITA class (1908)
ORION (1872). See LYRA class (1872)
Oscar Lehtinen. See SUMAC (1903)
P.E. Romanzoff. See JASMINE (1935)
PALMETTO (1909). Slso see LAUREL (1915)
PALMETTO (1917), 98
PANSY (1878), 43
Pattona. See JOSEPH HENRY (1880)
PHAROS (1854), 7
PHAROS (1872) launch, 38
PIERCE, FRANKLIN (1853), 5
Pike, General (1852)◆, 150
PINE (1918)*, 102

PINK (1878), 45
PINK (1898) launch, 72
Plymouth. See IRIS (1899)
POE, GENERAL (1870), 30
POINCIANA (1930). See ALTHEA class (1930)
POINSETTIA (1919), 103
POLARIS (1872). Scc LYRA class (1872)
Polar Star. See CACTUS (1865)
POPLAR (1939). See GOLDENROD class (1938)
POPPY (1923) launch, 111
PRIMROSE (1922)* launch, 110
Prospect. See CACTUS (1865)
PUTNAM, GENERAL (1865), 18
PUTNAM (1869). See GENERAL PUTNAM (1865)
PYXIE (1923), 115
Q-7, USA. See POPPY (1923)
Queenstown. See JESSAMINE (1881)
RANGER (1857), 12
Red's Baby. See POINCIANA (1930)
RHODODENDRON (1935), 135
RICHARD RUSH (1840)*, 3
RODGERS, JOHN (1883), 52
Roger B. Simons, EPA. See MAPLE (1939)
ROSE (1870), 30
ROSE (1892). See GRACE DARLING (1883)
ROSE (1916), 97
RUBY (1890), 59
RUSH, RICHARD (1840)*, 3
S.A. McCall. See DANDELION (1872)
S.D. Mason, USA. See FERN (1915)
Salvager. See ELM (1919)
Sea Inspector. See MYRTLE (1932)
SEQUOIA (1908)* See MANZANITA class (1908)
SEYMOUR (1867), 22
Sharit, Enrietta (1900)◆, 150
SHARPIE (1885), 53
Shortest Service as Lighthouse Tender.
     See AGUACATE (1901)
SHRUB (1920), 106
SHUBRICK (1857), 14
Sidney (1893-1894, 1903-1904)◆, 151

SKYLARK (1856), 11
SNOWDROP (1897). See WATER LILY class (1895)
South Wind. See AMARANTH (1892)
SPEEDWELL (1923), 112
SPEEDWELL class (1923), 112
SPRAY (1853), 4
SPRUCE (1923)* See SPEEDWELL class (1923)
STEERS, GEORGE (1854), 8
SUMAC (1903)*, 77
SUNBEAM (1852), 3
Sunbeam. See DANDELION (1872)
SUNDEW (1924)*, 115
SUNFLOWER (1907), 84
SUNRISE (1867), 22
SUNRISE class (1867), 22
SUNSET (1867). See SUNRISE class (1867)
SUSAN (1867). See SUNRISE class (1867)
Suwanee, USS. See MAYFLOWER (1897)
TAMARACK (1934), 134
The Knight. See WM. R. KING (1853)
THISTLE (1890), 59
THISTLE (1927)*, 117
Three Brothers (1905)◆, 151
Tiffany. See BLUEBONNET (1939)
Townsend, W.J. See DRIFT (1894)
Trinity I. See LARCH (1926)
TULIP (1869). See J.N. SEYMOUR (1867)
TULIP (1908). See MANZANITA class (1908)
TWO MYRTLES (1908), 88

U.S. Army/War Department Vessels:
Big Chief. See IRIS (1899)
Captain Edwin Long. See SUNDEW (1924)
Captain A.M. Wetherill (1923). See PYXIE (1923)
Colonel Charles L. Williard.
     See MADRONO (1885)
Colonel Fred G. Hodgson.
     See COL. HODGSON (1922)
Colonel Albert Todd. See LOTUS (1924)
Colonel John V. White. See SPEEDWELL (1923)
General R.B. Ayres. See PYXIE (1923)

Gen. George Gibson. See GEN. GIBSON (1922)
General Edmund Kirby. See ILEX (1924)
General W.P. Randolph. See LUPINE (1927)
General John P. Story. See ACACIA (1927)
General G.N. Whistler. See SPRUCE (1923)
General Ludington.
    See GEN. LUDINGTON (1923)
Heather (FS-534). See HEATHER (1903)
Heroine. See HEROINE (1853)
Junior MinePlanters.
    See SPEEDWELL class (1923)
LeClair. See COTTONWOOD (1939)
Q-7. See POPPY (1923)
S. D. Mason (FS-551). See FERN (1915)
Wakerobin. See WAKEROBIN (1927)
Willow. See WILLOW (1927)

U.S. Coast Guard Cutters (USCGC):
Azalea (WAGL-262).
    See COTTONWOOD (1939)
CG-72013-D. See LOCUST (1931)
Hydrangea. See MAYFLOWER (1897)
Ida Lewis (1996). See GRACE DARLING (1883)
Juniper. See JUNIPER (1940)
Mayfair. See PANSY (1878)
Red Beech (WLM-656). See OAK (1921)
Salvia (WAGL-400). See MAGNOLIA (1904)
Spruce (WAK-246). See SPRUCE (1923)
White Pine. See WAKEROBIN (1927)
Also see U.S. Revenue Cutter Service

U.S. Coast Survey Vessels (USCSS):
A.D. Bache. See BACHE (1869)
Bibb. See BIBB (1864)
Daisy. See DAISY (1873)
Drift. See DRIFT (1894)

U.S. Dept. Of Environmental Protection (EPA)
Roger R. Simons. See MAPLE (1939)

U.S. Navy Ships (USS):
Adario (YNT-25). See ZIZANIA (1888)
Big Chief (IX-101). See IRIS (1899)
Cactus. See CACTUS (1865)
Christiana (IX-80). See AZALEA (1891)
Coeur de Leon. See VAN SANTVOORT (1857)
Daffodil. See ARBUTUS (1871)
Elmasada (SP-109). See COSMOS (1919)
F. Mansfield (SP-691). See SHRUB (1920)
Fern. See FERN (1871)
Gardenia. See GARDENIA (1888)
Geranium. See GERANIUM (1865)
Gopher. See FERN (1871)
Granite. See GRANITE (1860)
Heliotrope. See HELIOTROPE (1865)
I.N. Seymour. See SEYMOUR (1867)
Iris. See IRIS (1865)
Maine. See MANGROVE (1897)
Niagara (SP-263). See POINSETTIA (1919)
Putnam. See GENERAL PUTNAM (1865)
Shubrick. See SHUBRICK (1857)
Suwanee. See MAYFLOWER (1897)
William G. Putnam. See GEN. PUTNAM (1865)
YAG-32. See AZALEA (1891)

U.S. Public Health Service (USPHS):
Henry Carter. See PYXIE (1923)
Wistaria. See WISTARIA (1882)

U.S. Revenue Cutter Service (USRCS):
Forward. See MANGROVE (1897)
George M. Bibb. See BIBB (1864)
Mohawk. See LARKSPUR (1903)
Richard Rush. See RUSH (1840)
Shubrick. See SHUBRICK (1857)
Tyler. See BIBB (1864)
William Aiken. See GOV. AIKEN (1855)

VAN SANTVOORT (1857), 13
Venture. See LINDEN (1931)
VERBENA (1870)*, 29

VERBENA class (1870), 29
Victor Lynn. See JESSAMINE (1881)
VIGILANT (1856)*, 11
VIOLET (1871), 31
VIOLET (1930), 124
VIOLET class (1930), 124
W.J. Townsend. See DRIFT (1894)
WAKEROBIN (1927), 120
WALNUT (1939)* See HOLLYHOCK class (1937)
Wanderer (1901-1903)♦, 151
War Department Ships. see U.S. Army
WARRINGTON (1871), 32
WASHINGTON, MARTHA (1867), 23
WATCHFUL (1857). See SKYLARK (1856)
WATER LILY (1887). See GOLDENROD (1888)
WATER LILY (1895), 69
WATER LILY class (1895), 69
WAVE (1853), 4
WAVE (1861). See DELAWARE (1856)
Wetherill, Capt. A.M. (1923). See PYXIE (1923)
Willet Rowe. See IRIS (1865)
WILLIAM R. KING (1853), 5
William F. Martin (1869)♦, 151
William G. Putnam.
    See GENERAL PUTNAM (1865)
William B. Shubrick. See SHUBRICK (1857)
WILLOW (1927)*, 121
WISTARIA (1882), 51
WISTARIA (1933). See LINDEN class (1931)
Wisteria Island. See WISTARIA (1882)
WOODBINE (1914)*, 94
Wright No. 1. See HOLLY (1881)
YERBA BUENA (1907) launch, 82
Yojoa. See WALNUT (1939)
Zendrico. See FRANKLIN PIERCE (1853)
ZINNIA (1939), 141
ZINNIA class (1939), 141
ZIZANIA (1888), 57

The lighthouse tender, *Lilac,* passes America's most famous navigational aid on the way to a shipwreck in New York Harbor.

U.S. Coast Guard photo c. 1911